Do-it-yourself Yearbook

Popular Science

Do-it-yourself Yearbook

1988

Popular Science BOOKS

Published by
Popular Science Books, New York, NY

Distributed to the trade by
Rodale Press, Emmaus, PA

Published by

Popular Science Books
Grolier Book Clubs Inc.
380 Madison Avenue
New York, NY 10017

Distributed to the trade by

Rodale Press, Inc.
33 East Minor Street
Emmaus, PA 18049

ISSN: 0733-1894

ISBN: 1-55654-018-3

Manufactured in the United States of America

introduction

Here it is—the sixth annual compendium of the best do-it-yourself articles from the pages of *Popular Science,* augmented by an unprecedented number of original articles created expressly for this Yearbook. You'll also find four very special articles reprinted from *HOME, The Homeowner,* and *WORKBENCH* magazines. This added material fills out Pop Science's editorial coverage. Since it's dubbed "The What's New Magazine," *PS* is tightly oriented toward new products and techniques. The magazine rarely has space for service features, such as the one on page 18 that shows you what to look for when shopping for an affordable house to fix up yourself. Yet such instruction belongs in a how-to book of this scope—especially when it comes from as experienced a do-it-yourselfer as Phil McCafferty.

All of the articles you'll find here are written by the top how-to writers in America. Many of these names appear each month on the *Popular Science* masthead, as consulting editors. And at least three of these writers have served as president of the National Association of Home and Workshop Writers—a post currently held by the aforementioned McCafferty.

The year of the home

You'll probably notice, as you page through this volume, that the emphasis in this year's selection is on the home—on remodeling rather than on freestanding projects you'd build in a workshop. That area is far from neglected, though, with furniture projects and shop techniques both well represented. There's also a brand new section on home electronics and wiring. There's good reason for the home emphasis: Home improvement continues to be a national passion, with more money invested in fixing up and expanding existing housing than is spent on new construction. Picking up on my series of articles for *Popular Science* under the umbrella label "Room at the Top," this Yearbook presents a 12-page section on two different ways to raise your roof—for homes on tight lots, where the only way to expand is *up.* This volume also gives you ideas for other add-ons, such as air-lock entries or a passive-solar spa wing. Or for finding new space in your home by finishing off the attic or basement.

And what about those furniture projects and shop techniques? Well, feast your eyes on the red-oak hutch on page 64, or the elegant Queen Anne writing table on page 71—both by master woodworker Cy Wedlake. Then there's "The Ultimate Workbench" by the prolific Mr. McCafferty—with ideas gleaned from the likes of Tom Jones, R. J. DeCristoforo, A. J. Hand and other craftsmen. Or "Build Your Own Custom Carport" by Nick Engler, proof positive that practical needn't be boring.

Nothing beats a band saw for power, speed, and accu-racy. Surprised? Then read "Cris" DeCristoforo's "Bandsaw Basics," page 126. It's loaded with his step-by-step techniques for getting the most out of this versatile power tool. And if strong, elegant woodworking joints appeal to you, don't miss "Two New Approaches to Finger Joints" on page 130. Master woodworkers Cy Wedlake and Tom Jones detail a unique finger-joint machine you can build—and a nifty new jig you can buy.

What distinguishes the bulk of these projects from those you'll find in other home project books is not only the crisp, modern design (again, that "What's New" approach) but the quality of the construction drawings. *PS* hires only top technical artists such as Carl De Groote and Eugene Thompson, and its editors work closely with these draftsmen to be certain the reader will have all the information he'll need to adapt the project to his own home.

Where the information is peculiar to a specific house (as is mine on the special techniques and materials used in our showcase "Upside-down House," or Elaine Gilmore's report on a high-tech house that has everything), we make certain the *principles* are fully explained. You'll find this is true even when specific construction details would be of little practical use.

Cars and computers

The principles of how things work are especially important when you try and service today's ultra-sophisticated, computerized cars. So are the kind of hands-on procedures laid out for you in Ken Zino's article on troubleshooting oxygen sensors—a vital component of your car's engine-management system. You'll also find tips from Bob Cerullo on tracking down irksome short circuits, in addition to his articles, "What to Know Before You're Towed" and "How to Buy a Used Car." If you've wandered into a new-car showroom lately, you can imagine why the latter piece is of interest to so many folks these days. Whether your car is new or not-so-new, these tips can help you keep it running smoother, longer.

Ultimately, it's my job at the magazine to assure that whenever a reader sits down before a PS project, he or she doesn't get up hungry. Since both the magazine staff and our regular freelancers work so hard toward that end, we're all delighted to have our best efforts reprinted in this more permanent form. It makes it all doubly worthwhile. And you, as the Yearbook buyer, benefit from the fact that most of this material has been "reader-tested." You can count on its accuracy and thoroughness.

May the final benefit be reflected in your home!

Alfred Lees
Home and Shop Editor
POPULAR SCIENCE

contents

sun valley supertech

This will be one of the most visited rooms in the home," predicts Eric Thiel, project manager for Grabher Construction, the company that built this 8,000-square-foot house in Sun Valley, Idaho. It is a remarkable statement, considering we are in the basement mechanical room and the house above is one of the most beautiful I've ever seen.

Still, Thiel has a point. Though the soul of the house is surely its striking architecture and exquisite detailing, its heart and brain are down here where a fascinating profusion of pipes, tubes, and wires converge. The house is primarily a family retreat, but secondarily it is an experiment to advance the state of the art in energy conservation and solar-heating technology. Among its features:
● Evacuated-tube, heat-pipe solar collectors.
● Windows that combine low-emissivity film and argon gas; some are the most energy efficient ever installed.
● Passive-solar heat retained in high-thermal-mass materials.
● A clever evaporative cooling system that employs a decorative pool and fountains.
● A computer, accessible by telephone link, that controls and monitors energy systems, alarms, and lighting.

This seamless integration of architecture and technology resulted from the collaboration of architect Arne Bystrom of Seattle, Washington, and the ENSAR Group, energy architects and mechanical engineers, of Lakewood, Colorado.

The impetus—and many of the ideas—came from the owners, a couple from the San Francisco area who requested anonymity. I'll call them Mr. and Mrs. Greene for convenience. Mr. Greene, a venture capitalist by profession, is an electrical engineer by education. "In 1950 I could design a pretty good circuit using vacuum tubes and relays," he says with a grin. "There's not much market for that today." But he retains a keen interest in technology. That's the main reason Thiel predicts heavy traffic through the mechanical room.

Ted Prythero, Gregory Franta (an engineer and an architect, respectively, with ENSAR), and Bystrom began designing the Sun Valley house in 1982. Construction started in 1983 and continued through last winter. Workers joked that they were beginning to feel like those medieval craftsmen who spent whole lifetimes building one ca-

thedral. Indeed, the house is almost cathedral-like in the richness of its details, all designed by Bystrom.

The passive house

The east-west profile of the home's copper-clad roof mimics the slopes of the mountains behind it. Its north-south slope matches the angle of the sun at midday on the winter solstice. Around midmorning the sun begins streaming into the house (which faces somewhat west of south). Soon the temperature climbs to shirt-sleeve comfort. David Friedland, the live-in caretaker (cook and mechanical whiz) introduces me to the house.

In the sun-warmed entry he shows me the windows: conventional in appearance but not in performance. Those on the south wall have a layer of low-emissivity plastic film between two layers of glass; the spaces between are filled with argon gas. The film, Southwall Technologies' Heat Mirror, reflects radiant heat back into the sunspace. The argon gas conducts heat less readily than does air. The windows are made by Alpen, Inc., of Boulder, Colorado, and boast an impressive R-5 insulation value.

Even more impressive are the north windows in the living room and master bedroom. They have *two* layers of Heat Mirror and *three* spaces filled with argon. Result: an R-value of 6.7. Though ENSAR recommended against using large north windows, Bystrom insisted on them because of the view. The compromise: these experimental

Heat-pipe solar collectors are suspended from sanded and oiled redwood rafters (left). Interior detailing, including the circular staircase (top), was designed by architect Arne Bystrom. Cabinets, doors, and stairs were custom-made in small cabinet shops. Laminated redwood columns with Asian-inspired joinery (above) support the roof.

windows, specially fabricated by Alpen. "They're the most efficient ever installed as far as we know," says Friedland.

Friedland points to a fat white pipe that soars nearly to the top of the 30-foot-high sunspace, its top sliced at an angle showing a vibrant red interior. "When the temperature up there reaches eighty degrees, a fan goes on and pulls hot air through the pipe and into a rock bed below the spa/game room," he explains. Warm air from the rock bed is delivered to the room as needed.

Direct and indirect passive solar energy will provide the majority of heat for the house. Most of the remaining space heat, and heat for the spa and domestic water, will come from the active solar heating system.

Two 500-gallon hot-water tanks dominate the mechanical room; they're bright red. A synthetic hydrocarbon called Braco 888, made by the Bray Oil Co., circulates in a closed loop between the tanks and solar collectors, thus charging the tanks with heat.

The collectors, made by Philips of the Netherlands, consist of individual glass tubes, vacuum-sealed to reduce heat transfer. "You can change them like light bulbs," notes Friedland. In the center of each is a heat pipe.

Heat pipes are very efficient heat-transfer devices be-

cause the working fluid inside (a refrigerant in this case) changes phases: When it vaporizes, it absorbs a great deal of heat, called latent heat. When the gas condenses, it releases the latent heat. In the Philips collectors the heat is transferred to the oil at the headers. The box below explains all of the passive and active systems and how they work.

A computerized building-management and control system made by Andover Controls Corp. in Andover, Massachusetts, virtually tends the house. "It monitors more than eighty parameters, including temperatures of collectors, radiant slabs, and water tanks, and the incident solar radiation," ENSAR's Prythero tells me. "It analyzes the input data and controls pumps, valves, windows, and blinds."

The computer has a built-in modem and telephone. "Using a computer and modem in his office in California, the owner can call and tell the computer he's coming in on Friday," Prythero says. "If he wants the hot tub at a hundred degrees and the window shades open, the computer will see to it."

The computer also has a vocabulary of fifty words. "If the security or fire alarm is triggered, the computer will

Heating and cooling the supertech way

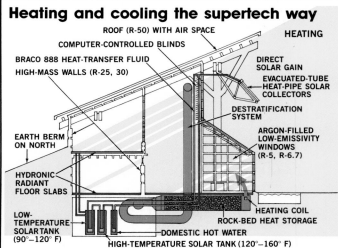

HEATING

ROOF (R-50) WITH AIR SPACE
COMPUTER-CONTROLLED BLINDS
BRACO 888 HEAT-TRANSFER FLUID
HIGH-MASS WALLS (R-25, 30)
DIRECT SOLAR GAIN
EVACUATED-TUBE HEAT-PIPE SOLAR COLLECTORS
DESTRATIFICATION SYSTEM
ARGON-FILLED LOW-EMISSIVITY WINDOWS (R-5, R-6.7)
EARTH BERM ON NORTH
HYDRONIC RADIANT FLOOR SLABS
LOW-TEMPERATURE SOLAR TANK (90°–120° F)
DOMESTIC HOT WATER
HEATING COIL
ROCK-BED HEAT STORAGE
HIGH-TEMPERATURE SOLAR TANK (120°–160° F)

COOLING

COMPUTER-CONTROLLED BLINDS, WINDOWS
AIR SPACE IN ROOF MINIMIZES HEAT GAIN
NORTH WINDOWS FOR CROSS-VENTILATION
COOL-AIR INTAKE BENEATH BERM
EVAPORATIVE CHILLER
HEAT EXCHANGER
AIR HANDLER
DECORATIVE FOUNTAINS
TERRACE POOL

DRAWING BY ADOLPH BROTMAN

In winter, the sun enters through the south glass, and its heat is stored in concrete walls. When the temperature high in the sunspace reaches 80° F, a fan draws air from there through a decorative column and delivers it to a 500-cu.-ft. rock bed, where heat is stored until needed. A second destratification duct (not shown) delivers hot air from the top of the sunspace to an air handler for redistribution. Computer-controlled blinds track the sun to maximize solar gain. An air space in the roof keeps the copper rooftop cold to prevent ice dams; an earth berm on the north wall shields the house from winter winds.

The active solar heating system uses evacuated-tube heat-pipe collectors. These transfer heat to oil-filled headers. From there the oil circulates in a closed loop, delivering heat to a domestic-hot-water tank and to two water-

filled solar tanks (one is shown in the photo at right). The high-temperature tank provides heat for the spa, small radiators, and "quick-heat" coils in the air handler and rock bed. The low-temperature tank provides heat for radiant floor slabs. All are closed-loop systems. Two small Weil-McClain VHE boilers supply backup heat.

In summer, shading and venting provide most of the cooling. High south windows, motorized and computer-controlled, open when sunspace is above 80° F. Automated blinds block the sun. Water in a terrace reflecting pool is sprayed through decorative fountains, promoting evaporative cooling. Cooled water is circulated through a heat exchanger where it cools the water that circulates through hydronic floor slabs. An evaporative forced-air cooling system serves as backup.

call the proper number and explain the problem," Prythero notes. Well proven in commercial buildings, this is the system's first installation in a residence.

A low-voltage, programmable lighting system will be linked to the computer. "You can have lights come on at a preset time, to a preset intensity," Friedland tells me. "And you can program them to change during dinner."

Idea house

ENSAR's calculations indicate that the house will be 85 to 90 percent self-sufficient in heat and hot water. A thorough monitoring program will test that prediction.

"Whatever the energy saving turns out to be, it'll never pay for the systems, even if my wife and I live to be 3,000 years old," Greene cracks with good-humored candor. "But I think some interesting ideas will come out of this that others can use in more cost-effective ways."

Despite the current abundance, Greene hasn't forgotten that oil is a nonrenewable resource. "Somebody has to do experimental work to find alternative energy sources," he says. Then quickly adds: "If we'd known what we were getting into, I'm not sure we'd have volunteered to do quite so much. But it really has been a ball"—*by V. Elaine Gilmore. Photos by Jeff Austin. Drawing by Adolph Brotman.*

Redwood kitchen cabinets feature fir inlay trim (top). Cabinets (even the door handles) were designed by architect Bystrom. Living room (right) has a sunken fireplace—and north-facing windows with an R-value of 6.7.

upside-down house

No skimping on amenities here: (1) Patio door in master bedroom gives onto a private deck. (2) West wall's large bumpout has a glass roof that's a skylight for the shower. (3) Smaller bump-out is the kitchen's greenhouse bay. (4 and 5) Partition walls (except around bedrooms) stop short of the cathedral ceiling to add spaciousness. (6) Dormer is a sun scoop for the living-room ceiling.

E xcept for its concrete-tile roof, the single-story 1,278-square-foot house looked conventional enough when I drove up to it this past summer through a gathering crowd. Yet when I joined Doug Sutherland, the mayor of Tacoma, Washington, in snipping the ribbon that opened the *Popular Science* display house to the public, we opened the floodgates to what would total nearly 4,000 visitors before the home was closed a month later—and sold at once for $88,000.

What was the secret of the house's broad appeal? Well, it didn't hurt that Tacoma's energy department had computed total heating costs at $60 a year (an average of $5 per month)— and that's without any major solar input, active or passive, since the Puget Sound area isn't noted for sunny days. But the area isn't noted for frigid winters or high fuel costs, either, so there had to be more to the appeal than energy efficiency.

What had initially attracted me to the project was that its vigorous, progressive young builder, Steve Rich (president of Commencement Bay Construction Co.), had combined in a single house the best aspects of new building-technology of recent years. Choosing one of the twenty-one plans from the American Plywood Assn.'s "Build a Better Home" portfolio, Rich had engineered the house to meet all the goals of Tacoma's own Super Good Cents energy program, based on conservation standards of the Bonneville Power Administration. This also qualified the house for Owens-Corning's Thermal Crafted Home label, and packed the project with construction innovations:

● An all-wood foundation, with a raised wood floor on special trusses.
● A new airtight drywall approach (ADA) that eliminates air infiltration.
● Zones heating with forced-air electric wall heaters.
● Advanced framing techniques with

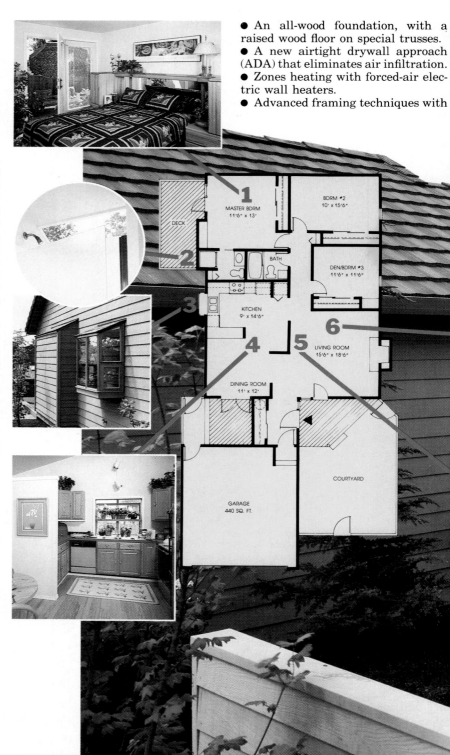

all structural members 24 inches on center (OC), saving 20 percent on lumber costs and creating larger cavities for insulation—for ratings of R-19, R-30, and R-38 in walls, floors, and ceilings, respectively.
● Wide use of oriented-strand board (OSB) sheathing for the walls, floor, and roof deck.
● Showcasing new low-maintenance roofing and siding products.

In conventional building, the roof is often wood shingles over a truss-supported plywood deck. Here, truss-supported panels form the *floor* of the house as well and tie into a permanent wood foundation.

At the opening ceremonies, I asked Rich how many of these innovations he'd retain in future projects.

"I plan to stay with wood foundations and the airtight drywall," Rich told me. "As far as cost effectiveness goes, I think ADA runs about equal to tacking up polyethylene.

"I expect that each time we build an ADA house, installation will go faster. Drywall hangers aren't crazy about the system because they have to use screws rather than nails to keep the panels snug against the gaskets.

"The system does, of course, make for a very tight house, so I include an air-to-air heat exchanger. And the fireplace I installed has its own outside combustion air. I'd say the tightness of our envelope has to be the main contributor to our $5-a-month heating cost."

Another contributor may be less popular with some homeowners—windows have been kept to a minimum. Note on the floor plan that the rear wall is totally blank, and the only windows in the right wall bring a bit of daylight to the two bedrooms. This can help fuel economy if these "blind" sides of the house are sited north or into prevailing winter winds. The other two walls are more open, and skylights are cleverly used.

All-wood foundation, truss-supported floor

Pouring footings for this house was a simple one-day job, and then the foundation went up, despite a spell of nasty weather, in one more day. What speeded the process? Preengineered trusses set on pressure-treated sill plates bolted to the perimeter footings and to a central footing strip down the middle of the floor plan. Because this plan is a simple rectangle, the trusses go up fast—24 inches OC—and are quickly clad in pressure-treated ply (for the foundation walls) and OSB (for the platform floor).

This novel approach, called the Bowen system after the Alaskan company that designed it, creates a raised wood floor with a crawl space beneath—the type of floor most home buyers prefer (over slab-on-grade) for comfort and energy efficiency. A raised wood floor is easier to insulate and loses no heat through direct contact with the ground. The system is manufactured and sold throughout the United States by local roof-truss plants, and can be adapted to more complex floor plans.

This new system is practical because of preservative treatments that make lumber and plywood virtually rot-proof. (Note APA's term: *permanent* wood foundation.) The system also provides the ideal platform for advanced framing techniques, which minimize lumber costs and maximize insulation by using 2 × 6 studs and special roof trusses all set 24 inches OC. Because each structural member sits directly atop the supporting member below (roof truss aligned with stud, aligned with floor truss), expensive "load-transfer" members, such as doubled top plates, built-up headers, and cripple studs, can be omitted.

Most of this foundation will be bu-

ried in backfill, so installation is critical to avoid ground-water leakage. Before the treated plywood is nailed on, beads of waterproof sealant are run along the mud sill and uprights where panels butt.

OSB is an upgraded version of waferboard, where alternating layers of strandlike wafers are laminated at right angles, like the veneer grains in plywood. The long edges are tongue and groove.

Drywall system eliminates vapor barrier

Perhaps the greatest innovation in the *Popular Science* house is one you can't see. When I visited the site during construction, I watched the work crew tapping drywall ceiling panels through gaps between the top plate of the partition-wall framing and the roof truss above. After the panel was in place, they cut a snug hole in it for the plumbing stack, then carefully caulked around the pipe they dropped through.

"The drywall must be continuous in any ADA project," builder Rich ex-

plained. "The trick is to avoid every seam you can—and to seal every penetration."

ADA is the brainchild of Joseph Lstiburek, president of Toronto's Building Engineering Design Corp. "ADA uses gypsum board and various components of the building envelope as the air barrier system," says Lstiburek. "The function is prevention of through-the-envelope air leakage to reduce energy consumption

Drawing at right and these six photos show how the floor is erected on a wood foundation and the Bowen truss system: (1) Concrete is only used for footings, which must be level since preengineered trusses sit atop them. (2) Trusses tip up one by one and are nailed in place top and bottom. (3) Beads of adhesive sealant are run along the footing plate and uprights before preservative-treated plywood is nailed with stainless-steel fasteners. Joints between panels are caulked. (4) OSB subflooring is glued and nailed to the joist chord of each truss. (5) Wood foundation can be installed in wet weather. Here gravel is shoveled atop drain tile. (6) Felt is laid atop gravel so backfilled earth won't filter down.

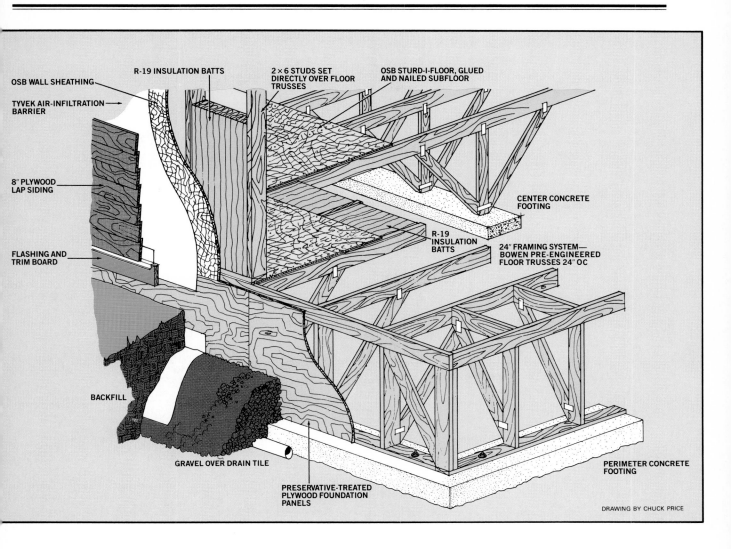

OSB WALL SHEATHING

TYVEK AIR-INFILTRATION BARRIER

R-19 INSULATION BATTS

2 × 6 STUDS SET DIRECTLY OVER FLOOR TRUSSES

OSB STURD-I-FLOOR, GLUED AND NAILED SUBFLOOR

8" PLYWOOD LAP SIDING

CENTER CONCRETE FOOTING

R-19 INSULATION BATTS

24" FRAMING SYSTEM— BOWEN PRE-ENGINEERED FLOOR TRUSSES 24" OC

FLASHING AND TRIM BOARD

BACKFILL

GRAVEL OVER DRAIN TILE

PRESERVATIVE-TREATED PLYWOOD FOUNDATION PANELS

PERIMETER CONCRETE FOOTING

DRAWING BY CHUCK PRICE

and condensation problems. If the movement of moisture-laden air into a wall assembly is eliminated, movement of moisture by vapor diffusion is not likely to be significant."

To prevent air leakage, drywall panels on all walls that face the weather are set against foam gaskets. (Sill plates for these walls are already laid on double beads of caulk.) Gasketing is applied, as well, around every window and door opening. Because the gaskets are compressed, any later shift of the wall just lets them expand to keep all joints sealed. Lstiburek claims that this procedure makes it unnecessary to apply a standard vapor barrier under the drywall as long as you apply several coats of a low-permeability paint. (Some brands, such as Glidden's Insul-Aide, are promoted as vapor-barrier paints.)

There remains some controversy about eliminating a polyethylene vapor barrier, however. Lstiburek makes a distinction between a vapor barrier and an air barrier because any material or system that's used as an air barrier must be continuous. Any seam-gap or void in the material defeats its purpose. Vapor barriers, on the other hand, don't have to stop diffusion completely to be effective.

Lstiburek points out that while sheet polyethylene is a good "vapor diffusion retarder" (a term he prefers to "vapor barrier"), it is a poor air barrier. ADA is an effective air-barrier system but still requires a vapor diffusion retarder, which could be sheet polyethylene or aluminum foil, instead of three coats of low-perm paint.

"I used no polyethylene barrier in this house," Rich told me. "The ADA system is simpler to get right. You avoid having to staple six-mil film to the studs, caulking all overlap joints, and trying to seal the film around punctures for electrical outlets and rough plumbing"—*by Al Lees. Photos by Strode Photographers. Drawings by Chuck Price.*

How to order house plans

You can buy complete construction plans by sending a check to American Plywood Assn., Dept. PS 12/86, Box 11700, Tacoma, WA 98411. Specify *PS*

Energy House and the number of sets wanted: One set is $94; four sets, $150; eight sets, $195. Allow four weeks.

SUPPLIERS' ADDRESSES

The following suppliers were chosen for participation in this project: **Bowen System,** 5520 Lake Otis Pkwy., Anchorage, AK 99507 (floor trusses); **Bruce Hardwood Floors,** 16803 Dallas Pkwy., Dallas, TX 75248 (flooring); **Cochrane Northwest,** 1916 Marc St., Tacoma, WA 98421 (WilsonArt laminate); **Domestic Supply Co.,** 6750 S. 180th St., Seattle, WA 98188 (Merillat cabinets); **Marley Electric Heating Co.,** Orting, WA 98360 (wall heaters); **Monier Roof Tile,** Box 5567, Orange, CA 92667 (concrete roof tile); **Owens-Corning Fiberglas Corp.,** Fiberglas Tower, Toledo, OH 43695 (insulation); **JCPenney Co.,** 1301 Ave. of the Americas, New York, NY 10019 (interior furnishings); **Perma-Door by American Standard,** 9017 Blue Ash Rd., Cincinnati, OH 45242 (entry door); **Preway,** 1430 Second St. N., Wisconsin Rapids, WI 54494 (heat-circulating fireplace); **Quantum Wood Windows,** 2720 34th St., Everett, WA 98201 (windows); **Senco Products,** 8485 Broadwell Rd., Cincinnati, OH 45244 (construction fasteners); **Thermal Efficiency,** Box 1869, Seattle, WA 98111 (air-to-air heat exchanger).

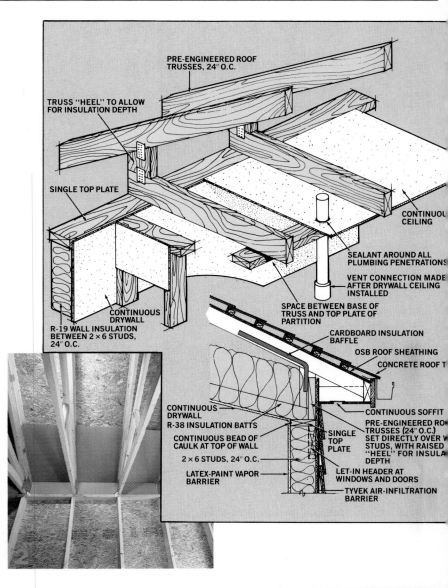

ADA is detailed in drawing above and in photo three. (1) Preassembled gable ends and trusses are lifted onto top plates by crane, then tipped up one by one and nailed. (2) OSB roof and wall sheathing is complete, ready for batt insulation; cardboard baffles will keep the air channel clear from soffit to ridge for attic ventilation. (3) Foam gasketing is applied to the frame of the kitchen greenhouse bay—part of the airtight system; when drywall is screwed onto studs, the gaskets compress. (4) Concrete roof tiles are nailed to the dormer, one nail through a hole provided at top of each tile; note other tiles stacked on the main roof. (5) Lap siding is applied 6 inches to the weather, right over the Tyvek wrap.

new-generation foam homes

I opened my eyes and peered up through triangular skylights into an azure Florida sky. At the zenith of the bedroom a pentagonal cupola formed a loft, and from there white walls curved gracefully down. The paucity of right angles seemed vaguely strange. I had never awakened in a dome before.

This 40-foot-diameter geodesic dome is the office and model of American Ingenuity, Inc., of Melbourne, Florida. It is also home to Michael and Glenda Busick, company president and vice president, who had invited

Previous page: American Ingenuity's geodesic dome is made of polystyrene-foam triangles. The foam is cut in the factory and covered with reinforced concrete. Lower rows of panels can be placed by two or three workers. (A panel weighs between 100 and 345 pounds, depending on dome size.) Upper panels are placed by crane. Framing is temporary shoring: wood 2 × 4s attached to metal hubs. When the dome shell is finished, the framing comes down. Above: Prototype house made using High Tech Homes' technology is also made of polystyrene foam and concrete.

me to spend the night and "experience dome living."

I was intrigued with the geometry of their house and with the materials of which it is made: triangular panels of flame-retardant expanded-polystyrene foam covered on the outside with concrete. The company makes the panels, builds foam domes in the area, and sells dome kits, mostly to owner-builders.

The day before, some 100 miles south in Palm Beach County, I had seen other polystyrene houses, built using a system developed by High Tech Homes, Inc., of Coral Gables, Florida. When finished, these houses are indistinguishable from their neighbors. But see one going up, and you may do a double-take: Walls and roof are stark-white foam blocks, which serve as formwork for sprayed concrete; they stay in place to become the insulation.

Houses built with both of these systems are claimed to have superior fire, termite, and rot resistance and excellent strength, and to require little maintenance. And both produce superinsulated houses that cost no more to build than R-ordinary houses.

After a six-year stint as a fighter pilot in the Air Force, Michael Busick, an electrical engineer, moved to Florida to start an electronics business. His immediate need: a building for his company. "I didn't want to spend $400 a month on air conditioning," he recalled, "so I decided to forget all I knew about buildings and just ask, What is the best way to build?"

His research led him to domes. "A dome has less surface area for a given interior volume than any other shape," Busick noted. "And when you reduce surface area, you reduce heat transfer, keeping heat outside in summer and inside in winter. Also, a dome is inherently strong. So it can be built using fewer materials."

But why foam? "Foam is a beautiful-material to work with," Busick said. "It cuts easily and cleanly, and I believe polystyrene foam is the best insulation on the market for the price."

Busick designed his first dome in 1976. Requests for similar domes put him in the contracting business. "Each time we'd build a dome, we'd try something new," he related. "In the housing industry, most people just keep doing what they've been taught. But I come from the electronics industry, where if you sleep late one morning, your competition is ahead of you."

A few miles from the Busicks' home, two other domes form a double blip on the flat Florida landscape. This is American Ingenuity's factory.

Inside the linked domes I saw stacks of triangular foam panels with beveled edges: building blocks for future domes. Some already were covered in the center with a mesh of galvanized-steel reinforcing topped with a thin cost of special concrete (containing fibers and additives to improve its strength, resiliency, and water resistance, Busick explained).

When the panels are all in place to form a dome, the beveled seams are slathered with concrete, forming ribs three inches thick (see photos). A coat of paint finishes the exterior. "The concrete shell requires no expensive sealing to reduce air infiltration," said Busick. "And it's totally resistant to aluminum-siding salesmen and roofing contractors."

Inside, ½-inch drywall is glued directly to the foam. Cutting drywall into triangles and taping and spackling the seams is a tedious process, Busick admits. "But it's not difficult. And we tell builders how to cut the drywall so there is no waste."

American Ingenuity (3500 Harlock Rd., Melbourne, FL 32935) makes two-story domes in 30-, 34-, 40-, 45-, and 48-foot diameters. The polystyrene panels are available in seven- and nine-inch thicknesses, giving insulation values of R-28 and R-36. Base price for dome kits ranges from $5,920 to $12,995. Door and window dormers, skylights, cupola, and screened porch are extra. Transportation is about $1 a mile.

One owner-builder, Robert Bryan of Palatka, Florida, says his 40-foot dome will cost around $25,000, complete. That does not include any labor cost, however. Bryan, his brother, and his father did all the work.

In east central Florida, American Ingenuity builds the domes for $32–$38 per square foot, turnkey. "And that's what you pay for a conventional house with the same space, the same plumbing, the same carpeting and doorknobs," Busick said. "But you can heat and cool ours for one-third the cost."

The Busicks paid about $110 for air conditioning in 1986; heating (minus some wood they burned in the fireplace) was $5. An efficient groundwater heat pump gets part of the credit for those rock-bottom numbers.

Dome's skin sister

On a corner lot in a section of Palm Beach County known as Wellington sits an L-shaped house with white stucco walls and a red tile roof. Though unremarkable-looking, it is another polystyrene-and-concrete structure, a prototype built by High

Tech Homes, Inc. (2121 Ponce de Leon Blvd., Coral Gables, FL 33134).

Nearby, I saw a second High Tech house under construction. Outside, its gray concrete skin awaited a stucco topping. Inside, the foam walls and roof were still visible. The foam panels are cut in the factory to form channels for sprayed-concrete columns and rafters, I learned from J. Mike Schram, vice president of construction. "The heaviest panel here weighs only sixty pounds," he noted.

On site, pressure-treated 2×4s go up first. "Neither the foam nor the wood is structural," Schram told me. "You could rip out everything but the concrete and still meet all building

codes." The drawing shows how a High Tech Homes house is built.

A few other building systems use foam blocks for walls, though their structures are different. "Some of them have conventional wood-framed roofs—where you most need the extra insulation," Schram pointed out. "And they use sprayed concrete inside as well as out. We use standard drywall inside. That's a lot less expensive."

High Tech Homes' patented building system was inspired by foam houses one of the principals in the firm saw in Europe. Company president Leonard Oboler, an electrical engineer, adapted the technology to meet American building codes.

The company licenses builders to use the system, and licensees can sublicense others. That's how C.K.&W. Construction Co. of West Palm Beach, Florida, got involved. (Coincidentally, Douglas Whalen, vice president of marketing for C.K.&W., bought the High Tech Homes prototype.)

In a pony area across the road from a polo club, I saw C.K.&W.'s first foam project, a condo—for horses. The long building stood glaringly white against a slate-gray sky. The impetus behind building stables of foam was not so much the comfort of the horses as the training of a construction crew.

A few weeks later, C.K.&W. was to begin a 93-unit town-house development using High Tech Homes' foam system. "With it we can use an eight-man crew and build a single-family house, start to finish, in forty-five days—maybe thirty if all goes well," said C.K.&W. president Thomas

DOME FLOOR PLAN

SCREEN DOME
28' × 21'

DINING ROOM
11' × 15'

BEDROOM
10' × 15'

KITCHEN
10' × 12'

SUNKEN LIVING ROOM
14' × 14'

BATH
9' × 10'

UTILITY
10' × 7'

FIREPLACE

SEATING
9' × 9'

BEDROOM
10' × 14'

GARAGE
26' × 26'

ENTRY
9' × 10'

FREEZER

PANTRY

PORCH

FIRST FLOOR

When the dome shell is assembled, the beveled seams of the foam panels are filled with concrete (top left). A double layer of wire mesh reinforces the seams. Screened geodesic porch (top right) covers the patio and a balcony off the second-floor master suite in the Busicks' dome. Floor plan of their first floor is shown above. Both house and garage domes have second floors. The Busicks chose to emphasize the geometry of the dome (right), but because interior walls are non-load-bearing, any arrangement is possible.

Hughes. "At that price, I don't need a construction loan."

Speed also reduces labor costs, but the cost of materials for a foam house is greater than for standard frame or concrete-block construction. Thus, total costs are similar.

Labor and materials for the shell of the High Tech Homes prototype cost $7 per square foot, Schram reported. Whalen paid $110,000 for the completed 2,000-square-foot house, including a large lot, landscaping, and many deluxe features. "That's what conventional houses [which are generally concrete block] cost around here," he said. "And hours has R-50 insulation in the roof and R-42 in the walls." Conventional 2 × 4 frame houses have R-11 walls and R-19 roof; and a block house has about R-3 walls, unless insulation is added.

Is so much insulation important in a climate like South Florida's? "You bet it is," Whalen maintained. "Our electric bills—and that includes hot water as well as air conditioning—were around $100 a month in the summer, about half what we were paying in our previous house. And we're talking two teenage boys here. That's money in the bank"—by *V. Elaine Gilmore. Photos by Greg Sharko. Drawings by Adolph Brotman.*

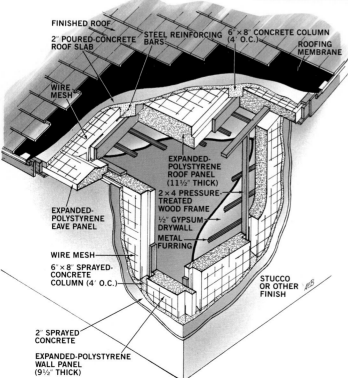

Polystyrene-foam panels (top right) wait to become walls and roof of High Tech Homes' horse stables. Wall panels are 4 by 8 feet by 9 inches thick. Roof panels are 4 by 16 feet by 11½ inches. After foam shell is up and mesh reinforcing placed, a High Tech Homes house is sprayed with concrete (top left). First, channels in the foam are filled to form concrete columns, then walls are sprayed. Concrete for the roof is pumped. Inside the foam shell, metal furring strips run horizontally between 4-foot-OC wood framing (above). Drywall will be attached to the furring. Interior walls are non-load-bearing; here, metal studs will hold drywall partitions.

FINISHED ROOF

STEEL REINFORCING BARS

6" × 8" CONCRETE COLUMN (4' O.C.)

2" POURED-CONCRETE ROOF SLAB

ROOFING MEMBRANE

WIRE MESH

EXPANDED-POLYSTYRENE ROOF PANEL (11½" THICK)

2 × 4 PRESSURE-TREATED WOOD FRAME

½" GYPSUM DRYWALL

METAL FURRING

EXPANDED-POLYSTYRENE EAVE PANEL

WIRE MESH

6" × 8" SPRAYED-CONCRETE COLUMN (4' O.C.)

STUCCO OR OTHER FINISH

2" SPRAYED CONCRETE

EXPANDED-POLYSTYRENE WALL PANEL (9½" THICK)

How it's built: A concrete slab is poured, and pressure-treated 2 × 4s are attached every 4 feet; pressure-treated 2 × 6s at the same spacing frame the roof. Foam panels are placed and braced temporarily. Metal furring strips are attached to the inside of the 2 × 4s tying together the structure. Next, rebars are added to the column and rafter spaces in the foam. (They're tied to lag bolts in the wood framing.) Wiremesh reinforcing is attached to the outside of the foam. Sprayed concrete creates wall columns and skin, which is screeded to a 2-inch thickness. Pumped concrete forms roof rafters and deck, also screeded to a 2-inch thickness. Exterior walls are generally faced with stucco. Roof is covered with shingles or tiles. Drywall finishes the interior.

a skylight for all seasons

Tube-shaped skylights are aligned from east to west. Between them, motors are hidden in "mechanical penthouses."

The clock strikes midnight, and the new year begins—January 1, 2000. Inside an enormous house in the woods of northern Virginia, seven 16-foot-long barrel-vaulted skylights are hidden behind movable insulated panels. At night the panels seal off plastic-glazed housings that are exposed to the cold winter sky.

The hours speed by. It's 1 A.M., 2 A.M., 3 A.M. Finally, it's daybreak. In unison, the panels concealing the skylights open by a crack, slowly spilling cold air into the house. After 15 minutes they quietly rotate up into the skylight bays, where they face the northern sky. Direct sunlight beams into the house from the south and helps heat it throughout the day, while the insulated panels reduce heat loss from the skylights' colder northern side. The clock races onward, and night falls. Like giant eyelids heavy with sleep, the skylights' panels slowly rotate down until they're closed.

I'm standing in an upstairs hall-way, facing the computer that directs the movements of these special skylights, called Roto-Lids. The date and time are displayed on the computer monitor. But according to my 1987 wristwatch, the first day of the year 2000 lasted only two minutes. That's because I'm watching a computer program that compresses time to simulate the operation of the Roto-Lids during a variety of daily and seasonal conditions. August 16, 2000, for example, is an extremely hot day. The skylight bays overheat, and an emergency exhaust system automatically expels hot air.

The purpose of any skylight is to bring daylight into a building, and most skylights perform that task adequately. Unfortunately they also lose heat on cold winter nights and gain heat on hot summer days, so they may waste energy and make a house uncomfortable. The Roto-Lid is far more sophisticated than most skylights because it's designed to optimize both lighting and heating. It does so using a computer system that collects information about temperature and light levels outside the house, then automatically adjusts the positions of insulated panels inside the skylight housings. Left to its own devices the computerized system will operate the Roto-Lids until the year 2000—and beyond. If necessary, the computer program can be tailored to suit individual tastes, or the Roto-Lids can be operated in a manual mode.

The nerve center of the Roto-Lid system is an IBM PC-compatible computer. It's wired to a light sensor and thermistors, which measure ambient air temperature, on the outside of the house. The information from these sensors passes through analog-to-digital boards that convert it into data the computer can understand.

The computer also receives information from potentiometers installed in the ends of the skylights. These tell the computer the angle of the lids. "They're the computer's eyes," says Dixon Cleveland, vice president of

Inside the Roto-Lid system

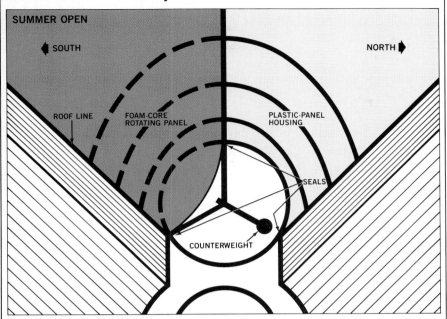

SUMMER OPEN

◀ SOUTH   NORTH ▶

ROOF LINE   FOAM-CORE ROTATING PANEL   PLASTIC-PANEL HOUSING

SEALS

COUNTERWEIGHT

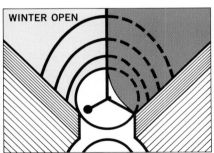

WINTER OPEN

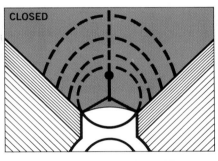

CLOSED

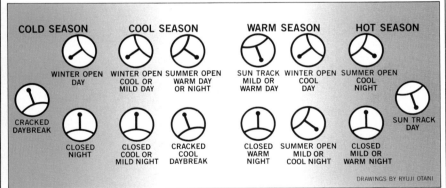

| COLD SEASON | COOL SEASON | | WARM SEASON | | HOT SEASON |

WINTER OPEN DAY — WINTER OPEN COOL OR MILD DAY — SUMMER OPEN WARM DAY OR NIGHT — SUN TRACK MILD OR WARM DAY — WINTER OPEN COOL DAY — SUMMER OPEN COOL NIGHT

CRACKED DAYBREAK — CLOSED NIGHT — CLOSED COOL OR MILD NIGHT — CRACKED COOL DAYBREAK — CLOSED WARM NIGHT — SUMMER OPEN MILD OR COOL NIGHT — CLOSED MILD OR WARM NIGHT — SUN TRACK DAY

DRAWINGS BY RYUJI OTANI

In its automatic mode the computer's strategy (drawings above) divides the year into six two-month seasons, beginning with December 15: cold, cool, warm, hot, warm, and cool. Throughout each day it determines whether the outside temperature is cool (under 65° F), warm (more than 80° F), or mild (somewhere in between). It also decides whether it is day or night—based on whether the light level is above or below a programmed threshold. Then the computer elects a lid position.

For example, the "summer open" position (top) blocks solar gain from the south but lets in diffuse northern light. The "winter open" setting (middle left) lets in direct light from the south to heat the house. When closed (middle right), the panel meets the house's roof line, isolating cold air in the bay. On very hot days the curved lid tracks the sun to prevent any direct light from entering, even when the sun is overhead. Astronomical equations used for sun tracking are stored in the computer.

Light and temperature parameters can be edited at any time. For example, a homeowner who prefers to have his Roto-Lids close late in the evening and open at the first hint of sunrise selects a low light threshold.

LCTechnologies. He and his brother, Hunt, wrote the program for the computer control system.

After gathering all this information, the computer chooses an optimal lid position and activates $1/80$-horsepower motors. "The reason the motors can be so small is that the panels are balanced by counterweights," explains Jim Adamson, the inventor of the Roto-Lid and a partner in Jersey Devil, the architectural group that designed and built the skylight-capped house.

"Normally, the skylights are closed at night," Adamson tells me. "But if the owners want to look at the stars, they can switch to the system's manual mode." They can also use the manual controls for demonstrations.

"Go ahead, try moving a lid," Cleveland encourages me. I lean over the keyboard and move a cursor on the screen to a box that says COMMAND ANGLE. Then I type in an angle for lid number five—350 degrees. I hit a key, and the lid above me begins rotating to a new position. Its six companions don't budge.

In the automatic mode, the computer uses a command strategy programmed into the system (see drawings) to determine the best position for the lids, depending on outdoor light and temperature levels. Fans turn on if the temperature inside the skylight bays reaches 160°F.

Adamson got the idea for the Roto-Lid while Jersey Devil was drawing up plans for a solar-powered warehouse. "The problem was finding a thermally efficient source of year-round lighting," he recalls. He obtained funds from the Department of Energy's Appropriate Technology Small Grants Program and built a prototype. The movable panel he invented forms seals in three positions—where the edges of the lid make contact with the structure of the skylight's housing.

Adamson doesn't expect his design to be used in many homes. "In a house, you don't have a problem with daylighting," he says, "so a skylight this size is a luxury." The mechanical and electronic equipment needed to drive the foam-core lids is expensive, so it's best suited to a large-scale application, Adamson says. He envisions using the Roto-Lid to light warehouses and malls. "I've always thought of it as an industrial skylight," he explains. "It could easily be sixty feet long." And Cleveland claims the computer program that now controls seven lids could easily handle 100 more—*by Dawn Stover. Photos by Kenneth Wyner.*

diy-er's guide to the "handyman special"

If you've been shopping for a home lately, you have probably found that well-kept, nicely located places are priced out of this world. Even the slightly worse-for-wear places seem too high. In many communities it seems to be a seller's market. Interest rates are uncertain. Realtors and lenders are aggressive.

And if you find that great place and dally for a few days adapting to the price shock and trying to figure how you will ever be able to afford it, the property will most likely be gone. Probably snapped up by folks who figure they'd better bite the bullet because prices will be even higher later on. If history is a guide, they may well be right.

But rather than buy that creampuff at a seemingly premium price some do-it-yourselfers will diligently poke around and wheel and deal until they find a more attractively priced home that indeed requires some fixing up. Enter the "handyman special." Some people will buy them for a song and end up with a superb home worth a lot more than they put into the place. Some will plunge into a renovation project, become discouraged, and never quite pull it off. And others will plainly lose their shirts. While they may end up with a nice place, they will have poured more into it in cash and sweat than it will ever be worth, even at today's prices.

Those who do well will probably have done so because they bought right, planned well, and were willing and able to work long, hard hours.

The opportunities

Suppose you buy your handyman special in an affluent suburb. Though $80,000 may seem like a lot to some people, you know that it's dirt cheap for a house in this locale. You put another $40,000 into it in materials and in labor you can't perform yourself, plus a good deal of your own time and effort. What you end up with is a house worth $165,000 in this upscale neighborhood—or $45,000 more than you put into it. But there's more to it than that.

Suppose now that you had borrowed that extra $45,000 and bought a $165,000 house to begin with. Depending on interest rate and life of the mortgage, what you would actually pay off on that $45,000 would be closer to *$90,000.* To have $90,000 net after federal, state, and local taxes, you'd have to gross something on the order of $175,000. If your actual gross salary is $40,000 per year, the DIY time

and effort you've spent has accomplished the same result as nearly *4 1/2 years* of work on your regular job!

The competition

Perhaps many people don't consider the fact there can be value to DIY effort beyond the actual time spent, as described above. But don't kid yourself into thinking you're the only one who ever thought of getting a bargain on a rundown property and fixing it up. There will be other DIYers looking at the same properties as you are. And in practically every community there will be at least a few people making a good living by *speculating*—searching out these diamonds in the rough, buying them, then quickly fixing them up and reselling them.

You can learn some lessons from the people who do this for a living. First off, they look for location, location, location. Through experience and doing their homework they will seem to know almost instinctively about how much it will cost them to fix up the place as soon as they inspect it, so they will know about how much they can pay and still turn a profit. And they are always on the lookout for things they know make a home more appealing, and hence ultimately worth more. Perhaps the three most basic considerations are the arrangement of the rooms, particularly the kitchen; the appeal of the bathroom; and the amount of closet and storage space.

The ground rules

The assumption is that you are looking for a way to get more home for less, and that you are willing to work hard to accomplish that goal. The home you choose may be old or relatively new. The common thread is that even though it is in a neighborhood you'd be happy to live in, the home has been neglected for one reason or another, and your opportunity lies in making it into something substantially better than it is by investing a reasonable amount of time and money.

While the principles described here are valid for adding rooms and garages, and making improvements such as fireplaces and swimming pools, they should be evaluated separately from strictly rehab projects. That's because many of these luxury items won't add as much to the value of the home as they cost—even if you do the work yourself. When evaluating a property, however, it's wise to deter-

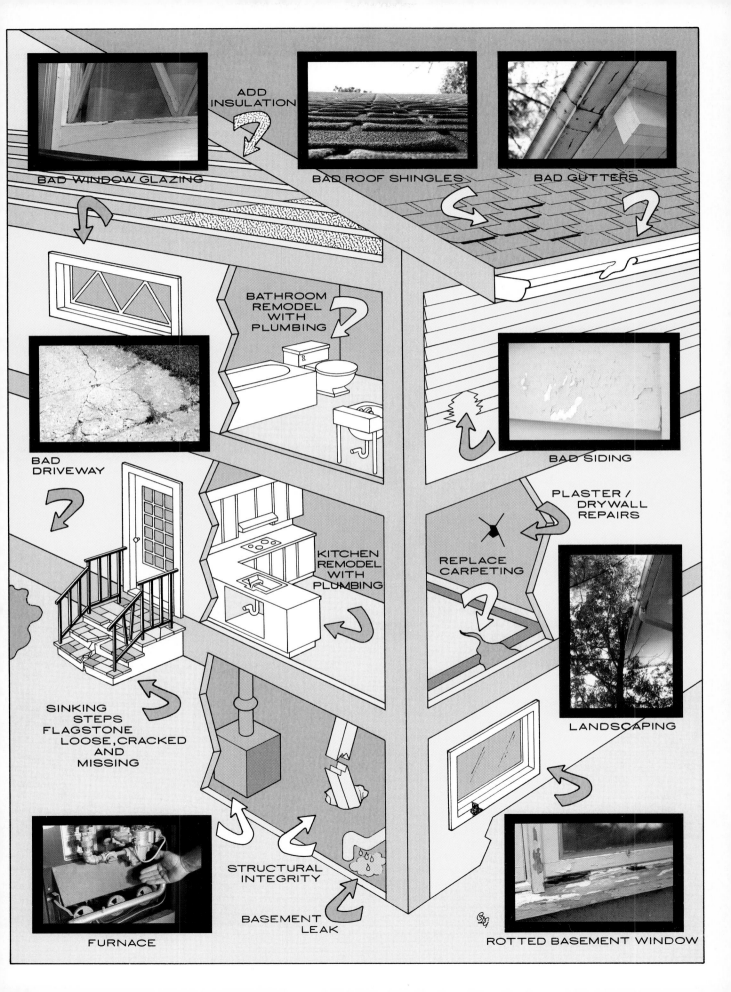

mine whether it is structurally sound and suitable for addition at some future date. If you are in doubt, hire an experienced builder to give you an opinion.

Finding the money, and other pitfalls

The pitfalls of investing in a handyman special include taking on more work than you can handle, overestimating your DIY skill level, inability to handle the finances, underestimating the costs involved, and overestimating the value of the renovated home. Financing a fix-up property may present some special problems, particularly if you need financing immediately for the purchase of the property and then need to finance the improvements a little later on.

As soon as you decide you want to pursue the DIY home-buying route, start talking to lenders about what you have in mind. Prepare a little plan that describes the price range of property you are looking for, a ballpark estimate of what you'll need to finance, and how much you think you'll need to pay for material and for contract work to improve the property.

You may find lenders ready and willing to suggest creative ways to handle your particular financing needs. But keep in mind that to qualify, your monthly mortgage and tax payments *cannot exceed 33 percent of your monthly gross income.* Some people try to get around this by overstating their incomes and "making themselves look good on paper." More often than not, these people are biting off far more than they can chew—particularly with adjustable-rate mortgages, should the interest rate rise faster than their salaries. Again, know ahead of time whether you can swing a property financially.

Where to find them

The perfect fix-up home opportunity is not likely to come up and hit you in the face. Be prepared to explore dozens of candidates to find the right one for you. The harder you look, the more likely you are to find it.

Pick a realtor you trust and feel comfortable working with. Share in detail with the realtor what you are looking for, the kind of spread between cost and ultimate value you can handle, and the kind of a contribution you are willing to make to take the place from as-is to dream-home status.

Search the ads. Look for clues such as "needs work," "must sell to liquidate estate," "handyman special," "older home in a nice neighborhood," and the like. Also look for prices that appear to be lower than you would expect for the neighborhood. Advertisements published by government guarantee agencies announcing sales of repossessed homes are also worth investigating. So are sheriff's tax-sale announcements.

Call several lenders in your area. They may be aware of repossessions that would interest you. And don't hesitate to spend the $100 to $500 it may cost to get a value appraisal on an interesting home *before* you lay down serious money.

Estimating rehab costs

When you find a property that looks promising enough for you to consider making an offer, thoroughly inspect it and make a list of *everything* that needs to be fixed. The finer the detail, the more accurate your estimate will be. Then prepare an estimate sheet for each item on your list that ends up summarizing material costs, DIY labor hours, and contactor fees, if any, envisioned for each task.

Material costs are relatively easy to determine. For example, a phone call to a building supply store explaining

Shingles that are swollen, cracked, or broken signal need for roof replacement. Material for DIY job $500–$800.

Rusting or leaking rain-gutter systems should be replaced to bring the home up to par. Material for minor repairs $10–$50; for replacement $250–$500.

Siding may only need repainting, but be sure to check for deterioration that could require replacement. DIY minor repairs $50–$100; complete siding replacement, materials and paint $1,000–$1,600.

Reglazing is easy, but it may be wise to replace windows if they are deteriorating, to save energy and to improve appearance. About $10 for reglazing; replacement double-hung window units $30–$150 each and up, depending on the size.

Examine all wood for rotting and possible insect damage. Areas such as basement windows are particularly vulnerable. Single-sash windows $30–$80 each.

that you need shingles, building paper, and nails to do a roof of so many square feet will get you a quick price. The same is true for carpets, paint, cabinets, sod, and windows. And don't forget to mention that you'll be handling the work yourself; you could get contractor discounts of up to 15 percent or so. You'll find materials estimates for some common DIY jobs within the photo captions. Costs represent those for a typical gable-roofed, 1,200-square-foot ranch with attached two-car garage.

If you've done some DIY work before, you probably have a pretty good idea of how long it will take to do many of the projects. Ask friends who may have taken on projects you have yet to encounter. Many home centers can also be helpful in telling you about how long it should take to perform a particular task.

If you explain truthfully to a contractor what you are planning, most will be happy to give you a ballpark estimate on the phone, which should be accurate enough for planning purposes. In fairness to the contractor, you should promise to include him as a bidder should you later need the work done.

By totaling up the sheets you should have an excellent plan, and a very good idea of what it will cost you to accomplish the job in both money and time. Don't forget to account for the travelling time, which could be significant if the place is a long way from where you now live.

If you're not sure about what needs to be fixed or replaced, don't hesitate to hire a qualified house inspector to evaluate the place for you. The cost will easily be offset by the trouble you'll avoid down the line.

By being that thorough, you may loose a property. So be it. There will be another, better one—even in today's real-estate rat race.

How much can you handle?

When you make up the task list for estimating purposes, be honest. Try to evaluate as accurately as possible your ability to handle each one. If there are aspects of the work you can't handle for health reasons, lack of time or skill, or maybe because you just don't have the necessary tools or equipment, put them in the "contract out" column right now. It is much better to recognize this up front so you can plan on the higher cost contracting out will likely entail.

The accompanying box rates the difficulty of common DIY home improvement tasks.

There may be jobs you would like to do, but can't because of local building codes. Rewiring, for example, requires a license in many areas, though in some communities you may be allowed to wire your home if you pass a competency test. If you recognize a weakness in a certain skill, consider signing up for a short course at a local vocational school. And if you don't have the tools, consider renting them for a particular project—but don't forget to add the rental cost to the estimate.

Are you psyched?

Depending on how much renovation your future dream home needs, the commitment can be substantial.

Now that you have a good idea of the time involved, you need to estimate how you want to spread it out. If it works

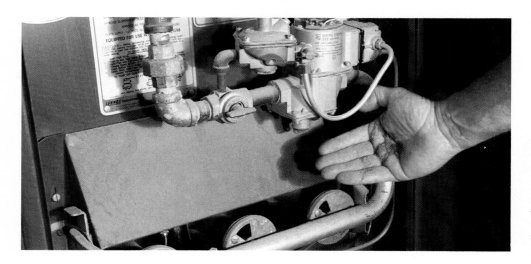

Determine the age of the heating, cooling, and water heating systems. Accumulations of dust, rust, and evidence of leaks may indicate a need to replace the furnace. DIY replacement $800–$1,500; professionally installed, $1,000–$2,200.

Codes, Permits, and Certificates of Occupancy

Building codes and the associated permits are meant to insure durable and effective building practices. Be it a city, village, township or county, some governing body will likely require you to get permits to do many of the things involved in fixing up a home. And of course the work you do must comply with the codes they specify. After the work is completed, an inspection will be required before the job is approved (and in some cases there are in-process inspections, too).

If you contact some of the work, such as plumbing or electrical work, your contractor is generally expected to apply for the necessary permits and subsequently arrange for inspections. Failure to get a permit and carry through the procedure to completion can result in fines and serious delays.

Basically what the building people want to know is what you are going to do, along with a reasonable estimate of what it will cost, since in most cases the permit fee is based on the cost of the project. Some people try and low-ball the cost to pay less for the permit or avoid an increase in their property taxes. Whatever the case, the building people are usually wise to this, so the best advise is to play it straight.

Before you start the project, list the various tasks you intend to do, the basic specifications—such as the type of roofing you intend to apply—and estimate the cost of each task. You won't need professional drawings, but the building officials will want fairly well scaled sketches of projects that can't be understood from descriptions. The building department should be able to give you copies of the codes or at least tell you where to get what you need. They will also spell out what inspections are required.

Now comes the important part, a document generally called a "certificate of occupancy." It certifies that it is okay to occupy the home after the permit work is complete or perhaps partially complete. This is particularly important because you will likely want to move into your project home as soon as possible. Typically the things that would prevent you from moving in if undone include wiring problems, plumbing fixtures not installed or sewer connections not capped off, and the bathrooms not enclosed from the rest of the home.

In some states or communities you'll also have to have an inspection to make sure the home meets code as the property changes hands. If it does, you will get a certificate of occupancy. Where this is a requirement, lenders will probably insist on it before they put through a loan. Be sure to check this out early on with the realtor, the lender, and the community government. Even where their is no such regulation, a lender may require his own inspection.

Shrubs and trees that have grown too close through neglect offer a quick and easy shot at making the place look better by pruning or removal and replacement. $0–$100 for pruning and minor reseeding; $500–$1,500 for major replanting, sodding, and curbing.

Depending on how bad the deterioration, driveways can be resurfaced with asphalt or may require removal and replacement. $1 per square foot for DIY materials; contractor cost to remove and replace driveway, $2–$5 per square foot.

Renovating Jobs— Arranged According To Difficulty

EASY

Insulation	Painting
Wallpapering	Landscaping
Electric fixture replacement	Concrete/asphalt repairs
Carpet cleaning	Floor refinishing
Basement leak repairs	Drywall/plaster patching
Window reglazing	

MODERATE

Interior trim work	Tile replacement
Gutter replacement	Cabinet replacement
Siding replacement	Countertop replacement
Installing windows	Hanging doors

DIFFICULT

Drywall hanging and taping	Trim and soffit work
*Rewiring	Carpet laying
*Plumbing	*Heating/A.C. replacement
Roof replacement	Concrete/asphalt replacement

Codes may require licensed installer to do work.

Dealing With Contractors

There may be home renovation tasks you can't do, or situations where your limited time might be better spent elsewhere. Examples might be plumbing, heating, rewiring, concrete work, or replacing shingles on a very steep roof. Contractors therefore can become vital. A call to your local home builder's association should help you find contractors for specific jobs. It is normal to ask a contractor for work and financial references. When possible, get at least three or more bids.

Once you have selected a contractor you feel is most likely to do the best job for you, draw up a written proposal to provide a clear understanding of what is expected, including a specific list of the work to be done, the time schedule, and payment terms. Keep in mind that it is not unusual for a contractor to ask for progress payments, nor is it normally out of line to make it clear that you will withold 5 percent of the money to be sure the job is completed to your liking. You may also want to ask for a year's warranty on materials and workmanship. And be sure it is understood who does or pays for the cleanup.

To protect yourself, consider these safeguards:
● Don't pay in advance.
● Don't pay the contractor's supplier directly for material. Pay only the contractor with whom you have a contract.
● If a progress payment is for material, ask for an itemized invoice. And make sure the supplies are physically on your property and checked for completeness.
● Review with your attorney the possible need for a *lien waver,* which may be necessary to protect you from a supplier to the contractor seeking payment for materials that have not been paid for.
● Ask the contractor to save labels, model numbers, warranties, instructions, etc., for all products that go into your job so you will have them for future reference.

And always keep in mind that a contract involves two parties. So be prepared to work together. Review progress regularly, daily if necessary. Delays may crop up. Unexpected problems may surface. The better the relationship you have with the contractor, the better will be your chances of working things out satisfactorily.

out to 500 hours, are you are willing to force yourself into working 25 hours a week for 20 weeks to do it? Or if you estimate 1,000 hours of work and you are only willing to spend 10 hours a week, can you (and your family) put up with an unfinished project for two years?

Ask yourself hard questions about what happens if you can't finish the job. Do you have a tendency to not finish tasks? Are you facing a divorce, a possible job layoff, a serious illness, or perhaps a transfer?

How are you at handling stress? There can be a lot when things don't go right—and almost certainly some things won't.

How are you at financial management? You'll probably be handling a lot of money. You'll also be handling all the supplies, coordinating delivery dates, and dealing with the supplies themselves. If you have trouble in these areas, now is the time to take that into consideration.

On the positive side, a major project like this can also alleviate day-to-day tensions as it brings you and your family together toward a common goal: a house everyone will enjoy living in, and showing off.

Taking the plunge

Once you've defined the commitment you'll be facing—as well as the risks involved—you can go to your trusted realtor or appraiser and say, "Here is what it will cost to buy the place. Here is what I want to do with it. Now tell me, what will my home be worth when I've finished?" As a cross-check on the appraisal, remember that the value of a home is determined primarily by the neighborhood. Find out what similar homes in top-notch condition have sold for recently.

If initial cost plus the cash you estimate it will take for the transformation is less than the estimated final value, and the difference divided by your labor hours gives you a reasonable hourly pay for your time, you may want to take the plunge. If home prices continue to escalate, your DIY efforts could be even more rewarding over the years—*by Phil McCafferty. Drawing by Carl De Groote.*

two ways to raise the roof

raise high the ranch roof

I can't believe you did that," crackled the disembodied voice above. It had come from the general direction of the lone TV cameraman thrust up between the denuded rafters of the ranch house. I'd driven to the Boston suburb of Reading, Massachusetts, (eighteen months before today's return visit) to observe a taping of an early sequence for a new season of the Public Broadcasting System's how-to series *This Old House*—and to check out this project for my own *Popular Science* Room at the Top series.

Room is certainly what they were creating up there, as I watched from the front lawn with nervous homeowner Mary Jane Fernino. The broadcast comment we'd just heard was directed at TV host Bob Vila, who had just helped Mary Jane's husband toss a big section of old roof deck off the eaves for the cameraman. A strip of still-attached shingles had acted as a hinge, sending the scrap mass crashing against the picture window below.

"Oh, well," Mary Jane muttered stoically, "we were going to replace that window anyway." Seeing that they were taking a break up top to assess damage, she and I moved in to drag the debris off her protesting shrubbery and carry it to a waiting dumpster.

The electronically amplified voice we'd just heard was that of producer-director Russ Morash, whom I had already visited around back in his makeshift studio tucked into a basement workshop (lined, I'd noted, with shelves of back issues of *Popular Sci-*

ence). The small, expert crew that creates this show does all its recording at each successive remodeling site, huddled in some dark, quiet corner around a TV monitor and com-

BEFORE

BEFORE

Owner Mary Jane Fernino stands at the head of her new stairs. Behind her is the second-story sunspace projecting from the upper hall (partially hidden by bedroom deck in top photo). "Before" and "after" photos at left show how the added story boosts the house's curb appeal. The old roof to the left of the chimney was stripped off, and the chimney was extended past the new ridge.

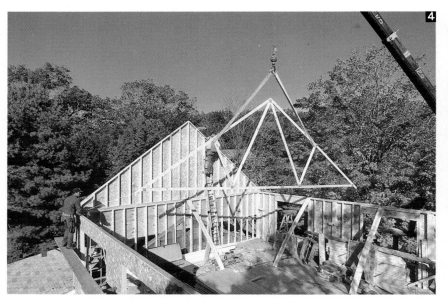

(1) Shingled roof deck is pried up in sections after being cut with a circular saw. (2) With ridge and rafters removed, the attic joists are covered with a tarp to prevent weather damage before the new floor is laid. (3) Preassembled gable end is lowered onto new wall framing and held in place with braces, as are the walls. Note garage at old roof height.

(4) One by one, new trusses are dropped in place by a crane and spiked to top plates of the new walls. Once the connecting ridge board is in place, a new roof deck will be applied. (5) Norm Abram staples shingles over Deck-Dri.

municating with the "performers" and cameraman elsewhere on the project via remote hookups. Each performer wears a concealed microphone to pick up his comments for the tape. All the action being shot would be edited later into a smooth compression. Obviously, the "I can't believe you did that"—and the goof that prompted it—would be cut before this segment was aired.

As we walked back from the dumpster, Mary Jane shook her head in continuing disbelief at the spectacle of her home being torn apart. "It's been inadequate for us since our

daughter started school," she told me. "But we love the neighborhood and the pool out back—so we didn't want to move. Of course, the pool's being there meant we couldn't expand *back,* and the house is already at allowable distances from our *side* lot lines, so we concluded that the only way to go was *up.* Every time we watched them creating new living space on *This Old House,* my husband and I would look at each other and moan 'We need you, Norm!'"

Her reference was to the show's star carpenter, Norm Abram, who was above us now, slicing through an-

other section of shingled roof deck so his helpers could sledge and pry it loose to toss onto the shrubbery. Mary Jane shaded her eyes, gazing upward: "And there at last Norm really is—on *my* roof!" She shook her head again and beamed me her megawatt smile: "And as a bonus, *Popular Science* is helping fill our dumpster. With such an auspicious start, this project is bound to turn out right!"

Now, a year and a half later, I'm back to check. The TV exposure (which had come in response to Mary Jane's letter to the show, but which treated only the first phase of this

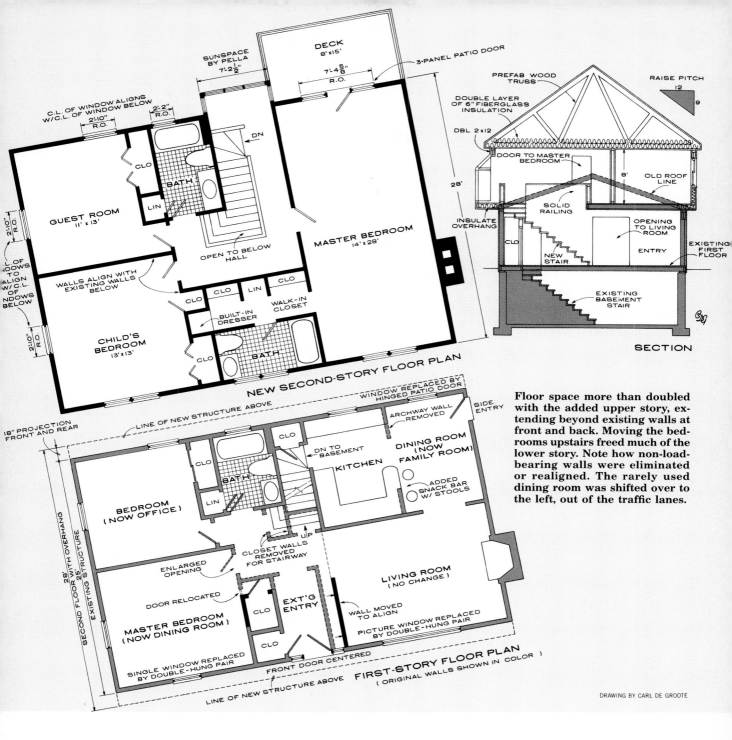

NEW SECOND-STORY FLOOR PLAN

SUNSPACE BY PELLA 7'-2½" R.O.

DECK 8'×15'

7'-4⅝" R.O.

3-PANEL PATIO DOOR

C.L. OF WINDOW ALIGNS W/C.L. OF WINDOW BELOW
2'-10" R.O.
2'-2" R.O.

CLO

BATH

LIN

GUEST ROOM 11'×13'

C.L. OF WINDOWS TO ALIGN W/C.L. OF WINDOWS BELOW

2'-10" R.O.

DN

OPEN TO BELOW HALL

MASTER BEDROOM 14'×28'

WALLS ALIGN WITH EXISTING WALLS BELOW

CLO
CLO
LIN
CLO

BUILT-IN DRESSER
WALK-IN CLOSET

CHILD'S BEDROOM 13'×13'

CLO
CLO

BATH

2'-10" R.O.

SECTION

PREFAB WOOD TRUSS

RAISE PITCH
12
9

DOUBLE LAYER OF 6" FIBERGLASS INSULATION

DBL 2×12

DOOR TO MASTER BEDROOM

8'

OLD ROOF LINE

SOLID RAILING

OPENING TO LIVING ROOM

INSULATE OVERHANG

CLO

NEW STAIR

ENTRY

EXISTING FIRST FLOOR

EXISTING BASEMENT STAIR

28'

FIRST-STORY FLOOR PLAN
(ORIGINAL WALLS SHOWN IN COLOR)

LINE OF NEW STRUCTURE ABOVE

WINDOW REPLACED BY HINGED PATIO DOOR

SIDE ENTRY

18" PROJECTION FRONT AND REAR

CLO
CLO

ARCHWAY WALL REMOVED

DN TO BASEMENT

KITCHEN

DINING ROOM (NOW FAMILY ROOM)

BATH

LIN

ADDED SNACK BAR W/ STOOLS

BEDROOM (NOW OFFICE)

28' SECOND FLOOR WITH OVERHANG
25' EXISTING STRUCTURE

UP

CLOSET WALLS REMOVED FOR STAIRWAY

ENLARGED OPENING

DOOR RELOCATED

MASTER BEDROOM (NOW DINING ROOM)

CLO

EXT'G ENTRY

CLO

LIVING ROOM (NO CHANGE)

WALL MOVED TO ALIGN

PICTURE WINDOW REPLACED BY DOUBLE-HUNG PAIR

SINGLE WINDOW REPLACED BY DOUBLE-HUNG PAIR

FRONT DOOR CENTERED

LINE OF NEW STRUCTURE ABOVE

DRAWING BY CARL DE GROOTE

Floor space more than doubled with the added upper story, extending beyond existing walls at front and back. Moving the bedrooms upstairs freed much of the lower story. Note how non-load-bearing walls were eliminated or realigned. The rarely used dining room was shifted over to the left, out of the traffic lanes.

---

massive remodeling) is now a dimming memory. But Mary Jane's prediction was on target: The house has been transformed from a cramped suburban ranch with mismatched windows (see "before" insets on opening pages) into a gracious two-story house that now boasts real architectural distinction.

The Ferninos have been fortunate enough to get Abram back, between taping commitments, to help them with later phases of their remodeling. The interior of the first floor now bears little resemblance to what I'd seen on my earlier visit. As the floor

plan above indicates, walls have been shifted or removed and doorways widened. Both bedrooms have been moved upstairs and replaced by a home office and formal dining room. The kitchen has been opened to the old dining room, which is now an activity area where the family gathers during meal preparation. This new family room is separated from the kitchen only by a peninsula snack counter, and now sports direct access to the patio (where most summer dining takes place). Abram has returned to replace a back window with a hinged patio door.

To bring harmony to the front of the house, the windows of both downstairs rooms have been replaced to match the new upstairs windows. The entry door has been shifted to the right, to center on the window above it. These changes involved more than cosmetic improvement, because the living room's old single-glazed picture window was an energy waster and robbed the house of privacy from the street.

"The surprising thing," Mary Jane tells me as we climb the new stairs, "is that all this extra space didn't cost us a penny extra in heating costs last winter. All the new windows are double-glazed, of course—and we put twelve inches of Owens-Corning Fiberglas insulation in the new attic. We also resided the whole house in vinyl, weatherstripping and caulking as we went. That tightened it up a lot."

And the Ferninos need never worry about the ice damage that can plague houses in the Boston area. Along the eaves of the new roof deck and on up two feet beyond the new wall line, Abram applied a self-adhesive membrane strip from Owens-Corning Fiberglas Corp. (see photo). Called Deck-Dri, it's an asphalt sheet surfaced with polyethylene film that seals the deck from penetration by melting snow. Deck-Dri is also a vapor barrier, so it should only be used over vented spaces such as these soffit-vented eaves.

The space upstairs is impressive. You're welcomed at the head of the stairs by a delightful sunspace bay from Pella Windows & Doors that offers an embracing view of the pool and wooded backyard. Mary Jane takes her morning coffee here after getting her daughter off to school, and it's a cozy nook to settle into for some reading or sewing.

Next door, the new master bedroom is a luxurious 28-foot "floor through" with a three-panel patio door in the rear wall for access to the private deck. And private it is—a lofty retreat raised above the cares of the day, ideal for a cocktail chat while the children grab a final swim as the sun sets on a summer evening.

Near the other end of the long room, a walk-in wardrobe closet leads to a sybaritic master bath with—of course—a whirlpool tub. The original design placed this bathroom in a back corner of the house, but the plumber pointed out that all utility runs from the basement (supply and drain pipes) could go up through the smaller closet by the front entry. So the floor-plan switch made good economic sense.

The two other major gains upstairs are yet another bath—directly above the existing downstairs bath—and a badly needed guest room. The child's bedroom, too, is more spacious than the old one below.

But is this type of upward expansion practical for most small houses? After all, you're stacking up a lot of extra weight—will existing walls and foundations carry the load? In a well-built house with an excavated basement, there should be no problem—as long as the added story is carefully designed to distribute its weight onto load-bearing walls. Such houses are characteristically overbuilt for single-story structures.

If you have any doubts about the stability of your house's foundation, have it checked by a structural engineer. If you commission an architect to design your addition, checking out the structural feasibility will be part of his or her responsibility.

As we descend, Mary Jane displays special pride in the enlarged entry hall. "We did all this tiling ourselves," she points out. Those back issues of *Popular Science* in the basement are obviously not just for show. The Ferninos worked alongside the TV crew during the shooting and have continued to do much of the work on later phases of the job.

All told, the remodeling—which cost less than $50,000 because of the sweat equity—has added at least twice that amount in value.

But it's taken a year and a half's disruption. For all these benefits—twice the space, with no increase in heating and cooling costs—would the Ferninos go through it all again? "Never—unless we had Norm again," Mary Jane says firmly. "But it has let us stay where we want to live"—*by Al Lees. Photos by Michael Lutch. Drawing by Carl De Groote.*

vaulted showplace

Standing at the bottom of my attic stairs in the living room, I look up. All I see is blue sky—I've just finished ripping the roof off my small house. I hope clear sky is all I'll see for at least five days. Please, no rain till I get my roof back on. Now I know how Noah must have felt as he labored on his Ark, anticipating the Deluge.

A few years ago, my wife, Marion, and I bought a two-bedroom ranch with an eye to doing something with it in the future. The future came fast. Our son was born soon afterward, and we found ourselves in the same boat many Americans are in: We were cramped for space but didn't want to move. (A recent National Assn. of Home Builders report states that the number-one remodeling job has been room additions, indicating that the add-on-rather-than-move-out trend is in full force.)

To ease the crunch, we decided to build an upper floor, almost doubling our living space. Our design is applicable to any ranch-style house (see drawing). Going up instead of out to gain more room can be a sensible way to go for many homeowners. It can be cheaper than excavating to extend a foundation. Zoning restrictions or small lot size might even preclude outward expansion. Hooking up with utilities is easier when you stack-build. Splicing into your heating system is more convenient; in fact you usually don't have to upgrade your heating plant when you extend upward and have an open floor plan. And you can radically change the look of your house in the bargain. Our decision was based on solving a number of problems with one stroke:

● Space was tight, but so was money. I wanted to do most of the work to save labor costs, and I didn't want to tackle foundation work.

● In an apparent siting error, the living room faces north. Because it got no direct light, it always seemed dark and dreary. Removing the living-room ceiling and putting skylights on the south side of the roof would provide natural lighting.

● We wanted a second bath, but doing anything but hooking up to existing plumbing runs would have been prohibitive.

● We wanted more entertainment space, and hanging a second-level cantilevered deck off a family den would provide it—with interest.

● Existing head room in the attic was useless, so putting on a new, higher, roof would make the *entire* second-story floor space usable. (Most attic renovations make use of only a portion of the floor space.)

Original ranch (below) had an offset gable incorrectly spliced into the roof—it was beginning to sag. The renovated house has cleaner, more modern lines (right and above); the cantilevered balcony and asymmetrical roof provide architectural interest. Poor siting left the living room (double windows to left in photo below) facing north, with no natural lighting. Caradco skylights and glass door on south side (above) flood the living room (on opposite side of house, lower floor) with light.

BEFORE

AFTER

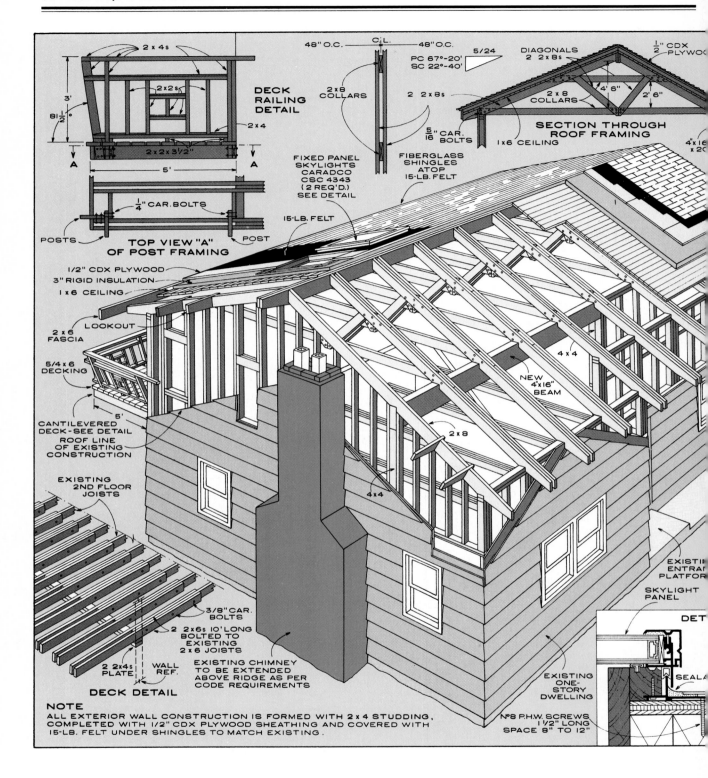

DECK RAILING DETAIL

2 x 4s
2 x 2s
2 x 4
3'
8½"
A
5'
¼" CAR.BOLTS
2 x 2 x 3½"
TOP VIEW "A" OF POST FRAMING
POSTS
POST

48" O.C.   C.L.   48" O.C.
PC 67°-20'
SC 22°-40'
5/24
2 x 8 COLLARS
2 2x8s
5/16" CAR. BOLTS
FIXED PANEL SKYLIGHTS CARADCO CSC 4343 (2 REQ'D.) SEE DETAIL
FIBERGLASS SHINGLES ATOP 15-LB. FELT
15-LB. FELT

DIAGONALS 2 2x8s
½" CDX PLYWOO
2 x 8 COLLARS
4' 6"
2' 6"
SECTION THROUGH ROOF FRAMING
1x6 CEILING
4"x16 x 20

1/2" CDX PLYWOOD
3" RIGID INSULATION
1 x 6 CEILING
LOOKOUT
2 x 6 FASCIA
5/4 x 6 DECKING
5'
CANTILEVERED DECK-SEE DETAIL
ROOF LINE OF EXISTING CONSTRUCTION
EXISTING 2ND FLOOR JOISTS

NEW 4"x16" BEAM
4 x 4
2 x 8
4x4
EXISTI ENTRA PLATFOR
SKYLIGHT PANEL
DET
SEAL

3/8" CAR. BOLTS
2 2x6s 10' LONG BOLTED TO EXISTING 2 x 6 JOISTS
2 2x4s PLATE
WALL REF.
DECK DETAIL
EXISTING CHIMNEY TO BE EXTENDED ABOVE RIDGE AS PER CODE REQUIREMENTS

EXISTING ONE-STORY DWELLING
N°8 P.H.W. SCREWS 1½" LONG SPACE 8" TO 12"

NOTE
ALL EXTERIOR WALL CONSTRUCTION IS FORMED WITH 2 x 4 STUDDING, COMPLETED WITH 1/2" CDX PLYWOOD SHEATHING AND COVERED WITH 15-LB. FELT UNDER SHINGLES TO MATCH EXISTING.

● The original roof needed structural repair anyway.

The result is a well-lighted living room with a 20-foot vaulted ceiling and an upstairs consisting of a 12-by-18-foot den area and 14-by-16-foot master bedroom (with 12-foot cathedral ceilings), a 7-by-11-foot bath, an office nook, generous storage space, and a cantilevered redwood deck running the length of the house.

With the old roof gone, we are about to begin framing for the new asymmetrical roof, which will have a ridgepole about 5½ feet higher than the previous 6½-foot-high ridge. This is turning out to be a big—and traumatic—job. A thick layer of debris surrounds

the house as if a violent whirlwind had ripped by; my vulnerable house with all my belongings yawns wide open; and butterflies flutter in my stomach as we set to our task.

One of the best reasons for going up is saving costs. You'll need to have plans made; you'll need a good framing carpenter to put up the basic

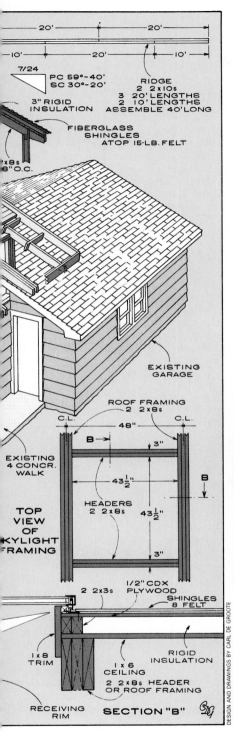

20'   20'
10'   20'   10'

7/24
PC 59°-40'
SC 30°-20'   RIDGE
3" RIGID   2 2x10s
INSULATION   3 20' LENGTHS
                    2 10' LENGTHS
                 ASSEMBLE 40' LONG

FIBERGLASS
SHINGLES
ATOP 15-LB. FELT

2x8s
8" O.C.

EXISTING
GARAGE

ROOF FRAMING
2 2x8s
C.L.   C.L.
48"
B →   3"
EXISTING
4 CONCR.
WALK   B
            43 1/2"   ↓
HEADERS
2 2x8s   43 1/2"
TOP
VIEW
OF
SKYLIGHT
FRAMING   3"

1/2" CDX
2 2x3s   PLYWOOD
                  SHINGLES
                  8 FELT

1 x 8
TRIM   RIGID
            1 x 6   INSULATION
            CEILING
            2 2x8s HEADER
            OR ROOF FRAMING
RECEIVING
RIM   SECTION "B"

DESIGN AND DRAWINGS BY CARL DE GROOTE

in a project like this. But I was able to sheathe and shingle the roof, side the house, and do most of the interior work myself, saving a bundle. Remember, however, that a job like this is tremendous, and the trade-off is time: Going this route takes endurance and months of hard work if you devote your weekends and vacation time to it. (General rule of thumb: Estimate how long something will take, then triple it. This way you'll remain only slightly behind schedule.)

Before you talk to an architect, know precisely what you want to accomplish, and have some ideas on how you want to do it. To a certain extent, our requirements dictated the project's design. For example, the south side of the addition would require head room of at least 7½ feet at the end wall. But I wanted to minimize the height of the ridge. Since a portion

of the north side would be open air space over the living room and head room wasn't as critical, we used an asymmetrical roof design—the pitch is shallower on the south side than on the north. Also, one of my primary goals was daylighting for the living room, so we put two large skylights on the south side. Because the house is in the Northeast, where winters are cold, the rest of the windows in the addition are smallish, and there are none on the north side.

Once you have drawings, you can submit them to local authorities for a permit. Then you can get to work.

A week of fourteen hour days sees us complete the framing and roof decking, but it is many more days before the roof is weathertight. A tarp helps me withstand a few rainstorms with only minor leaks—and no damage. The days fade into weeks, the weeks

PHOTOS BY THE AUTHOR

structure; and you'll probably need a plumber and an electrician. But if you're handy and don't mind hard labor, you can do all the other work yourself. I was lucky enough to have my father, a retired carpenter contractor with more than 40 years of experience, help me frame the structure. His kind of expertise is *essential*

Framing should tie in with original (top). Unforeseen circumstance: Garage roof juts into living space (right); we framed around it. Laminated beam (above) is framed into two sidewalls. Note: We used blocking instead of birds-mouthing rafters as in the drawing.

into months. Occasionally I get help from my father or my brother or my brother-in-law, but most of the work I do myself, mostly on weekends—insulating, sheathing, and shingling the roof; siding the house with a double layer of cedar shakes, underlayment and finish; the interior work . . . there is little free time anymore. Will I ever be done?

When it comes to framing, the walls should match the existing framework, in this case 2 × 4s. You can either rip out all old framing down to the top sill and frame the upper level anew, or, leaving the gable ends, tie into the old framing and cut down on waste. We chose the latter. The roof is an exposed-beam truss design, using double 2 × 8s 48 inches on center. All 2 × 6 floor joists are either doubled or tripled, depending on span, and the double joists for the cantilevered deck sandwich the existing floor joists and extend 5 feet into the house. The deck is made from California Redwood Association redwood.

An 8-foot Caradco patio door opens onto the long five-foot-wide balcony/deck with a beautiful view of our wooded property. I used 5/4 × 6 clear redwood for the decking; the double joists provide ample strength so 2 × 6 decking isn't needed, and I get a knot-free deck surface. The railing, made from 2 × 4s and 2 × 2s, is based on a four-foot modular design of my father's, with no space more than 6½ inches wide. The design avoids the boring ladder look of many deck railings, and it is pitched out slightly to provide maximum deck space.

An important part of the project design is the 4-by-16-inch exposed laminated beam traversing the width of the living room. This supports the long span of the roof over the open livingroom area. The roof is covered with three inches of Energy Shield rigid insulation from Owens-Corning Fiberglas; conventional fiberglass batts are used in the walls. I sheathed the roof and walls with ½-inch plywood and used Owens-Corning Chaparral II shingles on the roof. The exterior walls are sided with conventional striated cedar shakes to match the existing siding. Finally, the entire house was primed and painted beige (Richmond Bisque from Benjamin Moore).

Part II: The interior

Wielding my utility knife, I had just cut through the joint where the stairwell wall meets the living-room ceiling. I stood on my ladder, listening.

"This one's a four-footer."

My dad's voice came from somewhere above me on the other side of the ceiling. I measured four feet from the wall and cut a parallel line in the ceiling four feet long, then another line straight back to the wall. With some gentle persuasion from above, the four-foot square of gypsum board popped loose along its joint lines, and I pulled it free.

With only this small section of ceiling gone, the bleak living room brightened as light flooded in from the roof windows. In a couple of hours my father and I had peeled the rest of the ceiling and removed the joists. Blinking in the sunlight with the ceiling gone, I felt like Lemuel Gulliver, as though a colossal Brobdingnagian had lifted the lid of the dark little box in which I lived.

After completing the outside of the addition and hooking up with the plumbing and heating systems, my first job was to insulate.

I wanted the most insulation I could get in the walls with the least amount of wasted interior space, so I used 3½-inch Owens-Corning fiberglass batts between the studs with an extra ½ inch of Energy Shield rigid polyisocyanurate insulation on the interior—for an insulating value of more than R-15. (Three inches of Owens-Corning Energy Shield insulation had gone into the roof when I first built it, for about R-24.) After installing the foilcovered insulating panels—and before putting up the wallboard—I would seal the joints with plastic tape to maintain the vapor barrier. But before I could install the panels, I had to put in the wiring.

The electrical work was one of only two aspects of the job for which I hired a contractor (the other was extending the heating system): Complicated wiring can get tricky; it can also be dangerous if it's done incorrectly. And complicated it was, partly because I used a new product called TriCon wiring from Brintec Corp.

TriCon wiring contains the power, cable-TV, and telephone lines all in one three-part cable. In cross section, it resembles a Y, with the thick power cable being the tail and the TV and phone lines making up the arms, all joined at the center. With TriCon, every run to an outlet must be a direct home run back to the load center (because of the TV and phone lines), but the wiring's advantages are two-fold. First, you save labor by pulling only one cable instead of three. Second, you have the convenience of phone and TV jacks, as well as a power out-

let, at any TriCon receptacle. Want to relocate the TV or telephone? Just move it and hook up to any available outlet.

Not everything went smoothly with the wiring, though. When the local New York state fire underwriters' inspector came to check the electrical work, he wouldn't pass it because neither he nor his superiors in Albany had ever seen or heard of TriCon—even though it was Underwriters' Laboratories–approved. And I couldn't close up my walls until he gave his approval. Before the whole affair was straightened out, I had lost at least two months' working time at a critical stage in the project.

Tricks of the trade

Getting back on track, I installed the rigid insulation, then the drywall, using two-inch cement-coated nails to get at least an inch of penetration into the studs. But because I had built a wraparound wood ceiling (see photos), how would I finish off the top of the wallboard?

I borrowed a trick from my father, a retired commercial carpenter contractor. At the top of the walls, 10 inches down from the ceiling, the rigid insulation is flush with the wood, so I ran the wallboard 1½ inches above the wood-panel joint and capped it with metal J-mold. The result is an arrow-straight architectural shadow line that's easy to paint. There's no need to cut with a paintbrush at the top because the drywall is on a plane ½ inch out from the wood surface.

Another trick concerned the window treatment. I used Caradco windows throughout the addition, but I had two problems: Because of the Energy Shield insulation, the finished wall would be ½ inch out from the window frames; and I didn't want to create bulky-looking window trim. Solution: I brought the drywall even with the ends of the frames to create a ½-inch lip, then used corner bead around the perimeter. Spackling and painting the corner bead resulted in a neat-looking opening where only the wood of the window frame is visible.

Before finishing the walls and installing the floors, I had to set up the wood stove—a large catalytic wood-burner from Consolidated Dutchwest. I wanted a wood stove as an auxiliary heat source in the cavernous living area, and because the stove has glass doors, the visible fire provides a cozy atmosphere. (To break up the stratified layers of heated air bound to form in a room with a cathedral ceiling—and to provide cooling currents

The roof was raised and the livingroom ceiling eliminated in this ranch; sky windows admit the sun to change the atmosphere—and character—of the house. Roof framing was stained with Benjamin Moore Tahoe Brown; staircase was originally a closed-in stair leading to a 6½-foot-high unfinished attic.

BEFORE

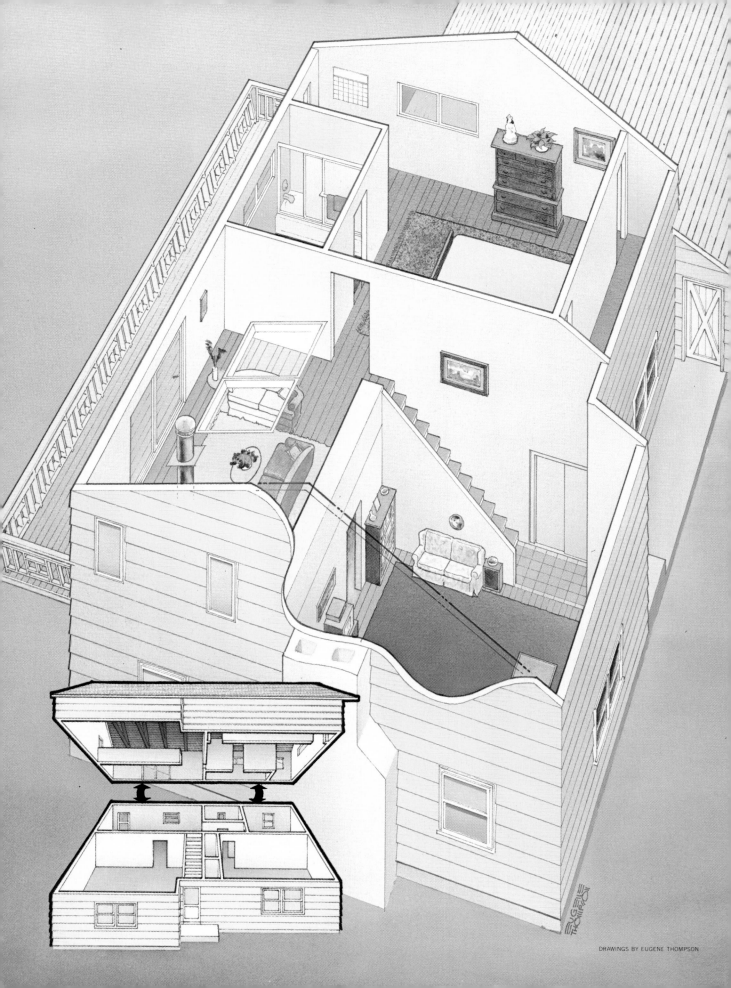

Bird's-eye cutaway (left) shows the addition's floor plan. Inset shows what was added to the existing ranch. Top and above: Wood stove is the centerpiece for the new den, while the half-wall bookcase adds to the warm atmosphere. Tops of the bookcase and shelves were laminated with Formica Colorcore; the rest was enameled. Master bedroom (right) and den sport Colony Plank oak flooring. A 16-foot closet is behind the bed; office and bath are to the right, out of view.

of air in the summer—I also installed ceiling fans from Beverly Hills Fan Co.'s new line of five-bladed "designer color" models. These range from high-tech chrome to rich pastel colors. I chose almond.)

In setting up the stove, I followed the guidelines provided by the manufacturer. Whenever you tackle a job like this, carefully read all the recommendations and installation instructions. I constructed noncombustible floor and wall shields using fireproof underlayment—with a one-inch airspace at the wall—and a new product from American Olean Tile Co. called Terra Pavers. These are a cross between ceramic-mosaic and paving tiles. Because Terra Pavers have a nonporous, easy-to-clean surface, they are ideal for use with a wood-burning stove, where ashes inevitably find their way to the floor.

Ah, the floor—that came next. A wood floor is not difficult to install once you get the hang of it, but it can be time-consuming, especially with random-width planking, which is what I used. Holes have to be drilled for the blind nailing to prevent splitting, and you have to take special care to make sure the wide boards are snugged and nailed properly.

The prefinished, dark-oak Chickasaw Colony Plank floor I installed is made by Memphis Hardwood Flooring; the planking comes in three-, four-, and six-inch widths. The tongue-and-groove design has beveled edges to give it a slightly rustic look; however, the beveling is not uniform, which made it difficult to get all the boards snugged properly. Also, an inordinate number of the 6-inch planks were very short, which made staggering the lengths difficult. The prefinished flooring saved finishing time, though, and the final appearance is perfect for a rural home like mine.

Once I had the floor in, doors, trim, and paint were all that were left. I hung solid-pine six-panel doors for the bedroom and bath (bifolds for the closet) and installed 2¼-inch pine colonial casing and 3¼-inch baseboard. Once you get to the paint in a job like

this, you know you're home free: After the drywall and trim got an undercoat of primer, a topcoat of Benjamin Moore Navajo White (flat for the walls and enamel for the trim) put the crowning touch on the project—*by Timothy O. Bakke. Photos by Greg Sharko. Design by Carl De Groote. Drawings by Carl De Groote and Eugene Thompson.*

LIST OF MANUFACTURERS' ADDRESSES
The following manufacturers were selected for this project. **American Olean Tile Co.,** 1000 Cannon Ave., Lansdale, PA 19446; **Beverly Hills Fan Co.,** 12612 Raymer St., North Hollywood, CA 91605; **Brintec Corp.,** 1600 W. Main St., Willimantic, CT 06226; **Consolidated Dutchwest,** Box 1019, Plymouth, MA 02360; **Caradco Corp.,** Box 920, Rantoul, IL 61866; **Formica Corp.,** 155 Rte. 46 CN980, Wayne, NJ 07474; **Memphis Hardwood Flooring Co.,** Box 7253, Memphis, TN 38107; **Benjamin Moore Paint Co.,** 51 Chestnut Ridge Rd. Montvale, NJ 07645; **Owens-Corning Fiberglas Corp.,** Fiberglass Tower, Toledo, OH 43659

four air-lock entries

Open your front door. Swish, a blast of cold air drives past you and into the house. Then, whoosh, the house compensates: A rush of warm air flows through the open door to the outdoors. It's an expensive exchange. In winter, your heating system must make up for the heat lost every time you open the door; in summer, it's your air conditioner that pays the price. But there's a solution.

You can eliminate those problems by adding an air-lock entry. The outer door prevents outside air from entering the house when the inner entry door is opened, and very little heated—or cooled—air escapes from the interior. And, during daytime winter months, the glass-encased air-lock entry works like a small greenhouse to absorb the sun's rays. Leave the inner door open, and some of this solar warmth enters the house. How well does an air-lock entry work? Last year it reduced my fuel bills by more than half, and I know that it more than paid for itself its first winter.

To cut the cost of materials, I built my air lock out of used materials I found at the lumberyard: a 36-inch-wide combination glazed and paneled door for $20; a pair of 30-inch-wide doors, for the sides of the portico, for $30; a 30-inch-wide 15-light French door, which is cut into two sidelights, for $10; and a glazed insert panel from a combination storm/screen door for only $2 (to be used as a transom above the operating door). Total: $62. New materials would have cost $500.

On the following pages I'll explain how I added an air lock to the portico on my home's entryway. You don't have a portico? Read anyway. You'll

Existing portico before adding air lock: Columns support the new framing.

get general ideas on how to add an air lock to your home. Then check the additional plans for specific information on adding an air lock to three other standard entranceways.

Door installation

The two stationary French doors are centered in the opening between the portico's supporting columns, so usually it's necessary to install blocking along the center line of the columns to support the studs that frame the openings for the doors (see drawings). Install 2 × 4 sole plates—preferably preservative-treated lumber—across the bottom of the openings. Run a double bead of caulking along the bottom face of the sole plates before toenailing them in place.

At the top of the door opening, nail on one or more 2 × 4 headers to fill the space between the top of the door and any existing structure (in my case, the top of the column moldings). Drill pilot holes and use 2½-inch wood screws to avoid damaging the portico.

The hinged operating door at the front of the portico is installed over a length of one-by-three-inch lumber, which also serves as a threshold in the door opening. I used a length of one-by-three-inch oak to reduce wear from traffic over the threshold, but preservative-treated pine is adequate. Caulk the bottom face of this board before putting it in place.

Next, nail vertical studs in place to frame the rough opening for the door and two sidelights. (No dimensions are given here because each installation will depend on the overhang and width of your portico.) If you position the horizontal 2 × 4 higher than the door because of molding on the columns (as I did), nail a 2 × 4 header about ⅛ inch above the top of the door, then toenail blocking at the same height in the openings for the sidelights.

My door came complete with a lock and doorknobs installed, so I had keys made to fit. If your door has no hardware, install a lockset early on in the project to keep the door steady while you work.

Sidelights, transom, sunburst

The sidelights are made from a 15-light French door (three vertical rows of five lights). They are installed in their openings in the same manner as the stationary doors at the sides of the portico (see drawings for cutting and installation procedures).

My transom is made from an old

storm-door insert, two feet wide by five feet high. Turned on its side, its 5-foot dimension was just right to span the opening above the door, but its original 2-foot width made it too high. I had to reduced the transome by removing the glass and carefully cutting the frame as shown.

Not all porticos have an arch formed in the front face as shown in the photos. If yours is a simple triangular portico with a straight edge along the bottom, your glazing job is complete. For my portico, I cut an accurate template from corrugated cardboard to fit the opening exactly, then transferred this pattern to a sheet of clear acrylic panel (such as Plexiglass).

For the curve of the sunburst, I measured the arc and cut a strip of ¼-by-½-inch pine to the correct length and nailed it to the underside of the arch directly above the center of the transom. I then nailed a second strip over the first to build the total

thickness to ½ by ½ inch. (I used two ¼-inch-thick strips because a ½-inch-square strip could break when bent to fit the curve of the arch.) In the workshop, I cut an ellipse about seven inches long by five inches wide out of ¾-inch pine, then cut it in half for assembly as shown in the drawing.

The finished sunburst is set in place against the stop nailed to the arch, and a second stop of two ¼-by-½-inch strips is nailed to the arch on the inside of the light to secure it in place. To complete the installation, short lengths of ½-inch-square pine are nailed along the bottom edge of the light at each side of the ellipse.

More cardboard templates

I own a profile transfer tool with sliding fingers that duplicate any shape. However, it is too small to duplicate the large moldings on my portico columns. But by using the same principle I found that it was quite easy to make cardboard templates that repro-

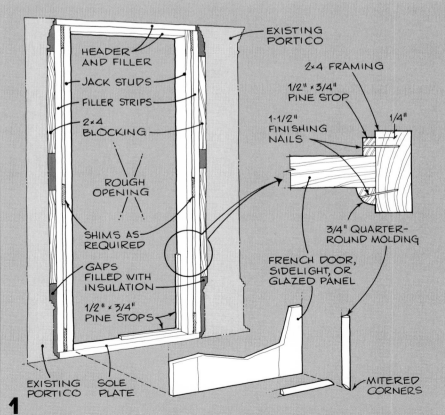

1 Enclosing a portico begins with rough openings that are ¼ in. wider and ⅛ in. higher than the door dimensions. Fasten 2×4 blocking and filler and jack studs to the portico columns with 2½-in. No. 10 flathead screws. Nail ½-by-¾-in. pine strips ¼ in. from the outside edge to serve as stops and weather seals around stationary doors. Molding holds the doors in place. The front door is hung on hinges using ¾-by-1¼-in. pine stops.

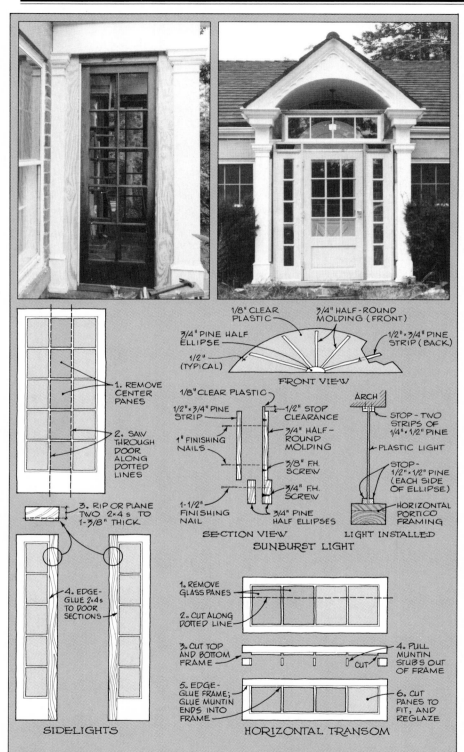

SIDELIGHTS

1. REMOVE CENTER PANES

2. SAW THROUGH DOOR ALONG DOTTED LINES

3. RIP OR PLANE TWO 2×4s TO 1-3/8" THICK

4. EDGE-GLUE 2×4s TO DOOR SECTIONS

SUNBURST LIGHT

FRONT VIEW

1/8" CLEAR PLASTIC

3/4" HALF-ROUND MOLDING (FRONT)

3/4" PINE HALF ELLIPSE

1/2" × 3/4" PINE STRIP (BACK)

1/2" (TYPICAL)

SECTION VIEW

1/8" CLEAR PLASTIC

1/2" × 3/4" PINE STRIP

1/2" STOP CLEARANCE

3/4" HALF-ROUND MOLDING

1" FINISHING NAILS

3/8" F.H. SCREW

3/4" F.H. SCREW

1-1/2" FINISHING NAIL

3/4" PINE HALF ELLIPSES

LIGHT INSTALLED

ARCH

STOP - TWO STRIPS OF 1/4" × 1/2" PINE

PLASTIC LIGHT

STOP - 1/2" × 1/2" PINE (EACH SIDE OF ELLIPSE)

HORIZONTAL PORTICO FRAMING

HORIZONTAL TRANSOM

1. REMOVE GLASS PANES

2. CUT ALONG DOTTED LINE

3. CUT TOP AND BOTTOM FRAME

4. PULL MUNTIN STUBS OUT OF FRAME

CUT

5. EDGE-GLUE FRAME; GLUE MUNTIN ENDS INTO FRAME

6. CUT PANES TO FIT, AND REGLAZE

Sidelights are made by cutting a French door. Rip ⅛ in. off two 6-ft. 8-in. 2×4s to bring them to 1⅜-in. thickness, and edge-glue them to door sections. Full-thickness 2×4 may be glued to the door and planed flush. Clear plastic sunburst is fastened with ¾-in. wood screws to the half ellipse at center. Arrange ¾-in. half-round molding in a pleasing pattern; screw the plastic to the molding, leaving a ½-in. gap at the top to clear the pine stop. Use ½-by-¾-in. pine strips and the other half ellipse for the inside of the sunburst; fasten to the outer sections with finishing nails driven through pre-drilled holes in the plastic. Transom above the door is made from a screen-door insert. Saw through the end frames and muntins, and reassemble the frame with resorcinol glue to fit the 17½-in. space between the two 2×4s above the portico columns. Cut the glass; secure it with the original muntin molding.

duce the shape of the molding in much the same way. These templates allowed me to transfer the molding pattern to the ¼-inch exterior-grade plywood used to enclose the air-lock-entry framing (see photo).

For example, for alongside the transom, I cut a piece of cardboard to an approximate fit inside the opening and held it in place with pushpins. I then cut ⅜-inch and ½-inch strips of cardboard, shaped one end to fit nicely against the molding, and taped it in position. By repeating this procedure with additional strips of cardboard, I eventually developed a complete profile of the molding. This was transferred to a piece of plywood, which I then carefully cut out on the jigsaw.

On long plywood pieces, such as those that cover the framing, I cut the cardboard to the width and length required, then trimmed away the areas adjacent to the molding. These areas are fitted to the molding using multiple cut-to-fit cardboard strips.

Before covering the inside of the openings with the plywood, stuff fiberglass insulation into all areas not filled by studs or blocking. Any small gaps that appear after the plywood is nailed in place with one-inch brads can be filled with wood dough.

Give the plywood and moldings a coat of primer; then paint the entire air-lock entry—portico and all—with an exterior paint of your choice.

Air locks for others

In addition to the overhanging canopy or portico entry door, there are many other types of entryways that can be easily enclosed with glazed doors to create an air-lock entry. The use of French doors or fully glazed doors with no muntins (for a more modern look) reduces construction to a simple 2 × 4 frame that forms the rough openings, and the large glass area contributes to the greenhouse effect.

The basic construction techniques are the same as those for a portico. But if you plan to buy new doors, take advantage of the many sizes that are available to fit the doors to existing spaces with a minimum of blocking. Framing can be brought to near-exact size by using 1 × 4, 2 × 4, and 4 × 4 lumber. And with no blocking to conceal, the framing can be left exposed and painted instead of covering it with exterior plywood.

The three idea sketches will stimulate your imagination and help you build a tasteful and compatible airlock entry for your home—*by Herb Pfister. Drawings by Eugene Thompson.*

Air locks for others

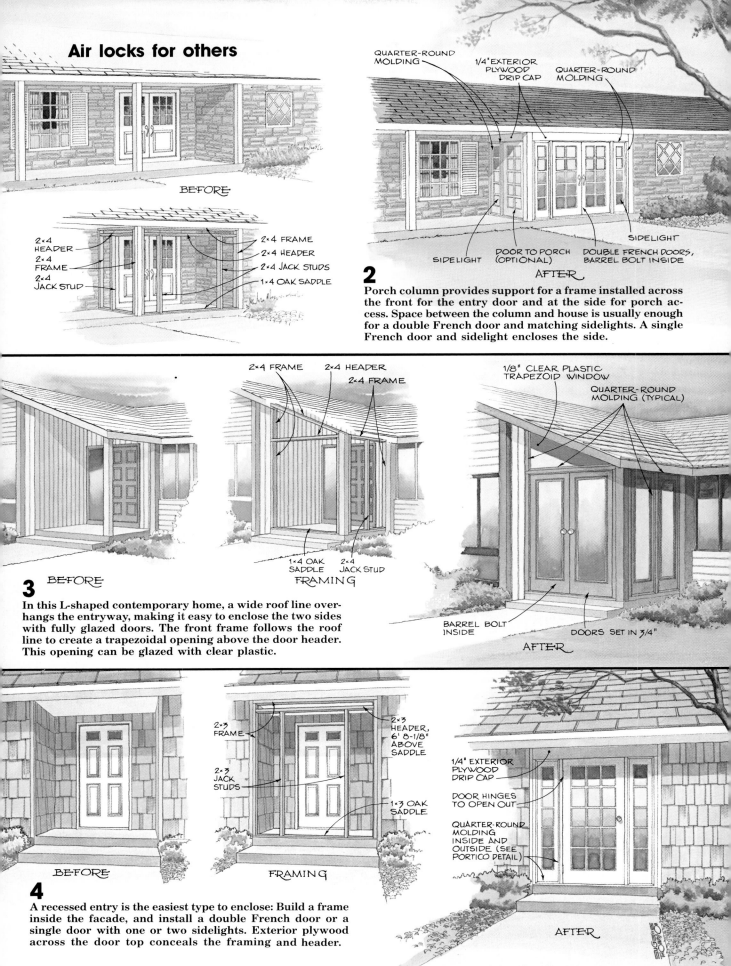

BEFORE

2×4 HEADER
2×4 FRAME
2×4 JACK STUD

2×4 FRAME
2×4 HEADER
2×4 JACK STUDS
1×4 OAK SADDLE

QUARTER-ROUND MOLDING
1/4" EXTERIOR PLYWOOD DRIP CAP
QUARTER-ROUND MOLDING

SIDELIGHT
DOOR TO PORCH (OPTIONAL)
DOUBLE FRENCH DOORS, BARREL BOLT INSIDE
SIDELIGHT

AFTER

2 Porch column provides support for a frame installed across the front for the entry door and at the side for porch access. Space between the column and house is usually enough for a double French door and matching sidelights. A single French door and sidelight encloses the side.

BEFORE

2×4 FRAME
2×4 HEADER
2×4 FRAME

1×4 OAK SADDLE
2×4 JACK STUD
FRAMING

1/8" CLEAR PLASTIC TRAPEZOID WINDOW
QUARTER-ROUND MOLDING (TYPICAL)

BARREL BOLT INSIDE
DOORS SET IN 3/4"
AFTER

3 In this L-shaped contemporary home, a wide roof line overhangs the entryway, making it easy to enclose the two sides with fully glazed doors. The front frame follows the roof line to create a trapezoidal opening above the door header. This opening can be glazed with clear plastic.

BEFORE

2×3 FRAME
2×3 JACK STUDS

2×3 HEADER, 6' 8-1/8" ABOVE SADDLE
1×3 OAK SADDLE
FRAMING

1/4" EXTERIOR PLYWOOD DRIP CAP
DOOR HINGES TO OPEN OUT
QUARTER-ROUND MOLDING INSIDE AND OUTSIDE (SEE PORTICO DETAIL)

AFTER

4 A recessed entry is the easiest type to enclose: Build a frame inside the facade, and install a double French door or a single door with one or two sidelights. Exterior plywood across the door top conceals the framing and header.

a spa in the sun

A plant-filled spa room is a wonderful place for enjoying the bubbly (above). Fixed windows and a sliding glass door are placed at the southern and eastern exposures to gain warmth from the winter sun (top), and the tiled slab stores heat for release in the evening. Solar gain is so effective that heat can be blown into the adjacent house to cut fuel costs. Overhangs at the eaves and gables prevent summertime overheating by shading the room from the midday sun.

One early summer day, two Pennsylvania homeowners stepped out onto their drab concrete patio slab and began thinking about improvements in their lifestyle. Several months and much sawing and hammering later, they stepped out onto the same spot, but this time lowered themselves into a bubbling spa tub surrounded by tile and plants and sunny windows. As snow fell outside, they could hardly remember the dull slab that used to be there.

Going from a useless "contractor's basic" to this kind of luxury was not problem-free. The homeowners wanted the spa addition to be on the same level as the existing ground floor of their house, but the old patio slab was a step down from the house. Also, the house was cantilevered at the second floor, and the spa room would have to be tucked under this overhand with an interior soffit. Lastly, although the homeowners wanted to use the spa year-round, they didn't want it to add to their heating load.

The solution to the first problem turned out to help achieve the last requirement. To make the addition level, the homeowners decided to pour another concrete layer. First they build a concrete block wall on the original patio as a form for the new slab. Then, using a concrete saw, they chopped a hole through the existing slab to take the spa they'd bought. The old slab was covered with a plastic vapor barrier, and on top of the barrier, they placed 2 inches of rigid-foam insulation. After they'd

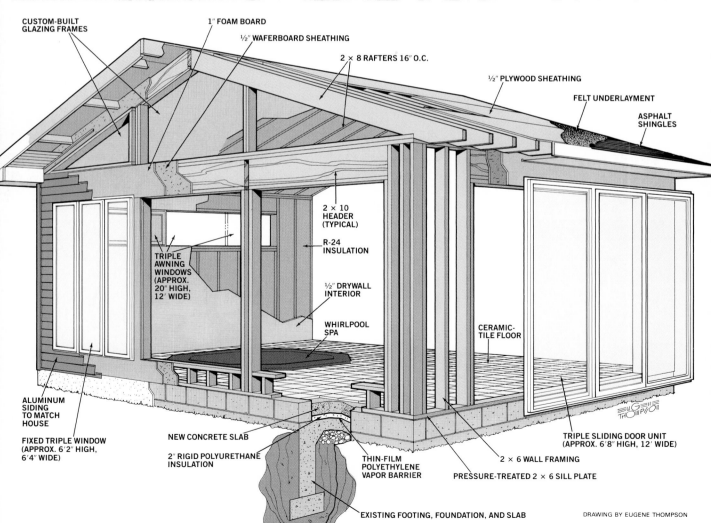

CUSTOM-BUILT GLAZING FRAMES

1" FOAM BOARD

½" WAFERBOARD SHEATHING

2 × 8 RAFTERS 16" O.C.

½" PLYWOOD SHEATHING

FELT UNDERLAYMENT

ASPHALT SHINGLES

2 × 10 HEADER (TYPICAL)

R-24 INSULATION

TRIPLE AWNING WINDOWS (APPROX. 20" HIGH, 12' WIDE)

½" DRYWALL INTERIOR

WHIRLPOOL SPA

CERAMIC-TILE FLOOR

ALUMINUM SIDING TO MATCH HOUSE

FIXED TRIPLE WINDOW (APPROX. 6'2" HIGH, 6'4" WIDE)

NEW CONCRETE SLAB

2" RIGID POLYURETHANE INSULATION

THIN-FILM POLYETHYLENE VAPOR BARRIER

TRIPLE SLIDING DOOR UNIT (APPROX. 6'8" HIGH, 12' WIDE)

2 × 6 WALL FRAMING

PRESSURE-TREATED 2 × 6 SILL PLATE

EXISTING FOOTING, FOUNDATION, AND SLAB

DRAWING BY EUGENE THOMPSON

Hole for the spa was cut with a concrete saw through the original patio (above). Before pouring the second layer, a wooden mold was erected around the hole. Rigid foam applied over sheathing is covered with aluminum siding.

leveled this new surface, the second concrete layer was poured. When it had set and the spa was in place, the surface was tiled. The resulting floor doubles as a heat sink that adds significantly to the passive-solar design. The 1/2-inch-thick earthtone tiles that cover the concrete capture heat while the sun shines on them, and hold it in the room. The tiles (from American Olean Tile, Lansdale, PA 19446-0271) aren't glazed, so they also provide some slip resistance. And because they're a solid color all the way through, the tiles won't develop wear patterns.

Though the homeowners knew passive-solar design was a good choice for their spa room, they were surprised to find that after construction was completed, their heating bills for the entire house dropped by almost 20 percent. They attribute this drop to several factors. The spa room is well insulated; according to the homeowners, the ceiling has an insulation value of R-36. This was obtained by using 2×12s in the construction and stuffing 11-inch fiberglass batts between them. The walls are constructed from 2×6 studs and filled with 6-inch fiberglass insulation.

Waferboard was nailed down on the studs, providing the structural strength for the roof support, then this sheathing was covered with foil-faced inch-thick polyurethane foam. This added insulation brings the wall R-value up to 24. The walls, as well as exposed wood such as the window headers, are faced with aluminum siding for easy maintenance—and to match the existing house.

In line with this passive-solar design, fixed gable windows are framed in the southern wall. All windows—both the custom models and commercial units—are double glazed to help

Sunlit spa room doubles as a casual all-season dining or entertaining area.

hold heat in the room. The western exposure has only three small, high windows for ventilation. The roof overhangs 18 inches on all three sides; the homeowners say this shades the sun room in the summer like the brim of a hat, avoiding overheating and the need for extra air conditioning. In the winter, when the sun is lower in the sky, the overhang does not impede warming rays.

But perhaps one of the most important energy-saving aspects of this sun room is tucked into the interior soffit. When the sunspace temperature creeps above 75°F, a thermostat-controlled fan built into the soffit switches on. Heat is carried out of the spa room through a duct running within the soffit and into the main house through a wall grille. Although the homeowners installed hot-water baseboard heating in the spa room, they rarely have to use this heat.

The spa tub itself is heavily insulated against heat loss, too. Before pouring the second concrete slab, the contractor built a wooden form around the hole chopped through the original slab. The tub, which had been factory-sprayed with urethane to prevent heat loss, was set into the hole and plumbed, then backfilled with sand. A separate gas heater outside the western wall of the sunspace heats the water for the spa, and all electrical controls are GFI-protected. The pumps and blowers for the spa are located in this same outdoor shed. For convenience, the water pipes run out to this pump house through a chase molded into the second concrete layer. According to the homeowners, this arrangement cuts down significantly on noise in the spa room. It also makes the plumbing easier to get to—no need to break up the floor when there's a leak or other problem. Also, in the interest of convenience, the underwater tub lights are not ordinary low-voltage pool bulbs. Instead, the bulbs are located in the pump house, and fiber-optic cables running through the plumbing chase bring light to special lenses in the tub. When a bulb goes out, this setup makes it easy to replace.

In the end, the homeowners have found that their versatile addition can be used for more than just water sports. Features like the ceiling fan and cathedral ceiling with exposed beams and track lighting over the spa make the room an attractive sun porch and party room. The aluminum siding was removed from the old south wall of the house, and this surface—now an interior wall—was refinished. The homeowners added a patio dining set, so their sunny spa doubles as an airy breakfast room—*by Naomi J. Freundlich. Drawings by Eugene Thompson.*

Follow these fast new tiling tips

Lay tile out in rented metal frame to determine best placement for trimming. Spread mortar with flat side of trowel.

Comb adhesive with notched side of trowel; use a frame to place tiles. Seat tile by striking with a wood block.

The next day, after mortar has set, spread grout diagonally; force it into joints with rubber-faced trowel.

Drag a towel damp with a latex grout film remover and water solution across the surface of set tile.

"Dress" joints with damp sponge. If grout residue remains, mix softwood sawdust with water and 5% acid,

using gloves. Make sure grout joints are set, then rub the mixture over the tile with a dry towel.

diy kitchen addition

Dark and crowded, narrow and confining—that's the way Leslie Clark says her kitchen used to be. It offered little in the way of conveniences, like many another kitchen of the immediate postwar era, lacking adequate dining space or even a door to the backyard patio. Dense evergreens behind the house contributed to the darkness of the Clarks' kitchen.

But space for expansion was limited because of a steep, close-in slope and the fact that the family didn't want to eliminate too much of their cherished patio space. It was a problem that designer Dan Ennis of Beaverton, Oregon, had to solve in order to give the Clarks the light-filled room they wanted. His solution was a prow-shape addition that knifes toward the slope without robbing too much outdoor living space. The angular lines of the new kitchen provide an interesting flow to the new space but meant that the old layout had to be totally dismantled and reordered.

Post-and-beam construction helped give Ennis the high ceiling he needed for a large skylight, and he carefully placed a number of windows to supplement the abundant light from overhead. Rewaining shadows were banished by installation of track lighting and other recessed fixtures.

Today, that cramped old kitchen seems like a dimly remembered dream. Leslie has new appliances to work with, sleek new cabinets with rich oak trim, a commodious pantry, enough room to do pirouettes around the work triangle on new vinyl flooring, and even a work desk—something the old setup simply could not accommodate. Add the cost of all of these new items to that for construction and interior renovations, and you begin to realize why the final bill came to about $29,000.

Leslie also now has a convenient and roomy dining area that nicely serves a family of six. And there's a new door that provides her four teenage sons with convenient access to the patio for barbecues and the like. In terms of square footage, the Clarks' addition may seem small—though the extra 140 square feet almost doubled the size of the original kitchen—but it looms as large as the Cascades from an enjoyment standpoint—*by Cathy Howard. Photos by Karlis Grants. Design by Dan Ennis.*

Reprinted by permission of THE HOMEOWNER magazine.

Wooden beam across the ceiling marks the boundary between old and new parts of the Clark kitchen (top, center). To the right is the old kitchen space, now partially occupied by the dining area. The door beyond opens to the patio. Note how the island's laminate countertop wraps itself around the peeled-pine post.

Surrounding pine trees and a steeply sloped lot at the rear of the Clarks' house created gloom and shadows, which were largely dispelled by installation of the kitchen windows and skylight. The addition (right) required sacrifice of part of the patio.

Convenient pantry cabinet occupies part of the old kitchen space (above) and contains all the canned, bottled and packaged items needed for normal meal preparation. It also has a pull-out rack for linens and a tray compartment.

Custom-made laminated cabinets, embellished with oak trim and brass handles, reinforce the kitchen's decorating theme. There's a small desk for menu planning and recipes (second, above). The Italian ceramic tile backsplash behind the range appears again behind a lowered counter (above) that serves as a baking center for rolling and kneading dough.

DINING ROOM

CUSHIONED BENCH

WINDOWS

COUNTER

COUNTER

14

SKYLIGHT ABOVE

RANGE

MICROWAVE OVEN

REFRIG.

20

KITCHEN

PANTRY

SINK

D/W

DESK

SHELVES

DUTCH DOOR

PEELED POLE

ISLAND

BREAKFAST NOOK

STORAGE DOORS

CLOSET

BENCH

BIFOLD DOORS

STORAGE SHELVES

PANTRY

UTILITY ROOM

STAIRS DN

SHADED AREA SHOWS SHAPE OF ORIGINAL KITCHEN

CARPORT

european-style master bath

A master bedroom is incomplete without a master bath. So when I drew up the plans for my new gable addition, I laid out a 9-by-12-foot space for that purpose. The bath occupies a corner of the new living space, up against a six-foot knee wall. Six feet doesn't offer much head room, so we put the vanity and toilet against that wall.

The heart of the bath is a 5-by-7-foot acrylic-faced fiberglass tub-shower unit from Acrylic Tub, Inc. (ATI, Box 90331, Nashville, TN 37209). This one-piece unit has smooth, pleasing lines, with no seams to leak or trap dirt. There's even a seat molded into the rear wall. And like many one-piece units, it has its own ceiling.

I framed a linen closet at the head of the tub to allow access to the plumbing. The plumbing, incidentally, is based on a Grohmix thermostatic pressure-balanced shower valve (Grohe America, Inc., 900 N. Lively Blvd., Wood Dale, IL 60191). You set the thermostat to the water temperature you want, and it will stay there, even if someone flushes a toilet or the temperature of your hot-water supply starts to drop.

The vanity is large enough to hold all the clutter that had been building up in our old master bath, plus towels and washcloths. I designed it in the popular European style, with full overlay doors and drawer fronts, no face frame, and no visible hardware. I also built a medicine chest to match.

Building the vanity

The vanity carcass has ³⁄₄-inch plywood bottom and uprights, with a half-inch ply back. Assemble all these parts with glue and screws, then add the ³⁄₄-inch plywood toe kick. Apply laminate to the ends of the carcass and to the inner faces of the two right-most verticals. Then laminate all edges except the edge of the right vertical and the edge of the bottom between the two right-most verticals. As shown in the sketch, these two surfaces receive ³⁄₄-inch-square ash strips. This will bring the edges out flush with the faces of the drawers when they are installed later. These are not attached until the drawers have been mounted in the carcass.

When constructing the cabinet doors, simply cut the plywood to size and laminate the two faces. After gluing on the decorative ash edge strips, laminate the top and bottom edges. Use a router and a straight bit to cut out a recess for the oak pulls. These pulls—also used for the drawers—are from The Woodworkers' Store (21801 Industrial Blvd., Rogers, MN 55374; catalog No. B1602). The best way to rout the necessary recesses is to make a template of plywood to guide the router. You'll need it for both of the doors and all the drawers.

Next comes the top. Cut it to size, glue on the edge buildup strips, then laminate as usual. Then take a ³⁄₈-inch rabbet bit and cut a ³⁄₈-by-³⁄₈-inch rabbet into the edge of the counter. To avoid chipping the laminate, make your first pass with the router a light one, and feed it with—not against—bit rotation. This is contrary to normal practice, but it will absolutely prevent chipping if you take a light cut only as deep as the laminate.

Next rip out ³⁄₈-inch-square strips of ash, miter the ends, and glue them into the rabbets. After the glue is dry, chamfer the strips with a piloted chamfer bit in your router. Make the backsplash in the same manner.

Now place the cabinet carcass in position and screw its back to a couple of wall studs. Screw the top in place, driving screws up through the corner blocks into the top. Screwing the top down will also lock the front edges of the uprights in position, so make sure they are properly spaced when you drive the screws home.

Now you install the drawers. I mounted mine on Blum slides (The Woodworkers' Store catalog No. D9665). These are easy to install straight and square using the gunlike Blum Minifix (also available from The Woodworkers' Store) as shown in the sketch. After the drawers are in place, install the drawer fronts. Here's an easy way to get them perfectly aligned: Start with the bottom drawer. Slide it in place and drill a pair of ³⁄₁₆-inch holes through the front. The position of these holes isn't critical, but roughly center them top to bottom, and drill them about eight inches apart. Take the front and place it in position. Check to see that it is level and right where you want it, then secure it with a pair of spring clamps. Open the drawer, and drive a ³⁄₄-inch screw through each of the two holes in the drawer front to secure the drawer face. Now remove the clamps and close the drawer.

Insert the next drawer and close it. Drill it as above. Lay a ⅛-inch-thick strip of wood atop the edge of the bottom drawer face. Rest the next drawer face on this strip, checking to see that it is aligned left to right, and secure the face to its drawer with two spring clamps. Open the drawer, and

Installing the one-piece shower-tub unit is easy. Just position it, frame stud walls around it, and cover with drywall.

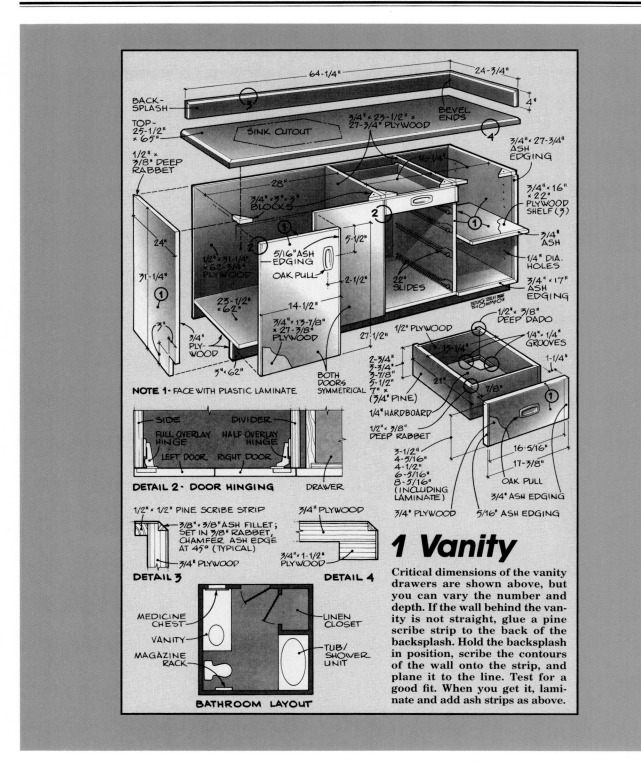

DETAIL 2 · DOOR HINGING

DETAIL 3

DETAIL 4

BATHROOM LAYOUT

1 Vanity

Critical dimensions of the vanity drawers are shown above, but you can vary the number and depth. If the wall behind the vanity is not straight, glue a pine scribe strip to the back of the backsplash. Hold the backsplash in position, scribe the contours of the wall onto the strip, and plane it to the line. Test for a good fit. When you get it, laminate and add ash strips as above.

screw through the front of the drawer into the face just as you did for the first drawer. Remove the clamps, close the drawer, and continue to the next one. Repeat until all of the faces are in place.

Hanging the doors

These go up with special European hinges. I used Blum hinges, available from The Woodworkers' Store. Use two catalog No. D9620 hinges for the left door (full overlay), and two No. D9621 hinges for the right door. You'll also need a special bit to install these. Follow the instructions provided with the hinges. The last step is to drill the two right-most uprights with 1/4-inch holes to accept shelf-support brackets. Then all you do is make up three or four shelves, and put them in place.

Medicine and magazines

The medicine chest is designed to sit between two wall studs. I used vinyl-faced particleboard for the case. Glue and screw the case together, then drill for the shelf-support brackets. Add the ash casing, and then make a few shelves.

Hang the door with a pair of Blum full-overlay hinges. To mount the cabinet in the wall, cut a 14½-by-24-inch

2 Medicine chest

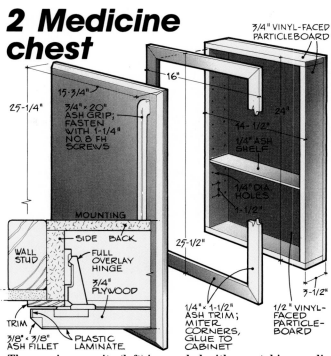

3/4" VINYL-FACED PARTICLEBOARD

25-1/4"

15-3/4"

3/4" × 20" ASH GRIP; FASTEN WITH 1-1/4" NO. 8 FH SCREWS

16"

24"

14-1/2"

1/4" ASH SHELF

1/4" DIA. HOLES

4-1/2"

MOUNTING

SIDE BACK

WALL STUD

FULL OVERLAY HINGE

3/4" PLYWOOD

25-1/2"

TRIM

3/8" × 3/8" ASH FILLET

PLASTIC LAMINATE

1/4" × 1-1/2" ASH TRIM; MITER CORNERS, GLUE TO CABINET

1/2" VINYL-FACED PARTICLE-BOARD

3-1/2"

The spacious vanity (left) is coupled with a matching medicine chest fashioned in an elegant European style. Together they hold all the clutter a bath gathers. The chamfered ash trim and pull of the medicine chest matches that of the vanity top. The sink, a hexagonal design from Kohler, is a self-rimming model, so it just drops into place.

3 Magazine rack

Complementing the trim used on the vanity and medicine chest, the magazine rack is constructed from light ash; the wall-mounted rack also helps eliminate bathroom clutter. A matching ash rack holds two towels within reach from the shower-tub unit. Although the bath is served by a heat pump, an in-wall electric heater provides extra heat for cold winter days.

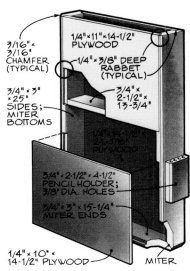

1/4" × 11" × 14-1/2" PLYWOOD

3/16" × 3/16" CHAMFER (TYPICAL)

1/4" × 3/8" DEEP RABBET (TYPICAL)

3/4" × 3" × 25" SIDES; MITER BOTTOMS

3/4" × 2-1/2" × 13-3/4"

3/4" × 2-1/2" × 4-1/2" PENCIL HOLDER; 3/8" DIA. HOLES

3/4" × 3" × 15-1/4" MITER ENDS

1/4" × 10" × 14-1/2" PLYWOOD

MITER

hole through the wallboard between two studs. Run a few beads of construction adhesive down the back of the cabinet, and then carefully press the unit into place.

Cut out the sides and bottom of the magazine rack, and rabbet them to accept the front panels. Cut out the compartment bottom; then, using miters at the bottom corners, glue the frame together. Add the two ash front panels, make up the optional pencil rack (for crossword fanatics), and finish with varnish or lacquer. To mount, run a few beads of construction adhesive down the back. Press in place on the wall, and secure with a prop for a few hours until the cement sets—*by A. J. Hand. Drawings by Eugene Thompson*

hang a hardwood ceiling

It was hard to heat and cool the family room shown in the photo, and it was impossible to insulate above the ceiling—so the homeowners installed a suspended ceiling. They chose Woodtech's insulated hardwood panels and stowed 3½ additional inches of insulation above the new surface. The panels were more difficult to install than a fiberboard system because the wood strips had to be carefully aligned with both side walls. But as you can see, the strikingly attractive new ceiling was worth the extra effort.

The standard 2-by-4-foot Woodtech panel drops into a 9/16-inch-wide suspended steel grid system (turn page for drawings). Parallel 1⁷/16-inch-wide strips of finished hardwood are mounted on the face of the panel. The ¾-inch-thick strips are spaced two inches on center and stapled to perpendicular back support strips made of hardwood lumber painted with a flat black enamel. The back supports extend enough beyond the edges of the panels so that they rest on the grid.

The backs of the panels are covered with black-faced one-inch-thick fiberglass insulation. The metal grid is the same color as the insulation and back supports—and the same width as the spaces between the facing strips—so it is nearly invisible after the panels are in place.

Because the basic panels weigh 15 to 20 pounds, depending on the type of

wood, you must use heavier hanger wire and screw eyes for Woodtech's grid than for a fiberboard system. The manufacturer recommends hanging the grid at least six inches, and preferably eight inches, below the existing surface. This gives you room to insert the panels. Also, you can stuff extra fiberglass insulation into the empty space.

At left, 2-by-2-foot panels in a sun room are arranged parquet-style. The wood is birch. Other wood species—such as ash, cherry, maple, poplar, red and white oak, and black walnut—are available. Right, oak strips are laid end to end to give a family room a new look. The basic panel is 2 by 4 feet, but you can order panels up to 10 feet long, in 1-foot increments. For curved wainscoting or columns, Woodtech's maker produces flexible-back panels. The company also offers custom-made rigid panels for broad, curved expanses. At bottom, the housing for recessed lighting is mounted on the back of the panel, with the finishing flange inserted into the face of the panel. Track lighting or conventional fluorescent panel fixtures made for suspended ceilings also can be used with Woodtech.

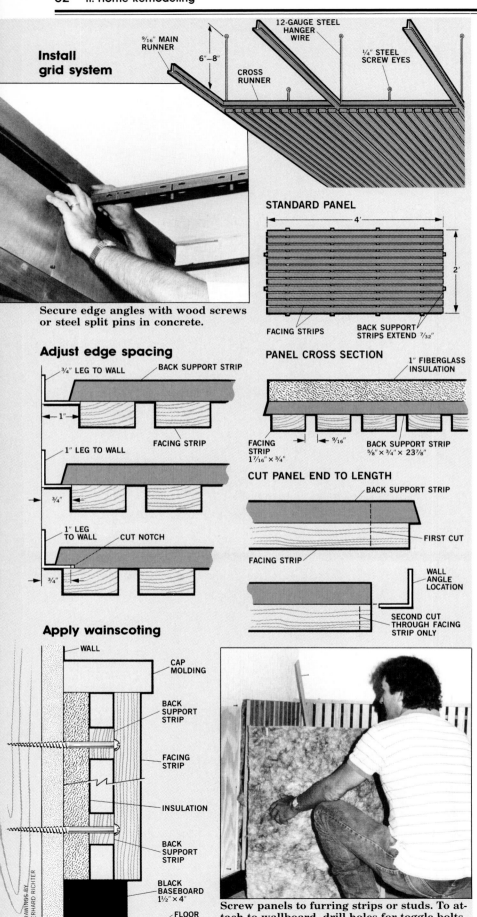

Install grid system

9/16" MAIN RUNNER
6"–8"
12-GAUGE STEEL HANGER WIRE
1/4" STEEL SCREW EYES
CROSS RUNNER

Secure edge angles with wood screws or steel split pins in concrete.

STANDARD PANEL

4'
2'
FACING STRIPS
BACK SUPPORT STRIPS EXTEND 7/32"

Adjust edge spacing

3/4" LEG TO WALL
BACK SUPPORT STRIP
1"
FACING STRIP

1" LEG TO WALL
3/4"

1" LEG TO WALL
CUT NOTCH
3/4"

PANEL CROSS SECTION

1" FIBERGLASS INSULATION
FACING STRIP 1 7/16" × 3/4"
9/16"
BACK SUPPORT STRIP 5/8" × 3/4" × 23 7/8"

CUT PANEL END TO LENGTH

BACK SUPPORT STRIP
FIRST CUT
FACING STRIP

WALL ANGLE LOCATION
SECOND CUT THROUGH FACING STRIP ONLY

Apply wainscoting

WALL
CAP MOLDING
BACK SUPPORT STRIP
FACING STRIP
INSULATION
BACK SUPPORT STRIP
BLACK BASEBOARD 1 1/2" × 4"
FLOOR

DRAWINGS BY GERHARD RICHTER

Screw panels to furring strips or studs. To attach to wallboard, drill holes for toggle bolts.

Prepare a perfectly rectangular opening for each panel. You can't cut a wedge out of a panel with a razor knife to compensate for out-of-square walls, as you might do with relatively inexpensive fiberboard tiles. Plan the job on paper before you begin the installation, with the center line running in the same direction as the facing strips.

The system is cleverly designed so that you won't need to split facing strips to make panels fit an odd-sized room width. Instead, you remove entire facing strips, trimming off the extra insulation and cutting the back support strips to leave 7/32-inch overhangs. If you find you must remove an odd number of strips, shift the grid layout one inch off center. You can make smaller adjustments by a combination of inverting the wall angle—which has a 3/4-inch side and a one-inch side—and notching or adding to the back supports (see drawings).

After you have sketched the grid layout, fasten the edge angles to the wall and install the grid. Then tilt the panels up through the openings and lower them into place.

To cut end panels to the proper length, measure the distance from the edge of the closest crossbar to the inside edge of the wall angle and add 1/2 inch. Cut off the remainder of the panel. Lay the panel in the opening, and mark a line on the facing strips where they meet the edge of the wall angle. Remove the panel, and saw through the facing strips along the line—don't cut the back support strips. If you make an error, don't worry. Extra back support strips come with the system.

Woodtech panels can be used for wainscoting as well as ceilings. The maker suggests using a black baseboard, which it supplies on request. If you order wainscoting specifically, the back support strips will be flush with the edges of the facing strips. If not, trim off the projections.

Set the panel on top of the baseboard, and attach it to your walls (see drawing). Woodtech furnishes flat black strips that you glue or tack between the panels to maintain the 9/16-inch spacing. Molding strips are available to cap the wainscoting and, if necessary, to frame the ends.

Ceiling and wall panels cost between $10 and $12 per square foot, depending on the wood selected. The Woodtech system is supplied by Architectural Surfaces, Inc., 123 Columbia Ct. N., Jonathan Business Center W., Chaska, MN 55318—*by Phil McCafferty. Drawings by Gerhard Richter.*

basement overhaul

Like a house within a house, this fully remodelled basement features entertainment and sitting areas, as well as master bedroom and bathroom. Inset photo shows conversational seating group with large-screen TV.

Remodeling a basement is probably the classic DIY home-improvement project. No matter what style or how old your house is, a finished basement can boost its value with added living space, convenience, and luxury.

A basement overhaul also brings new-home benefits to your current house without the expense and hassle of a move, and possible loss of an existing low-rate mortgage. And should you decide to sell, the "sweat equity" of doing as much of the work as possible yourself virtually assures that you'll get back 100 percent of what it cost you in materials. Contrast that with the 70 percent or so you'd get if you farmed out the work to a contractor.

These benefits appealed to Dave Firszt and his family as they got started on the drab and dingy basement of their northern Illinois home. Built in 1978, the house has a main basement area of 53-by-25 feet with a 7 1/2-foot height to the joists of the first floor. A lower walk-in storage area, about one-third the floor space of the main area, was left unfinished.

A series of mini-projects

Dave and his family knew a project of this scope was not going to be a quick and easy weekend effort. With that firmly in mind, they drew up a construction plan detailing

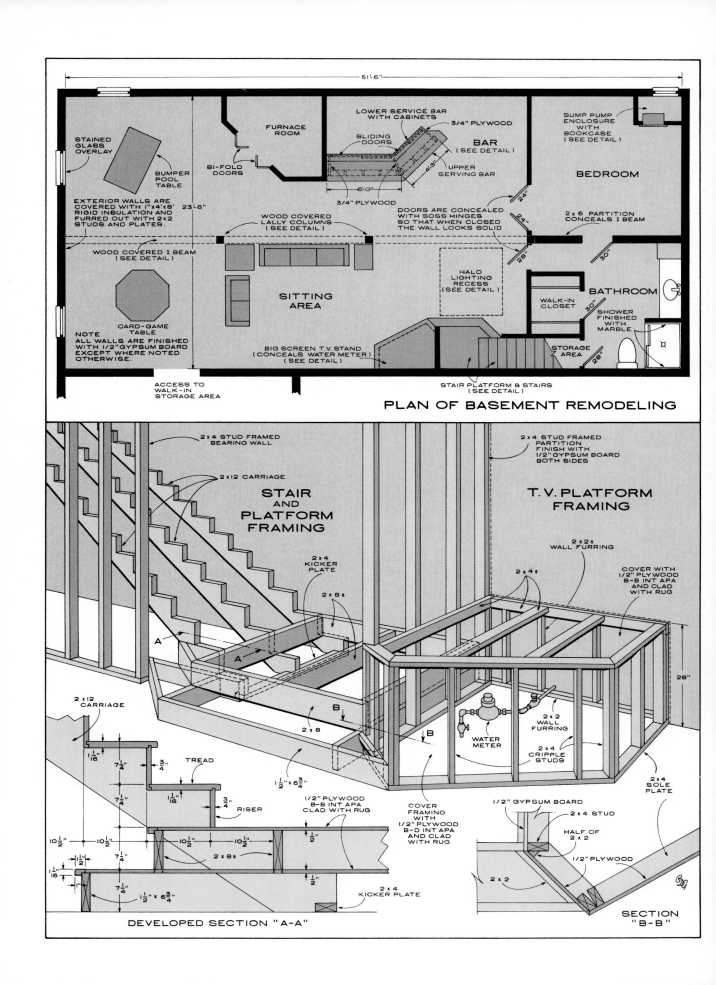

PLAN OF BASEMENT REMODELING

51'-6"

STAINED GLASS OVERLAY

BUMPER POOL TABLE

FURNACE ROOM

BI-FOLD DOORS

LOWER SERVICE BAR WITH CABINETS

SLIDING DOORS

3/4" PLYWOOD

BAR (SEE DETAIL)

SUMP PUMP ENCLOSURE WITH BOOKCASE (SEE DETAIL)

BEDROOM

EXTERIOR WALLS ARE COVERED WITH 1"x4'x8' RIGID INSULATION AND FURRED OUT WITH 2x2 STUDS AND PLATES.

23'-6"

UPPER SERVING BAR

4'-3"

3/4" PLYWOOD

6'-0"

2 x 6 PARTITION CONCEALS I BEAM

24"

24"

WOOD COVERED I BEAM (SEE DETAIL)

WOOD COVERED LALLY COLUMNS (SEE DETAIL)

DOORS ARE CONCEALED WITH SOSS HINGES SO THAT WHEN CLOSED THE WALL LOOKS SOLID

28"

30"

HALO LIGHTING RECESS (SEE DETAIL)

BATHROOM

SHOWER FINISHED WITH MARBLE

SITTING AREA

CARD-GAME TABLE

WALK-IN CLOSET

30"

STORAGE AREA

28"

NOTE
ALL WALLS ARE FINISHED WITH 1/2"GYPSUM BOARD EXCEPT WHERE NOTED OTHERWISE.

BIG SCREEN T.V. STAND (CONCEALS WATER METER) (SEE DETAIL)

ACCESS TO WALK-IN STORAGE AREA

STAIR PLATFORM & STAIRS (SEE DETAIL)

STAIR AND PLATFORM FRAMING

2 x 4 STUD FRAMED BEARING WALL

2 x 12 CARRIAGE

2 x 4 STUD FRAMED PARTITION FINISH WITH 1/2" GYPSUM BOARD BOTH SIDES

T.V. PLATFORM FRAMING

2 x 4 KICKER PLATE

2 x 8s

A

A

B

2 x 8

B

2 x 2s WALL FURRING

2 x 4s

COVER WITH 1/2" PLYWOOD B-B INT APA AND CLAD WITH RUG

28"

2 x 2 WALL FURRING

WATER METER

2 x 4 CRIPPLE STUDS

2 x 4 SOLE PLATE

2 x 12 CARRIAGE

7 1/4"

1 1/16"

3/4"

TREAD

1 1/16"

3/4"

RISER

7 1/4"

1 1/2" x 6 3/4"

1/2" PLYWOOD B-B INT APA CLAD WITH RUG

COVER FRAMING WITH 1/2" PLYWOOD B-D INT APA AND CLAD WITH RUG

10 1/2"

10 1/2"

10 1/2"

10 1/2"

10 1/2"

1/2"

1/2" GYPSUM BOARD

2 x 4 STUD

1 1/2"

7 1/4"

2 x 8s

1/2"

HALF OF 2 x 2

1/2" PLYWOOD

1 1/16"

1"

7 1/4"

1 1/2" x 6 3/4"

2 x 4 KICKER PLATE

2 x 2

DEVELOPED SECTION "A-A"

SECTION "B-B"

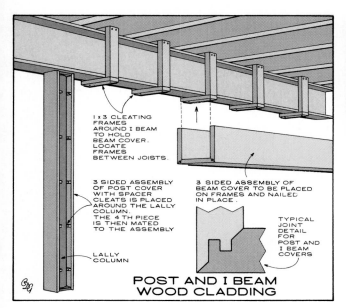

1 x 3 CLEATING FRAMES AROUND I BEAM TO HOLD BEAM COVER. LOCATE FRAMES BETWEEN JOISTS.

3 SIDED ASSEMBLY OF POST COVER WITH SPACER CLEATS IS PLACED AROUND THE LALLY COLUMN. THE 4 TH PIECE IS THEN MATED TO THE ASSEMBLY

3 SIDED ASSEMBLY OF BEAM COVER TO BE PLACED ON FRAMES AND NAILED IN PLACE.

TYPICAL JOINT DETAIL FOR POST AND I BEAM COVERS

LALLY COLUMN

POST AND I BEAM WOOD CLADDING

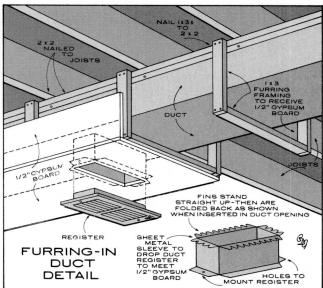

NAIL 1x3s TO 2 x 2

2 x 2 NAILED TO JOISTS

1 x 3 FURRING FRAMING TO RECEIVE 1/2" GYPSUM BOARD

DUCT

1/2" GYPSUM BOARD

JOISTS

FINS STAND STRAIGHT UP—THEN ARE FOLDED BACK AS SHOWN WHEN INSERTED IN DUCT OPENING

REGISTER

SHEET METAL SLEEVE TO DROP DUCT REGISTER TO MEET 1/2" GYPSUM BOARD

HOLES TO MOUNT REGISTER

FURRING-IN DUCT DETAIL

the individual stages that would make up their basement overhaul. Listing the different remodeling tasks allowed this large-scale project to be broken down into smaller jobs the Firszts could manage at their own pace.

Careful planning of the different stages allowed the work to progress in orderly fashion, while also permitting interruptions of the work and access to the basement for other needs such as storage. Dividing the remodeling project into segments also provided time and opportunity to rethink initial plans and work in new ideas for later stages as they went along.

Camouflaged furnace and other details

Rather than attempt to move basic home utilities and equipment typically found in basements, the family decided to leave the furnace, hot-water heater, water and gas meters, and sump pump in their original locations and camouflage them. The resulting uniquely shaped enclosures divide a large room into smaller, more intimate areas that are comfortable for one or two people, or as many as 20. A built-in bookcase and entertainment-equipment platform are also results of this decision.

The general plan included a main recreation room 40-by-25 feet with a walk-behind bar, seating group for conversation and watching large-screen TV, plus space for a pool table and board games. A 13-by-12-foot bedroom for a teenage son and a full 9-by-12-foot bathroom were also included (Figs. 1 and 2), along with a walk-in closet and generous under-stair storage area.

In addition to careful planning of the overall project, attention to smaller details helped make the remodeled basement an attractive and convenient living area.

The dropped acoustical ceiling features the latest products from USG Interiors, Inc. Newly introduced three-dimensional Tiffany Ceiling Panels were used with a new USG ceiling-grid system called Simplicitee. The sculptured design of the ceiling panels reduces noise levels and dramatically accents the main recreation room, bedroom, and bath with geometric modules that reflect light and shadows as the light quality and direction vary.

To mask the basement window wells, yet allow natural light into the basement, four Stained Glass Overlay panels were used as shown on pages 58 and 59.

The 62-inch-wide vanity top 1-inch-thick cultured marble. Each of the three walls of the 48-by-34-inch shower enclosure is an individual sheet of 3/8-inch-thick cultured marble. Kinkead Vista-Glide By-Pass Shower doors fea-

View from bathroom side door, through bedroom, and into the main room showing bar on north wall.

Shower and bath fixtures as seen from the northwest corner of the bathroom. Cultured marble vanity and patterned safety-glass shower doors are attractive yet practical features.

4

Bi-fold wood-and-glass doors hide furnace while allowing easy access.

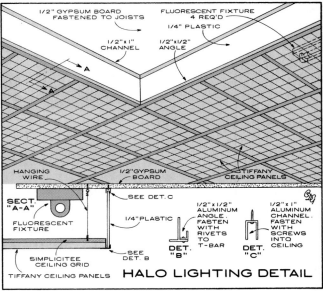

HALO LIGHTING DETAIL

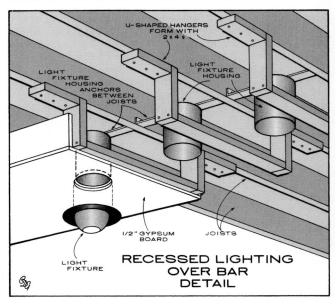

RECESSED LIGHTING OVER BAR DETAIL

ture brown-colored stripes on tempered safety glass. The gold frames, complete with a beige snap-on trim kit, highlight the shower area.

The mauve-colored carpet used throughout the basement has a *frizae* cut, which is a medium nap that has texture yet does not leave footprints.

Bi-fold doors with frosted-look glass inlay panels, as shown in figure 4, allow access to the water heater and furnace. The door louvers are functional and allow air flow to the furnace.

Double bedroom doors, bathroom doors, and access panels to the unfinished walk-in storage area boast concealed hinges and push-to-open closures that allow the finished door panels to appear as part of the wall when closed. The use of double doors for the bedroom is an example of the forethought that was used in planning this basement overhaul. Because of the wide entry, which makes it easy to bring in large pieces of wood or office furniture, this room easily can be converted into a workshop or home office.

Individual stages of construction

The first stage of the basement remodeling to be tackled was the framing of basement walls with 2×2 lumber. Polystyrene foam insulation sheets 1 inch by 4 feet by 8 feet were used and covered by gypsum wallboard.

Construction of the bedroom and bathroom at one end of the basement was the next step, and the most time-consuming. The bedroom presented no unusual situations, other than the use of concealed Soss hinges and press-to-open closures for the entrance doors—as shown in Figs. 5, 6, and 7—plus the construction of an enclosure to hide the

5

6

7

Mounting area in door is drilled out with a 1-inch boring bit. The same is done with the door jamb. Soss hinges are test-fitted into the door, (center) and a chisel is used to remove any excess wood. Shown at right is door and jamb with Soss hinge in place.

Every 4 feet, put a screw eye directly over the main T string. Wrap a length of wire through the screw eye and let it drop 3 inches below the string. Then bend the wire at a 90-degree angle about ¾ inch above the string.

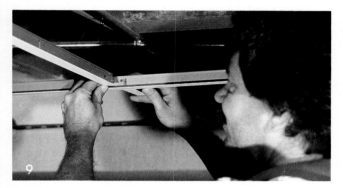

Simply snap the cross Ts into place, cutting with snips to make short sections for areas where a full ceiling tile won't fit.

Once the length of wall is measured, cut the metal wall angle to fit the space.

Wall angle is tacked in place using 6d nails.

sump pump with a swing-out bookcase for equipment access. The space for the bathroom already had plumbing drains installed when the home was first built, so this area needed only copper water pipes and finishing work.

Third stage of construction included the building and installation of enclosures to hide a support beam and posts. A standard metal I-beam runs the width of the basement. This horizontal beam and its vertical support posts are hidden by specially-cut pine boards that give the rich look of natural wood beam and posts (See drawing). Tongue and groove cuts in the boards allow the corner seams to disappear when the sides are mated.

The fourth stage focused on framing the furnace and water-heater area with 2×4 lumber covered by gypsum wallboard. The angular shape of this enclosure not only allows plenty of space to service either piece of equipment, but also provides a room divider and side wall for the bar. Double bi-fold doors were used to insure easy access.

Installation of the 6-inch-drop ceiling and ceiling recess for indirect lighting were key elements in the fifth stage.

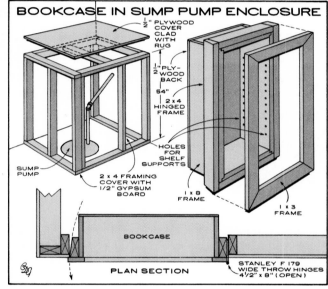

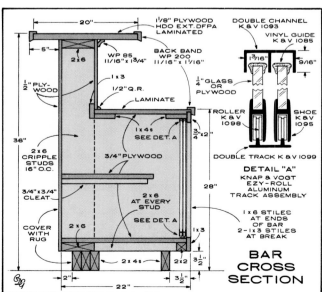

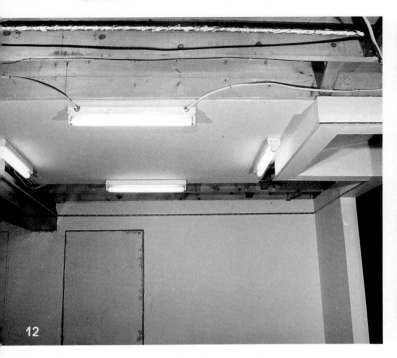

12

13

Halo lighting is provided by fluorescent lights mounted to wallboard 6 inches above where the new ceiling will be.

Cut a dado into each length of board to accomodate the thickness of the stained glass.

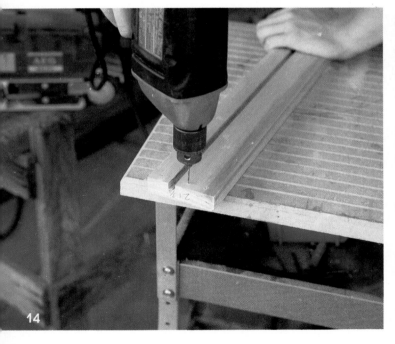

14

15

Nail pieces together but leave the top piece off for now.

Drill starter holes into the vertical sides of the window frame.

Once you determine where the main Ts of metal ceiling grid will go, run a string from that point—dropped 6 inches and perpendicular to the joists—across to the other end of the room. Then determine the position of the first cross T and run another string from one wall to the opposite wall—this time *parallel* to the joist and perpendicular to the string for the main T. This gives you a perfect square guide in which to hang the metal grid (Figs. 8 and 9).

In figures 10 and 11, wall angle for a corner of the ceiling is cut to size and then tacked into place with 6d nails.

Fluorescent lights provide dramatic halo lighting from each of the two areas of the ceiling recessed for the purpose. Once wallboard has been mounted to the joists above, lighting fixtures are mounted around the perimeter of the wallboard with toggle bolts as shown in figure 12.

Next came the wood frames for the stained-glass window overlays. Once you've cut the 1-by-3-inch clear lumber to size for each of the four windows, a ¼-inch dado is cut into each length of board to accomodate the thickness of the stained glass (Fig. 13). Sand each board smooth, then care-

Test window for fit, then attach the top of the frame.

Carpeting is stretched and tacked in place using an electric stapler and "kicker."

A good place to start any wallpapering job is along a straight door frame. This helps ensure that all subsequent pieces are straight.

Kicker stretches rug for additional tightening around post.

fully drill starter holes into the vertical sides of the window frame (Fig. 14). In figures 15 and 16, the pieces are nailed together with the top piece left off until the glass is tested for fit, as shown.

Finishing touches

For the Firszts, the final stage of the project was decorating their newly renovated basement. Color coordination was a paramount concern when selecting the textured wallcovering, wall-to-wall carpeting, and bar top. When putting up the wallpaper, Dave avoided alignment problems right from the start by using a door frame to butt the first piece (Fig. 17), so that subsequent pieces would be laid on straight.

The bar top with wood and brass inlays was custom-designed and made by a company that specializes in bar and table tops for restaurants. The Firszts saw to it that this craftsmanship was carried over to the carpeting on the bar and floor. Figures 18 and 19 show an electric stapler and "kicker" being used to stretch and tack the carpeting in place over the front of the bar and around a post.

Careful planning is the first and most essential step in completing a basement overhaul you can be proud of. With some forethought, even a major project like this can be started, interrupted, and then picked up again when time and money allow. The reward is sumptuous new living space for any home, and money in the bank should you decide to sell—*by Mike Bruening. Drawing by Carl De Groote.*

LIST OF MANUFACTURERS
Bar Top by Originals in Furnishings, 6050 West Oakton, Martin Grove, IL 60053; **Bathroom Wallpaper** by Seabrook wall coverings, 1325 Farmville, Memphis, TN 38122; **Bedroom Wallpaper** by CNA Wallcoverings, 23645 Mercantile Road, Cleveland, OH 44122; **Ceiling Panels and Grid** by USG Interiors, Inc., 101 South Wacker Drive, Chicago, IL 60606; **Shower Door and Trim** by Kinkead Division, USG Industries, Inc., 101 South Wacker Drive, Chicago, IL 60606; **Window Overlays** by Stained Glass Overlay, 151 Kalmus Drive, Costa Mesa, CA 92626.

attic entertainment center

f your house offers the option of finishing off an existing attic, it's the quickest way to avail yourself of "room at the top," without any structural changes.

Of course, if your overhead space is cluttered with the struts of a truss-supported roof, this solution isn't for you. But most older houses have attics that cry out for finishing. Don't write yours off just because the collar ties that span the rafters are too low to allow headroom. You can probably raise these, one at a time, to at least seven feet above floor height. Where they must be this low (for structural purposes), you can get a more spacious feeling by leaving them exposed, for a rustic beam effect; just run the drywall up past them to the peak.

If your attic has any floor at all, it's probably minimal. If there are boards laid across the joists, make certain they are properly nailed, and fill in any gaps before you cover them with sheets of 3/4-inch plywood or other underlayment. Then, after all your construction is complete, you can lay carpet or vinyl.

The major problem in the North Carolina house shown here was that the existing 2 × 8 rafters didn't create cavities deep enough to install eight-inch-thick insulation batts and still leave a space under the roof decking for air to flow from soffit vents under the three eaves up to the new ridge vent the homeowners installed. This circulation is essential to carry off heated air beneath the roof deck (in summer) and to prevent condensation buildup between deck and insulation (in winter). Moisture here can dampen the insulation, reducing its effectiveness, and cause rot damage.

So these homeowners attached 2 × 2s along the edges of all rafters passing through the insulated space (see photo) to deepen the insulation cavities. They used 2½-inch screws, spaced every 16 inches, driven with a screw gun.

In a windowless area such as this—with the ceiling angling down on three sides because of the hip roof—a skylight seemed essential. The one shown fit neatly between two joists.

It's best to nail the sills for your perimeter walls directly atop the subfloor. You'll want as much floor space as is practical, but don't push it so far toward the sloping eaves that your walls become less than 5 feet high. Shorty partitions like this are called knee walls. After marking out your floor space on the subfloor, figure out where you'd like bump-out bookcases and cabinets, so you can frame openings for them as you erect your walls.

If your rafters have their own support system, build your knee-wall framing around it. Since this framing will add support to the rafters, any existing system—except trusses, of course—can usually be removed once the new framing is in place.

Basically, this framing consists of 2 × 4 studs, 16 inches on center, between a sill and a top plate (also 2 × 4s), assembled with 16-penny nails. For better load transfer, it's a good

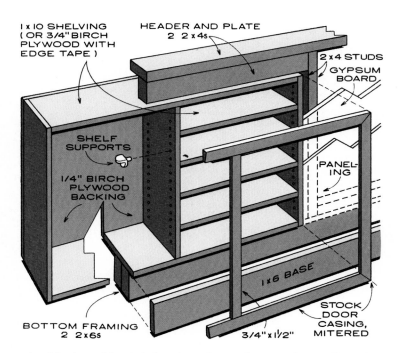

Recessed cabinets and bookshelves in the three knee walls—shown on following page—take advantage of space behind, without eating up floor space.

Frame them as shown above. In severe climates bump-outs should be wrapped in same insulation as walls to help avoid unnecessary heat loss.

idea to fit wedges between the top plate and each rafter.

With framing complete, run all wiring to baseboard outlets, ceiling lights, and fans. If you're extending heating and air-conditioning ducts to this area, now's the time to have them installed. Assuming local codes require an inspection before the walls are closed, schedule it at this point.

Standard insulation batts were installed between the rafters, with the paper (or foil) face down and the side flanges stapled to the rafters.

In many older houses, rafters are made of rough lumber that wasn't milled to a uniform width. So before you nail up your drywall ceiling, it's best to pull a string taut along the underside of the rafters to see if any low spots need shimming. The nailing pattern shown in the sketch was used with 1¾-inch gypsum-board nails. The same material was then installed on the knee-wall framing so that the wall panels supported the lower edges of the ceiling panels.

Most of the materials, including ¾-inch birch plywood for the bookshelves, came from Georgia-Pacific and cost about $5,000. The project added over $8,000 to the house's value—*by Al Lees. Drawings by Carl De Groote*

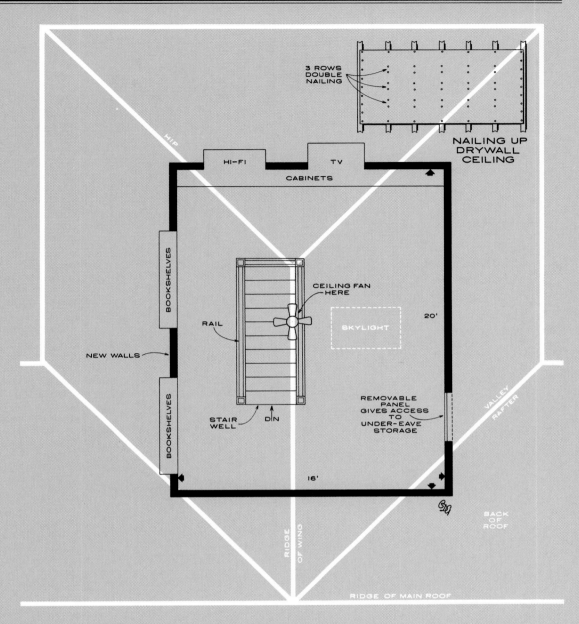

3 ROWS DOUBLE NAILING

NAILING UP DRYWALL CEILING

HI-FI
TV
CABINETS

BOOKSHELVES

BOOKSHELVES

NEW WALLS

RAIL

CEILING FAN HERE

SKYLIGHT

20'

STAIR WELL

DN

REMOVABLE PANEL GIVES ACCESS TO UNDER-EAVE STORAGE

16'

HIP

VALLEY RAFTER

RIDGE OF WING

BACK OF ROOF

RIDGE OF MAIN ROOF

Large diagram above shows how the finished floor plan fits within the eaves above the house's existing peninsula wing, and gives an idea what dimensions you can expect in your own attic. Existing stair was railed off on three sides with standard rail components and four corner posts bolted to floor frame. Sketch at top right shows the nailing pattern for fastening drywall sheets to rafters that are deepened by nailing on 2 × 2s (photo above, left).

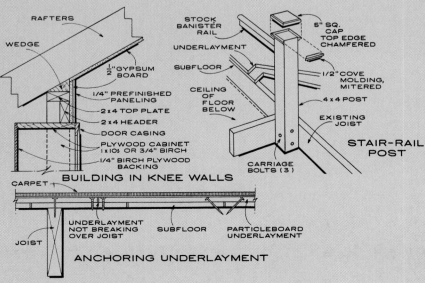

RAFTERS

WEDGE

1/2" GYPSUM BOARD

1/4" PREFINISHED PANELING

2 x 4 TOP PLATE

2 x 4 HEADER

DOOR CASING

PLYWOOD CABINET 1x10s OR 3/4" BIRCH

1/4" BIRCH PLYWOOD BACKING

BUILDING IN KNEE WALLS

STOCK BANISTER RAIL

UNDERLAYMENT

SUBFLOOR

CEILING OF FLOOR BELOW

5" SQ. CAP TOP EDGE CHAMFERED

1/2" COVE MOLDING, MITERED

4 x 4 POST

EXISTING JOIST

STAIR-RAIL POST

CARRIAGE BOLTS (3)

CARPET

UNDERLAYMENT NOT BREAKING OVER JOIST

SUBFLOOR

PARTICLEBOARD UNDERLAYMENT

JOIST

ANCHORING UNDERLAYMENT

red-oak hutch

Author fits doors to hutch. Here, a complete "dry" assembly before staining offers the first opportunity to truly evaluate the design—and the last to make changes.

In many households you'll find that the most costly single item of furniture is a hutch. Sometimes it is also the most ornate and can totally dominate a room. I wanted one that would be comfortable with furniture of almost any period, that would have just enough frills to avoid severity of design, and be easy to build.

Ours, if a few basics are followed, can be built by the home craftsman of average skill. It will blend with the decor of any period. It is massive enough to be imposing and look very expensive, yet it will not "own" the room it occupies. And, the builder can save a bundle over the cost of a store-bought hutch of equivalent quality.

Note that this project is large, with many parts. If you start out by cutting those parts with less than perfect accuracy the job will fight you every step of the way. For example, if the stiles or rails on those critical end panels are not cut to precise length, their corners can't be made square. Then you'll be building the whole buffet carcase with an invisible twist. You can't see it, but it's there. You may never know why you can't make the drawers fit right, or have to put a match book under one corner to prevent the unit from rocking.

You'll find, however, that there are no difficult cuts. And, while assembly of a complex unit often requires much ingenuity, this one is designed to go together easily and come into line automatically—if you cut the parts right. So check your equipment and adjust it for minimum error.

Selecting the wood

This hutch will look nice in just about any wood, from pine to cherry. I built it in red oak and later stained it to match the cupboards in our family kitchen. Just be sure that the wood you choose has been properly dried for your location. Choose planks where the grain runs parallel with the plank edge, with as much vertical grain as possible.

Incidentally, except for the single sheet of finish-plywood required, you probably won't be able to find the material you need at your friendly local lumber yard. If you do, you will pay through the nose for it. Go to a hardwood lumber specialist. Alternatively, most millwork shops will sell some of their material to the do-it-yourselfer.

Where to begin

The job starts with gluing up the top. The pieces, or *staves*, should be laid up "with the cup." This means that, observing the annular rings in the wood, you lay each piece on the bench bark-side down. This is generally recommended because wood tends to cup in the same direction as the curve of the rings. If you glue the wood up so that all pieces curve upwards, you can

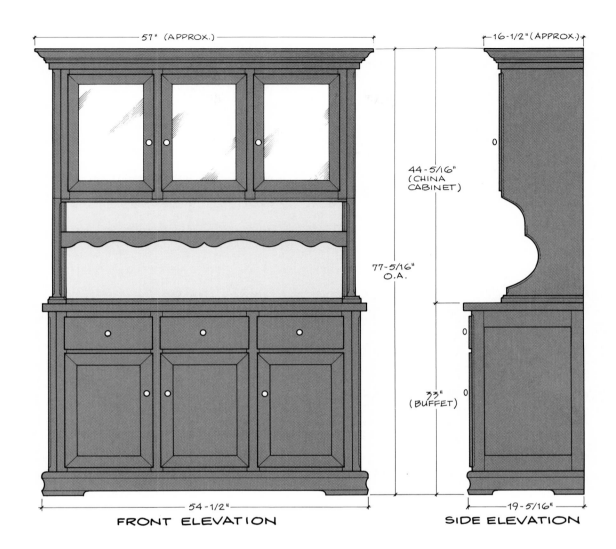

57" (APPROX.)

16-1/2" (APPROX.)

44-5/16"
(CHINA
CABINET)

77-5/16"
O.A.

33"
(BUFFET)

54-1/2"

19-5/16"

FRONT ELEVATION

SIDE ELEVATION

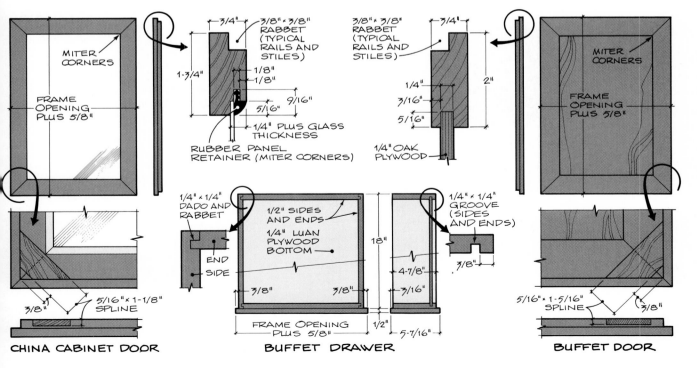

MITER CORNERS

FRAME OPENING PLUS 5/8"

3/4"

3/8" × 3/8" RABBET (TYPICAL RAILS AND STILES)

1-3/4"

1/8"
1/8"

9/16"

5/16"

1/4" PLUS GLASS THICKNESS

RUBBER PANEL RETAINER (MITER CORNERS)

3/8" × 3/8" RABBET (TYPICAL RAILS AND STILES)

3/4"

1/4"

3/16"

5/16"

2"

1/4" OAK PLYWOOD

MITER CORNERS

FRAME OPENING PLUS 5/8"

3/8"

5/16" × 1-1/8" SPLINE

1/4" × 1/4" DADO AND RABBET

END

SIDE

1/2" SIDES AND ENDS

1/4" LUAN PLYWOOD BOTTOM

3/8"

3/8"

FRAME OPENING PLUS 5/8"

18"

1/4" × 1/4" GROOVE (SIDES AND ENDS)

3/8"

4-7/8"

3/16"

1/2"

5-7/16"

5/16" × 1-5/16" SPLINE

3/8"

CHINA CABINET DOOR

BUFFET DRAWER

BUFFET DOOR

The rule for gluing the top: many clamps, moderate pressure. Apply a couple of 1/8-inch beads of glue to each part and flatten them with a thin wood paddle. Remove clamps before squeeze-out is completely dry and remove residue with a scraper.

In the rails, 3/4-inch is too much to take out in one pass, so do it in two passes or more. Rails were cut apart after grooving.

A pair of 1/8-inch cutters make an accurate groove for fitting the plywood panel. Width is adjusted by using paper washers as shims. A wood fence clamped to the router table controls groove depth.

fasten down at the edges and the top will remain flat even if its moisture content increases.

Of course it would be helpful if all your wood were blemish-free, with nice vertical grain, but in today's market that isn't easy. So if you have to turn a piece wrong way up to avoid a knot or dark streak, don't worry about it too much as long as most of the staves are right.

You can have all your material dressed to thickness and clamp the staves down as you edge-glue them, then sand and sand until the top is flat. Or, you can do as I did: simply dress the rough-sawn wood lightly on your jointer to flatten it and show the grain, glue it up, then have the millwork people finish-dress the blank in their big thickness planer.

Next, lay the finished top face-down on the bench and make a pencil layout of the carcase on the back. Now you can start cutting the rails. Cut the dadoes for the stiles all at the same time so you're sure of perfect alignment. Mark one end so you are sure they will assemble as you cut them.

Clamp the two top rails on your layout and mark the hold-down screw locations. Mark top and rails so that things go back together right. Countersink for the screw heads and drill through to spot-mark the top. Now you can go ahead and drill the top for the threaded inserts.

Our design calls for floating construction. This means that the top is allowed to expand or contract without warping or putting undue strain on the carcase. You drill the screw holes 1/4-inch oversize and tighten just enough to snug the top down. Some people even slot the hold-down screw holes to allow more movement, but I haven't run into any trouble by simply making the holes oversize (knock on wood).

Paneled ends

I used doweled construction here. Anything more elaborate, such as mortise and tenon, isn't necessary because the cleat for the bottom shelf support and the drawer slides will help hold things together. You can groove for the plywood panel on the saw by making multiple cuts or using an adjustable dado. I preferred grooving with a router on my trusty homemade router table. It's fast, the setup is simple, and I can easily stop the cut short of the dowel holes.

Don't glue the plywood insets into solid wood frames because of the differences in dimensional change between frame and panel with temperature and humidity. And if you go with the router, don't buy a 1/4-inch grooving cutter and expect it to give you a nice fit to your 1/4-inch paneling because the paneling will be well under nominal size. Get two 1/8-inch cutters. Their carbide tips will overlap so they nest at about 3/16 inch thickness. Then you can cut little paper washers to bring the cutting width up to the 7/32 inch or so you need to attain a proper fit.

Some people like to give the panels a coat of stain before assembly so that possible shrink in the frame won't cause a white line to show around the insert. All assembled parts that will show should be be sanded before assembly; it may be nearly impossible to do a good job afterward. Especially on oak, finish-sand all parts with the same grit of paper because the coarser the paper, the darker the stain will come out.

About an hour after you've glued up your panels you can remove the clamps and start your main carcase assembly. Glue the frame ends into that nice dado you cut in the end panel stiles, and glue the drawer slides onto the splines in the frame stiles. You can cut the bottom shelf and back now, too, and set them aside if you like. For the back and top of the china cabinet, I used 1/4-inch lauan underlayment. The wood is cheap and stains well.

Building the base molding

The next job can present problems, or it can be fairly easy; it all depends on the wood. For the base, be sure you have good, straight-grained material that will lay flat. The long convex curve is quite easy to make. It is done by cocking a 10-inch saw at a 60-degree angle to the piece and making multiple cuts, feeding the saw into the work 1/16 inch on each pass. On the radial arm saw there is a risk on this kind of operation of having the work drawn up into the saw and making the cut ragged. A simple hold-down, screwed to the saw table, is well worth the time it takes to make it.

Make sure the saw is angled to throw the work against the fence or it will try to get away from you. On the radial arm saw, particularly with oak

Check squareness of assembly when you clamp doweled parts together. If you've cut parts to the exact length and square on the ends, the assembly will be square without adjustment or machining.

Cutting the large convex radius into the base. Stock is being fed from left to right as the saw is adjusted down ¹⁄₁₆-inch at a time. A solid wood hold-down was screwed to the table to prevent the part from being drawn upward into the saw.

or cherry, be prepared to get a face full of wood chips. Goggles, or better yet a full face mask, are called for on this job.

On the table saw you don't have the chip or hold-down problem. Just clamp a wooden guide to the table at a 30-degree angle to the miter gauge slots. (It is clamped to the left of the saw). *Remember:* It's risky to push the work through with your hands. Use a pusher. The one from the jointer is ideal for this job.

Lay the pieces flat on the table for sanding. I have found that the best sanding block is one you can make from a simple piece of insulating foam board. Simply lay a sheet of coarse sandpaper face up in the groove and scrub the foam back and forth on it until it takes the shape of the groove. Then flip the paper over onto the foam and you have a perfectly contoured sanding block.

Cut the miters on the end pieces first and install them with an inch or so sticking out in back. When you cut these large miters leave ¹⁄₁₆ inch or so and take it off with shaving cuts to final size. Drill two oversize screw holes in the splines and install the screws with washers. Now you can adjust the molding position a little bit for fitting to the front piece. With the front molding fitted properly you can tighten the original screws and install another screw, with no washer, between them. Be sure to clamp and glue a 1¹⁄₂-inch-square glue block in each inside corner.

Install the top and back now, and you have a buffet that's about ready for drawers and doors. Proceed by making three plywood shelves, individually adjustable.

Building the china cabinet

The china cabinet sits loose on the buffet to make the complete hutch. Building it is straightforward just like

the buffet—until you come to the dentil and top crown moldings.

There are three ways to go with the dentil molding: You can use a molding head in your saw for those little curves; you can get a core box cutter with a full radius and make a setup to index the part past your router; or you can simply retreat and cut plain rectangular grooves with a dado cutter. Rectangular grooves are okay, but if you round them they will harmonize a little better with the cove cuts on the side panels.

More than 30 years ago, I bought the only molding head I could afford at the time—the one-tooth, 5-inch job pictured. I own two other molding heads now, but believe it or not, the old-timer runs with less vibration and makes just as smooth a cut. It feeds more slowly, but we home craftsman are not pushing for maximum production anyway.

Cut your dentil blank long enough to go across the front. Make it double-width plus a saw kerf to avoid making so many indexes and save a lot of time on hand sanding. Here's the way it goes: (1) cut grooves; (2) sand, with the paper wrapped around a ³⁄₄-inch dowel; (3) rout the cove on both edges of the blank; (4) dado groove for the flat portion; (5) saw the blank in two lengthwise.

Set the strips aside now until you have the big crown molding ready. You don't need fancy mitering equipment to cut the molding as long as you follow this procedure: First, cut the filler block to the proper width and angle. This will probably be about 55 degrees, depending on who made the molding cutters. Prepare a piece of scrap about 2 inches wide, ⁵⁄₁₆ inch thick, and 2 feet long. Set the filler piece on it and glue on the moldings. Use alligator clips and a few small finishing nails. You'll find it will be easier to drill for the nails if you're using hard woods.

Coarse sandpaper, pressed cutting-surface up into the groove, will quickly shape a piece of foam into a sanding block. Then, simply turn the paper over for fast, accurate sanding.

Now you can saw your miters, with the filler resting on the ⁵⁄₁₆-inch strips. Use the setup outlined for mitering the door frames, just as though the assembly were a simple rectangular block.

With the carcase assembly sitting on the carcase top on ⁵⁄₁₆-thick spacers, set dentils against the carcase resting on the molding assembly. Mark their position and install them with clamps and glue. Now lay the carcase assembly on its back and install the moldings. Screw the end moldings on first, leaving some stock sticking out in back for trim and adjustment. Cut this off with a hand saw later and sand flush.

Install the china cabinet feet and plate rail are next. Then install the finish-plywood back and the top with small nails. Sand the finish plywood before you install it.

Shelves in the upper cabinet are an option. Some hutches use the upper cabinet for display, and you can use a narrow plate rail as pictured in the assembly drawing. You can use a full-width shelf or three glass shelves as I plan to do.

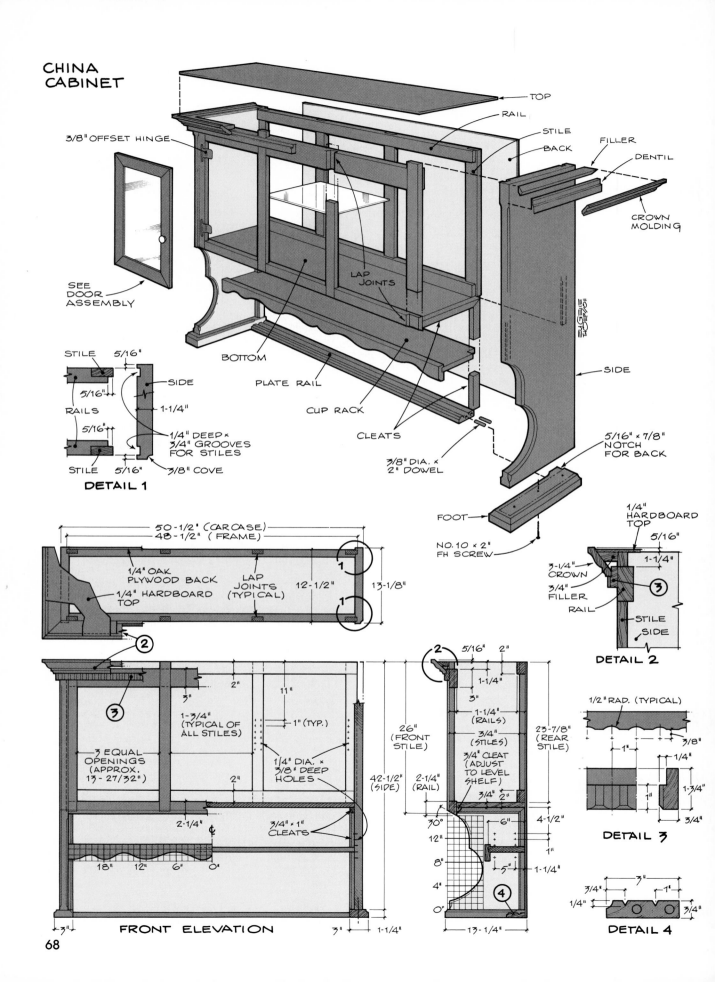

CHINA CABINET

TOP

RAIL

3/8" OFFSET HINGE

STILE

BACK

FILLER

DENTIL

CROWN MOLDING

SEE DOOR ASSEMBLY

LAP JOINTS

BOTTOM

PLATE RAIL

CUP RACK

CLEATS

SIDE

3/8" DIA. × 2" DOWEL

5/16" × 7/8" NOTCH FOR BACK

FOOT

NO. 10 × 2" FH SCREW

DETAIL 1

STILE
5/16"
SIDE
5/16"
RAILS
1-1/4"
5/16"
1/4" DEEP × 3/4" GROOVES FOR STILES
STILE
5/16"
3/8" COVE

1/4" HARDBOARD TOP
5/16"
3-1/4" CROWN
1-1/4"
3/4" FILLER
RAIL
STILE
SIDE

DETAIL 2

50-1/2" (CARCASE)
48-1/2" (FRAME)
1/4" OAK PLYWOOD BACK
LAP JOINTS (TYPICAL)
12-1/2"
13-1/8"
1/4" HARDBOARD TOP

1/2" RAD. (TYPICAL)
1"
3/8"
1/4"
1-3/4"
1"
3/4"

DETAIL 3

2"
3"
11"
1-3/4" (TYPICAL OF ALL STILES)
1" (TYP.)
3
3 EQUAL OPENINGS (APPROX. 13 - 27/32")
1/4" DIA. × 3/8" DEEP HOLES
2"
2-1/4"
3/4" × 1" CLEATS
18" 12" 6" 0"
3"

5/16" 2"
1-1/4"
3"
1-1/4" (RAILS)
3/4" (STILES)
3/4" CLEAT (ADJUST TO LEVEL SHELF)
3/4" 2"
26" (FRONT STILE)
23-7/8" (REAR STILE)
42-1/2" (SIDE)
2-1/4" (RAIL)
30°
12"
8"
4"
0"
6"
4-1/2"
1"
5"
1-1/4"
13-1/4"

3"
1"
3/4"
1/4"
3/4"

DETAIL 4

FRONT ELEVATION
3"
1-1/4"

BUFFET

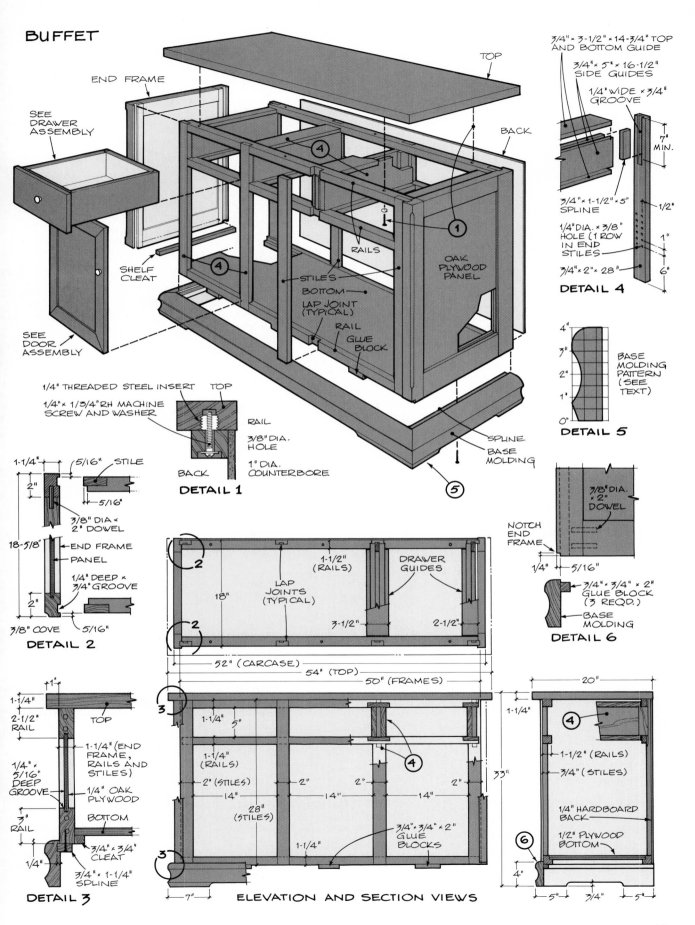

END FRAME

SEE DRAWER ASSEMBLY

SHELF CLEAT

SEE DOOR ASSEMBLY

TOP

BACK

RAILS

STILES

BOTTOM

LAP JOINT (TYPICAL)

RAIL GLUE BLOCK

OAK PLYWOOD PANEL

SPLINE

BASE MOLDING

3/4" × 3-1/2" × 14-3/4" TOP AND BOTTOM GUIDE

3/4" × 5" × 16-1/2" SIDE GUIDES

1/4" WIDE × 3/4" GROOVE

7" MIN.

1/2"

3/4" × 1-1/2" × 5" SPLINE

1/4" DIA. × 3/8" HOLE (1 ROW IN END STILES

3/4" × 2" × 28"

1"

6"

DETAIL 4

4"

3"

2"

1"

0"

BASE MOLDING PATTERN (SEE TEXT)

DETAIL 5

1/4" THREADED STEEL INSERT

1/4" × 1/3/4" RH MACHINE SCREW AND WASHER

TOP

RAIL

3/8" DIA. HOLE

BACK

1" DIA. COUNTERBORE

DETAIL 1

3/8" DIA. × 2" DOWEL

NOTCH END FRAME

1/4"   5/16"

3/4" × 3/4" × 2" GLUE BLOCK (3 REQD.)

BASE MOLDING

DETAIL 6

1-1/4"

5/16"

STILE

2"

5/16"

3/8" DIA × 2" DOWEL

18-5/8"

END FRAME

PANEL

1/4" DEEP × 3/4" GROOVE

2"

3/8" COVE   5/16"

DETAIL 2

1-1/2" (RAILS)

DRAWER GUIDES

LAP JOINTS (TYPICAL)

18"

3-1/2"   2-1/2"

52" (CARCASE)

54" (TOP)

50" (FRAMES)

1"

1-1/4"

2-1/2" RAIL

TOP

1-1/4" (END FRAME, RAILS AND STILES)

1/4" × 5/16" DEEP GROOVE

1/4" OAK PLYWOOD

BOTTOM

3" RAIL

3/4" × 3/4" CLEAT

1/4"

3/4" × 1-1/4" SPLINE

DETAIL 3

1-1/4"   5"

1-1/4" (RAILS)

2" (STILES)   2"   2"   2"

14"

28" (STILES)

14"   14"

1-1/4"

3/4" × 3/4" × 2" GLUE BLOCKS

7"

ELEVATION AND SECTION VIEWS

20"

1-1/4"

1-1/2" (RAILS)

3/4" (STILES)

1/4" HARDBOARD BACK

1/2" PLYWOOD BOTTOM

33"

4"

5"   3/4"   5"

69

With saw guard removed, you can see the one-tooth molding head that cut the dentil grooves. A long stick is clamped to the table as a guide, and the stock is advanced one groove at a time, aligning each edge with the edge of the stick.

Doors and drawers

I made drawers using the finger-joint machine described beginning on page 130. But there's a very simple and sturdy construction shown in the drawings.

Now about those doors. Some years back I was asked to do the kitchen for a well-known architect's home. There were 48 doors and I wanted to save work and cost. So I came up with splined corners as shown. My customer was enthused, and we are still friends. Here's the principle behind them:

I have always considered mitering among the most difficult woodworking jobs. A small angular error is doubled as it is repeated from one piece to that adjacent, so a perfect fit is called for. On the table saw, angularity is controlled by the miter gauge. To set it up right, dress one edge of a piece of scrap about 5 or 6 inches wide. Cut a 45-degree angle on each. Now press the dressed sides into a good carpenter's square. If there's a gap, adjust the miter gauge stop and keep going until the fit is perfect.

On the radial arm saw, the first thing to do is set the saw up so it will cut absolutely square with the fence. Then, lock the arm up tight and never move it again unless you absolutely must, because it won't come back to the same place twice.

Rarely will you have to cut an angle other than 45 degrees. So you make a pair of simple templates with 45-degree angles. To check the angles, use the same trick with the carpenter's square and scrap wood as suggested for the table saw. When you have it right, make a second template. This one you check by setting both against the fence, pointed ends together, and pushing the square against them. When the square touches both templates full-length, you have a setup for perfect mitering.

As you cut, don't turn the parts over and end-for-end to cut against the same template. Clamp both templates to the saw table and cut first against one, them the other. This way you will keep the crack-out on the back side of the frame. Cut all frame parts at the same time to the proper length. Clamp up your templates so that you saw off the ends of the blanks, leaving 1/16-inch flats at the end.

Now make the jig for routing the spline pockets. It comprises two pieces of wood about 3 inches wide, screwed to the edge of a piece of 3/4 plywood about 24 inches square. Use your carpenter's square to check that they are perfectly square with each other. Don't let them touch at the corners because you'll need a path for chips and sawdust to escape.

You'll also need a template follower on the router. Set up your first 45-degree guide, then, using a wood block as a width gauge, set up the other. You should use thick paper or cardboard under the guides so the frame parts can slide under them easily. Clamp the parts into the jig, two at a time, and rout the spline grooves. The inner groove should be cut first, using a travel direction that will hold the router against the guide.

I find the best way to make splines is to use thick wood, such as 2 × 4, and dress it to the thickness required to fit the groove. Then I cut off a strip, 1/32 inch thicker than I need for the groove, rejoint the edge, and cut another. *Remember,* you need a precise fit to the groove. If you go too tight, the wood will swell a bit from moisture in the glue.

Pull the splines down into the grooves with clamps, set quite loosely at first. Clamp across two corners and watch the parts slide down the spline to a perfect fit, then tighten the spline solidly into its pocket. Now you can remove the corner clamps, and in about a half hour with Titebond or Elmer's Professional you can take the four corner clamps off.

The plywood inserts are installed when you spline the corners in sawn or routed grooves. For the china cabinet doors I used a rubber glass retainer. I'm using plain glass now, but my wife plans to make her own leaded-glass inserts. It will be simple to pull the rubber retainer out and install the new glass panels. I got the rubber retainer by mail from the Woodworker's Store, 2108 Industrial Boulevard, Rogers, MN 55374. They offer it in two colors and gave me super service.

Make two accurate plywood templates for miter-cutting on the radial arm saw. Clamp them to the table. If the templates mate with a good carpenter's square, parts cut using the templates will mate with each other.

Spline pockets for door frames are routed using this jig. Only one side piece comes up to the joint. This allows chips to escape and provides a surface to "bank" the first piece against. Save the jig; you'll use it on many future jobs.

Finishing

You may have your own pet method in this department. I took the simple approach with a couple of coats of oil-wiping stain, both rubbed with steel wool. Then I put on a coat of sanding sealer, lightly sanded with 150-grit, then coated with about three coats of varnish.

When it comes to finishing materials, I'm leery about buying from the hardware store. Here the clerk probably knows a lot less about it than you do, but he will often proceed to advise you anyway. Go to a paint store and buy materials that all have the same brand name. They'll be compatible. Ask to see the manufacturer's specification sheet for the system you plan. It's under the counter in a looseleaf notebook. Then follow the manufacturer's recommendations.

If you work carefully and thoughtfully, you'll wind up with a great piece of furniture. It's rewarding to have your guests say with awe, "Did you *really* build this yourself?"—*by Cy Wedlake. Photos by Lakeside Enterprises. Drawings by Eugene Thompson.*

queen anne writing table

Long ago, when traveling was difficult and slow and there were no telephones, the lady of the house was responsible for keeping in touch with distant relatives and friends. Often a part of each day was set aside for correspondence, and the ladies' writing table was standard equipment in the more affluent homes.

Today, we may not write as many personal letters, but the writing table survives. Whether it's called a hall table or an occasional table, it is appropriate and useful just about anywhere in the house. It can sit against a wall, or out in the room. Ours will grace my wife's sanctum, where she corresponds with kids and cousins—and figures out how much my allowance must be cut next month.

For our table we chose Queen Anne period styling. This design era was characterized by elegance of line and form. The style was brought to its ultimate refinement by such masters as Thomas Chippendale, and its esthetic worth is demonstrated by its enduring popularity after more than 200 years.

Choosing your wood

The preferred material for this piece was originally mahogany. Superb American woods such as walnut and black cherry were later used. Oak is less favored for designs of this period, probably because it lends itself better to more rugged styling.

I made the unusual choice of maple for a couple of good reasons. For one thing, this fine-grained wood will take a glass-like finish and it was to be painted with a semi-gloss enamel to match and complement pieces already in the room. For another, maple is priced quite a bit less in our area than other suitable woods.

I like working this tough material. While it does cut more slowly than softer woods, it machines well with sharp tools. And you don't have to carpet your workbench to avoid nicks and dings.

Start with the legs

If you haven't built cabriole legs before, be of good cheer; they are not nearly as difficult as some other furni-ture-building tasks. They're just a bit more tedious.

The job begins with selection of the stock. Try for straight-grained stock that will finish to 3½ inches square. My source couldn't supply it, so I laid out the legs for 8/4 stock (2-inch rough sawn), which can be finished to 1¾-inch thickness and glued up.

Make a thin wood template from the drawing and trace its shape onto two sides of your blanks. You have to be very careful here because you always have rights and lefts in cabriole legs. Even though the shape is symmetrical, one side of the blank will have the grain parallel with the face, and the next will have edge or vertical grain. It looks bad to mix flat and vertical grain on the same side.

Lay two blanks side by side on the bench with flat-grain faces up. Lay your template on the left-hand piece, convex side out, and trace it down. Then flip it over, upside-down, onto the other blank. Now lay the template against one side (against the vertical grain), then trace it down with the inner, concave surfaces toward the workbench. Move it to the outside of the other leg without flipping it. The shapes should now appear just as you will view them in the finished piece.

You now have a band-sawing job.

Queen Anne writing desk is perfect for corresponding with distant loved ones. It also makes a neat little "office" for keeping household accounts—and fits in with the furnishings of most any room.

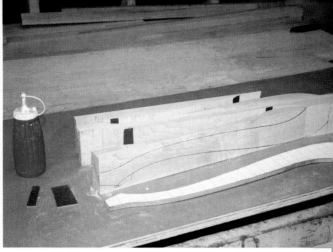

Cabriole legs are laid out in pairs, using a thin wood template, to get the wood grain right.

After the first two cuts the waste is glued back on using thin cardboard strips. These allow the finish-cut legs to be easily separated from the waste.

A vee-notch is cut into scrap 2 × 4 for a leg support. For the side radii, you'll need a second vee clamped to the top and a shim under the foot. Note that the radii are generated as a series of flats.

Feed slowly and carefully. After you make your first two cuts you'll have to put the waste back on. This is because you just cut your sawing pattern off on one piece and you need the other for a flat surface against the table for your next cut.

I've read a suggestion to tape the waste back on. It worked for the ears, but for the long leg I went back to the tried-and-true way. You glue little strips of paper material to one piece with a single bead of glue, as in the photo, then lay a bead of glue on the other side of the strip and lightly clamp waste and stock back together.

Fifteen minutes' clamping time is plenty with yellow glue. For the strips I use the thin gray cardboard that comes on the back of scratch pads. It is the right thickness to represent the kerf of the saw and splits easily with a wood chisel when it comes time to separate the finished pieces.

You have a good bit of hand shaping to do now. The ideal tool is the spokeshave. If you don't have one you might have to order one by mail because few stores stock them. You'll find that The Woodworkers Store—218. Industrial Boulevard, Rogers, MN 55374—sells them at a few dollars less than other mail-order outfits.

There's a simple trick for duplicating the radius from leg to leg. Cut a 90-degree Vee in one edge of a piece of 2 × 4. Clamp this to one edge of your workbench to hold a leg, and make a smaller vee board to clamp the leg down. Shim the foot for solid working support. Do *not* work back and forth around the piece to cut the radius. Instead, cut a series of carefully-gauged flats. The first flat is the most important. For a 1-inch radius this flat will be 7/8 inches wide at maximum. From where you stand, at the post-end of the leg, you can look down the flat and see its sharp edge following the gen-

eral contour of the leg, tapering toward the foot.

Don't complete the radius yet; wait until you've flatted all four legs. Then you can lay them side by side, and a glance will tell you if they are going to come out alike. Now you can go back and cut a flat on each side of your first flat. These will be 7/16 wide, and you will have cut your original, wide flat, down to 7/16 width as well.

After you take off the little peaks between flats, rub the leg down with coarse, then finer sandpaper until you have a true radius. You can flip the piece 90 degrees either way and do the smaller radii at the inside corners. At this stage you might partially finish-sand the entire leg.

The top

The drawing shows 3/4-inch finished thickness. I bought rough-sawn, 4/4 (1 inch) stock from a millwork shop. Hardwood sawmills usually cut a bit oversize of the full inch requirement for four-quarter. Mine was 1 3/16 or more. So that I'd get as much thickness as possible in the top, without paying the premium for 5/4 stock, I cut the pieces to length before I dressed them on the jointer. I dressed just enough to see the grain and spot any blemishes. Then I glued up.

I took my glued panel to the mill—which has a 24-inch thickness planer—and had them dress it for me. I wound up with a full inch thickness, instead of the 3/4 shown on the drawing, from my 4/4 stock. Next time you're in a furniture store, check the thickness of furniture tops. The more expensive pieces generally have thicker tops like like the one on mine.

Trim the top to size and lay it on the workbench bottom-side up. Particularly with the softer woods such as walnut, you should work on a clean, padded bench so you don't mar the

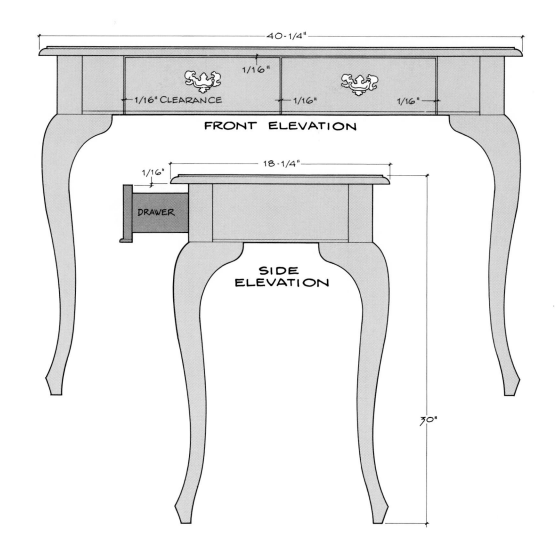

40-1/4"

1/16"

1/16" CLEARANCE   1/16"   1/16"

FRONT ELEVATION

1/16"   18-1/4"

DRAWER

SIDE ELEVATION

30"

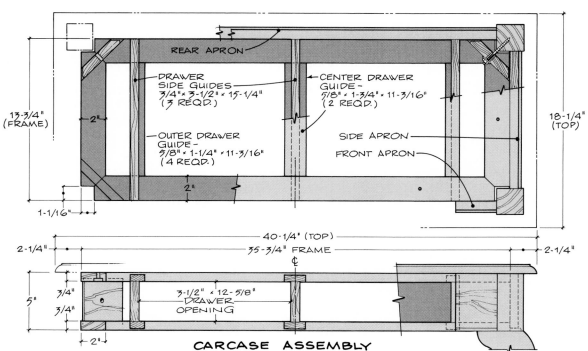

REAR APRON

DRAWER
SIDE GUIDES
3/4" × 3-1/2" × 15-1/4"
(3 REQD.)

CENTER DRAWER
GUIDE —
5/8" × 1-3/4" × 11-3/16"
(2 REQD.)

13-3/4"
(FRAME)

2"

OUTER DRAWER
GUIDE —
5/8" × 1-1/4" × 11-3/16"
(4 REQD.)

2"

SIDE APRON

FRONT APRON

18-1/4"
(TOP)

1-1/16"

2-1/4"   40-1/4" (TOP)   2-1/4"

35-3/4" FRAME

¢

5"

3/4"

3/4"

3-1/2" × 12-5/8"
DRAWER
OPENING

2"

CARCASE ASSEMBLY

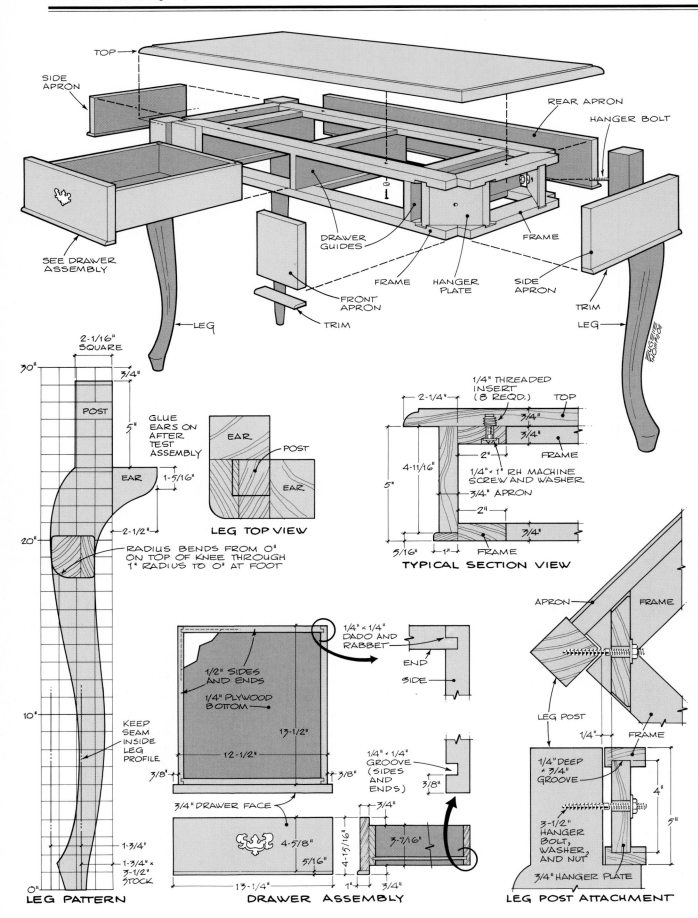

TOP

SIDE
APRON

REAR APRON

HANGER BOLT

SEE DRAWER
ASSEMBLY

DRAWER
GUIDES

FRAME

HANGER
PLATE

FRAME

SIDE
APRON

TRIM

LEG

FRONT
APRON

TRIM

LEG

LEG PATTERN

2-1/16"
SQUARE

30"

3/4"

POST

5"

GLUE
EARS ON
AFTER
TEST
ASSEMBLY

EAR

POST

EAR

1-5/16"

2-1/2"

LEG TOP VIEW

20"

RADIUS BENDS FROM 0"
ON TOP OF KNEE THROUGH
1" RADIUS TO 0" AT FOOT

10"

KEEP
SEAM
INSIDE
LEG
PROFILE

1-3/4"

1-3/4" ×
3-1/2"
STOCK

0"

1/4" THREADED
INSERT
(8 REQD.)

TOP

2-1/4"

3/4"

3/4"

2"

FRAME

4-11/16"

1/4" × 1" RH MACHINE
SCREW AND WASHER

5"

3/4" APRON

2"

5/16"   1"

3/4"

FRAME

TYPICAL SECTION VIEW

DRAWER ASSEMBLY

1/4" × 1/4"
DADO AND
RABBET

END

SIDE

1/2" SIDES
AND ENDS

1/4" PLYWOOD
BOTTOM

13-1/2"

12-1/2"

3/8"

3/8"

3/4" DRAWER FACE

4-5/8"

5/16"

13-1/4"

1/4" × 1/4"
GROOVE
(SIDES
AND
ENDS)

3/8"

4-15/16"

3-7/16"

3/4"

3/4"

1"   3/4"

APRON

FRAME

LEG POST

1/4"

FRAME

1/4" DEEP
× 3/4"
GROOVE

3-1/2"
HANGER
BOLT,
WASHER,
AND NUT

3/4" HANGER PLATE

4"

5"

LEG POST ATTACHMENT

Dado grooves for the hanger plates are cut into the rails with the radial arm saw, using a pair of plywood templates for lineup. This is the most accurate and fastest way to go.

wood. With the underside facing you, carefully make a pencil layout of the frame, aprons, and leg posts right on the top.

Making the frame

While my underframe is not authentic 18th century, it is sturdy and much easier to make than many of the other leg-mounting methods. Also, you can quickly remove the legs for transporting the piece.

Cut the eight rails using the drawing dimensions. If you use a radial arm saw, put in a new cutting fence and set your penciled cutting marks against the new saw cut. On the table saw I mount an extension on the miter gauge, set the saw for a deep cut, and cut the extension off. The sawn end of the extension shows you exactly where the saw blade will go when you cut the parts. These methods assure the accuracy you need for quick and easy assembly.

You can cut the miters a bit short of piece-to-piece contact. Placement of the dado groove for the leg braces is not critical as long as the grooves in adjacent pieces line up. On the table saw this is not much of a problem because miter gauges have adjustable stops that you can set for dead-on accuracy at 45 degrees.

It's different on the radial arm saw. Manufacturers can't seem to design an arm that will swing to an exact 45-degree angle and then come back to 90. So after you have carefully squared your saw to the fence, make yourself a pair of simple 45-degree jig

pieces from plywood. Work as accurately as you can.

When both pieces made, set them firmly against the fence and check them with a carpenter's square. The square should touch both angles full-length. If it doesn't, trim one template on the jointer until it does. Then, even if your 45 degree angle is off a hair, you will produce a miter that fits perfectly and delivers a 90-degree corner. Keep your 45-degree jigs. You will use them again and again.

When you have the rails cut, lay them down on the table, aligning with your layout. Mark them for the screws that will hold the top down, and drill for the screws. Many experts frown on the use of wood screws into the aprons with a solid-stock top, citing the inevitable expansion and contraction with humidity changes.

I usually use screw inserts for the hold-downs. Then I can drill 1/4-inch or so above the hold-down screw size so the top can creep a bit. This avoids having the aprons pull a warp into the top or throwing the table out of line. One guy I know tightens screws centered in the ends and pulls the long-side screws down only lightly until the top has had a month or so to stabilize in its ultimate environment.

You'll have to countersink the top rail for screw heads, at least in the center of the long side to clear the drawers. The center screws in the long side are offset about an inch to clear the center guide. Note that the holes run through top and bottom guides so you can reach through with a screwdriver.

Set the top up on 2×4s so you can reach under it with clamps and assemble the frame rails with the corner braces. I used glue and clamps, no screws. Check to make sure the rails, top, and bottom, are square and parallel. Now you can install the aprons, which you cut 1/16-inch longer than the frame rails, so the legs pull up tight to them. Temporarily install the legs, marking them so they will always go back in the same place.

The ear profiles are marked from the pattern first and the face curvature is marked from the legs. Then draw a line parallel with the face curvature to thin the piece. After sawing the face side, tape the waste back on and saw the curves that match the legs. Put a strip of waxed paper atop the rails and against the leg posts to catch any glue drips, and glue the ears to the legs.

I found that the mounted legs were easy to finish-sand. But they have to

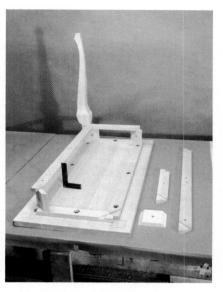

Parts for the Queen Anne table, except for the drawer structures. Line up top and bottom rails carefully with a square. Note placement of machine screw hold-downs. Lines on the table were used to align parts.

Ears are glued and clamped to the legs as shown.

come off to sand the knee and match the ears to the knees. A sharp block plane will come in handy here. Finish-sanding has to be done carefully, especially if you're using cherry or maple. The slightest scratch will show.

Original Queene Anne furniture drawers had hand-cut dovetails. The drawer structure I show is about the simplest I know of and it works. Of course you can choose from a dozen other structures if you prefer.

Apply your favorite finish and you now have a valuable piece of furniture that will give you great satisfaction and pride for a long time to come—*by Cy Wedlake. Photos by Lakeside Enterprises. Drawings by Eugene Thompson.*

country wall system

You don't need a chimney or fireplace to enjoy this versatile wall system. Put a back on the cabinets and these handsome units can stand alone in any room.

I doubt if this project was called a "wall system" back in the heyday of the country cabinetmaker. My grandfather, who was a country cabinetmaker and helped me build this, referred to them as "chimney shelves." They were so-called, he said, because they were designed to fill the space between a fireplace and a wall. But they are much more than that folk moniker implies. These "chimney shelves" also include cabinets, drawers, counters, and display space. They are, in fact, a country wall system.

Like most country-style projects, they are simple to build and easily adaptable to your needs. You don't need a chimney or a fireplace to put them up. Build one, two, or as many units as you need and attach them to any wall. Shorten or stretch the units to fill the available space. You can even make these units *movable* by putting a back on the cabinets and not attaching them to the wall.

Making the case

Select the stock you'll need to make the units. I suggest you use white pine with solid knots, to give this project a down-home look and feel. Many of the parts—the sides and shelves—are made from wider stock than what you can commonly find at a lumber yard, so you may have to join narrower boards edge to edge.

The case joinery is simple and straightforward—just dadoes and rabbets. These can be easily cut with a router. Clamp a straightedge to the stock when you rout it to serve as a guide (Fig. 1). Square off the ends of the blind rabbets and dadoes with a hand chisel.

Join the web frame (which supports the drawers) with tongues and grooves. These, too, you can make with a router. Mount your router to a worktable and pass the stock across the cutter as shown in figures 2 and 3. The rail and stiles of the front frame are doweled together. Use a doweling jig to accurately position the dowel holes, placing at least two dowels per joint.

Assemble the frames with glue. Then assemble the case—sides, shelves, back, web frame, and front frame—with glue and wood screws. Countersink and counterbore the screws, so you can hide the screw heads with wooden plugs.

Making the drawers and doors

Drawers and doors in this project overlap the front frame with a standard cabinet lip. Cut this lip in the door stock and drawer fronts with two passes of the router. Rout a rabbet on the back side of these parts, all around the edge. Then round over the front side.

The doors are made from solid slabs of wood, as indicated in the drawings. To keep these slabs from warping, brace them on the back sides with battens. *Don't* glue the battens to the doors. Instead, drill ¼-inch pilot holes for screws in the battens, and secure the battens to the doors with roundhead screws and washers. The oversize screw holes will let the door expand and contract with changes

1. When routing the dadoes and rabbets in the sides, use a straightedge to guide the router.

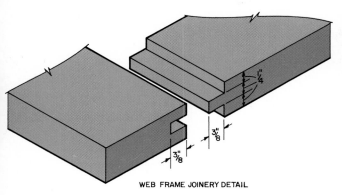

WEB FRAME JOINERY DETAIL

2. Use a rabbeting bit to make a tongue in the web frame parts.

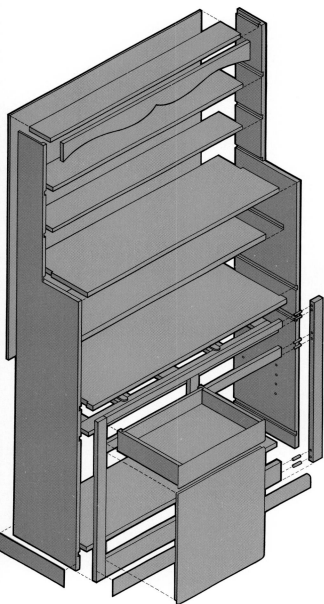

3. To cut the grooves in the web frame parts, use a straight bit. The router is mounted underneath a worktable.

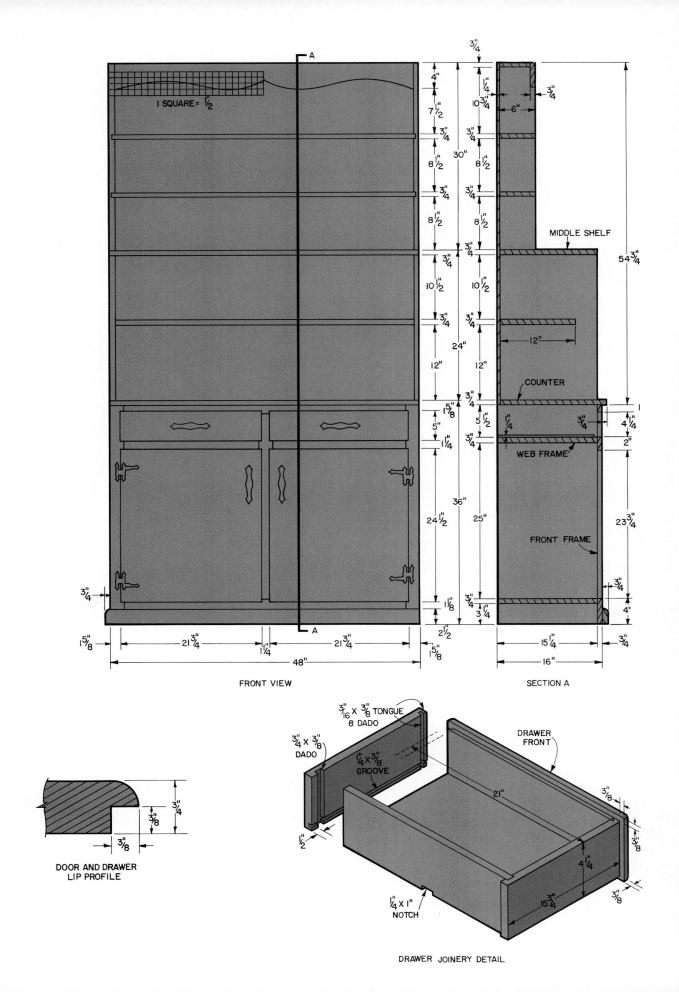

I SQUARE = 1/2"

MIDDLE SHELF

COUNTER

WEB FRAME

FRONT FRAME

FRONT VIEW

SECTION A

3/16" X 3/8" TONGUE
8 DADO

3/4" X 3/8"
DADO

1/4" X 3/8"
GROOVE

DRAWER
FRONT

1/4" X 1"
NOTCH

DRAWER JOINERY DETAIL

DOOR AND DRAWER
LIP PROFILE

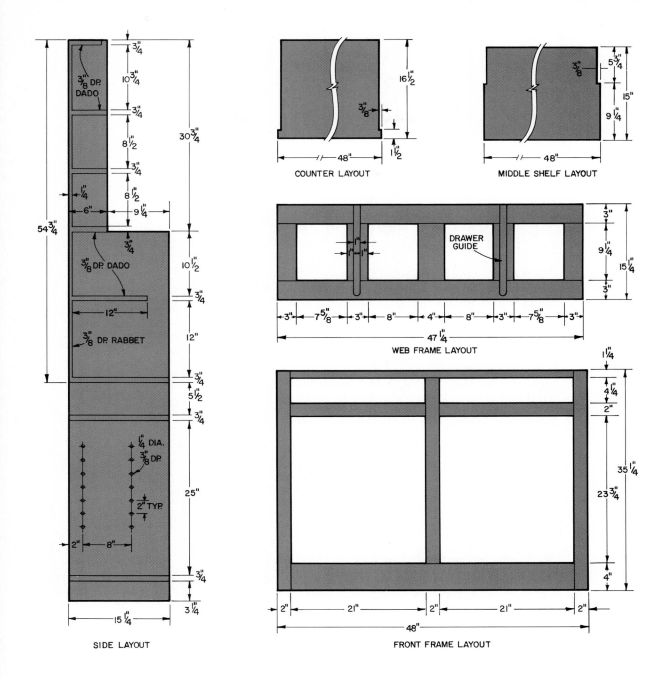

COUNTER LAYOUT

MIDDLE SHELF LAYOUT

WEB FRAME LAYOUT

SIDE LAYOUT

FRONT FRAME LAYOUT

in humidity. Mount the finished doors to the front frame with offset cabinet hinges.

The drawer parts are assembled with lock joints. Using your table saw, cut a tongue in the side edges of the drawer faces, and cut matching grooves in the drawer sides. Then cut grooves in the drawer fronts, sides, and backs to hold the drawer bottom, and notch the bottom edges of the drawer backs to fit over the drawer guide. Assemble the drawer fronts, sides, and backs with glue, but *don't* glue the bottoms in place. Just let them float in the grooves.

Finishing the wall system
Traditionally, country cabinetmakers gave their handiwork a hand-rubbed oil finish. That takes a lot of elbow grease, a bucket of linseed oil, and a few pounds of carnuba wax. You can duplicate the same finish (without the elbow grease) by using one of the many penetrating oil finishes on the market today. Apply as many coats of oil to the inside of the units as the outside; this will keep the completed project from warping. On your last coat, mix a little spar varnish in the oil to give the final finish depth and make it more durable.

Don't screw the finished units to the walls. Instead, hold them in place with molding. Install baseboard molding around the base, and cove or quarter-round molding up the sides and across the top. That way, if you ever want to move or rearrange your wall system, all you have to do is remove the molding—*by Nick Engler.*

contemporary breakfast stool

Here's a new variation on an old, old theme. This refreshingly different sitting stool is the handiwork of Tom Stender, a professional furniture designer/builder in Boston, New York. Tom's strong suit is classic furniture, but every now and then he works up a contemporary piece such as this one.

To duplicate this stool, select clear, straight-grained turning stock that's free of any defects. Turn the legs and rungs at slow speeds, using a gentle touch with the chisel to prevent the stock from "whipping". You may also need to use a *lathe steadyrest* to support the stock in the middle, especially when turning the legs (see photo).

The turnings are fairly simple to make. The legs have a gentle taper, and the front/back rungs have a slight bulge in the middle. All the turned parts have tenons, either at one or both ends. The only parts with any decoration at all are the side rungs. These have a single "bamboo" ring.

After you turn the legs and rungs, rip the bevel in the seat. Use your table saw with the blade tilted at 12 degrees to cut most of the way through the seat stock, as shown in the photo. Finish the cut by hand, and sand or scrape away any saw marks.

Drill the holes for the tenons in the seat and legs. The tenons must fit snugly in their holes. If there's any slop, the stool won't hold together. When you're satisfied with the fit, glue the parts together. Do any necessary touch-up sanding, then proceed to apply a finish of your choice—*by Nick Engler.*

Use a steadyrest to keep the long parts from whipping when you turn them.

To make the bevel in the seat, begin the cut on your table saw, cutting through as much stock as possible. Finish the cut with a hand saw.

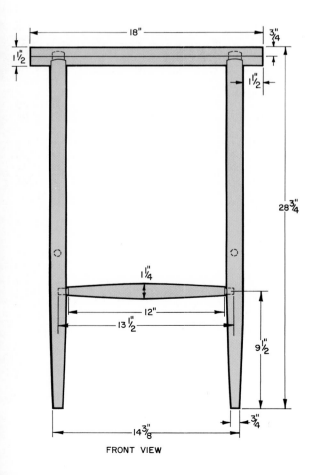

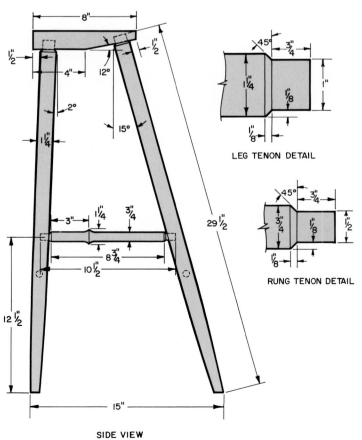

FRONT VIEW

SIDE VIEW

LEG TENON DETAIL

RUNG TENON DETAIL

take-apart
trestle dining table

Handsome yet practical, this table is also easy to make using straightforward cuts.

The trestle table is strong and solid and yet easily broken down into four pieces for moving. Just undo the eight screws which attach the legs to the tabletop, and knock out the wedges from the stretcher. The top is heavy, but can easily be negotiated through any door.

I rounded off all edges and corners to minimize injury to anyone who might fall against the table. And rounding over softens a piece, inviting people to run their hands over the rounded edges.

I built this table from 8/4 Honduran mahogany (actual thickness about 1⁷/₈ inches), but any hardwood would work. You need about 52 board feet for the table, but, depending on the quality of the stock, buy about 70 board feet to allow for waste, and to get what you need.

If you use thinner stock, make appropriate adjustments such as changing dimensions of mortise-tenon joints, moving the location of a wedged mortise joint, or using shorter screws. Remember, too, to allow the

tabletop to expand by screwing through the top support into the tabletop center board. You can also make slotted holes in the top support perpendicular to the tabletop grain, using a washer with each screw.

Tabletop

The first step for making a large, flat surface such as this tabletop is to plane the boards flat, removing the high surfaces and taking out any twists. Since the mahogany was too wide for my planer, I ran the boards

TRESTLE TABLE

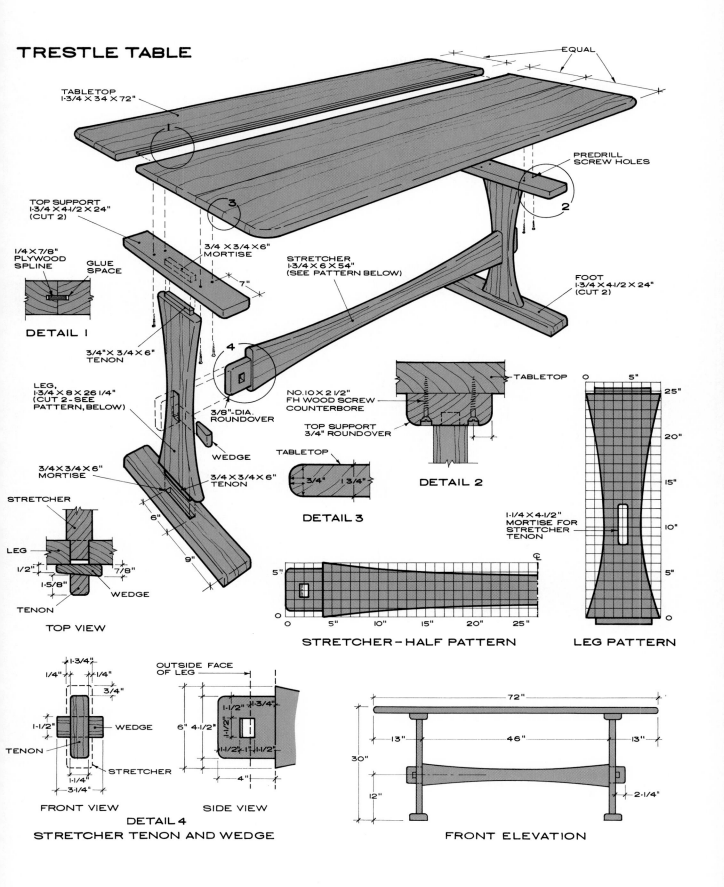

TABLETOP
1-3/4 × 34 × 72"

EQUAL

PREDRILL
SCREW HOLES

TOP SUPPORT
1-3/4 × 4-1/2 × 24"
(CUT 2)

1/4 × 7/8"
PLYWOOD
SPLINE

GLUE
SPACE

3/4 × 3/4 × 6"
MORTISE

7"

STRETCHER
1-3/4 × 6 × 54"
(SEE PATTERN BELOW)

FOOT
1-3/4 × 4-1/2 × 24"
(CUT 2)

DETAIL 1

3/4" × 3/4 × 6"
TENON

LEG,
1-3/4 × 8 × 26 1/4"
(CUT 2 - SEE
PATTERN, BELOW)

3/8"-DIA.
ROUNDOVER

WEDGE

NO.10 × 2 1/2"
FH WOOD SCREW
COUNTERBORE

TABLETOP

TOP SUPPORT
3/4" ROUNDOVER

TABLETOP

3/4 × 3/4 × 6"
MORTISE

3/4 × 3/4 × 6"
TENON

3/4"   1-3/4"

DETAIL 2

DETAIL 3

STRETCHER

LEG

1/2"

1-5/8"

6"

9"

7/8"

WEDGE

TENON

TOP VIEW

0   5"

25"

20"

15"

10"

5"

1-1/4 × 4-1/2"
MORTISE FOR
STRETCHER
TENON

5"

0

0   5"   10"   15"   20"   25"

STRETCHER – HALF PATTERN

LEG PATTERN

1-3/4"

1/4"   1/4"

3/4"

1-1/2"

WEDGE

TENON

STRETCHER

1-1/4"

3-1/4"

FRONT VIEW

OUTSIDE FACE
OF LEG

1-1/2" 1-3/4"

6"   4-1/2"

1-1/2"

1-1/2" 1-1/2"

4"

SIDE VIEW

DETAIL 4
STRETCHER TENON AND WEDGE

72"

13"   46"   13"

30"

12"

2-1/4"

FRONT ELEVATION

through a thickness sander to 1¾ inches thick.

Next, crosscut the boards for the top 1 to 2 inches longer than the finished table length, being sure to cut off ends that show checking (splitting). Rip the boards so they total about ½ to 1 inch wider than the finished table size. Joint all edges and lay the boards on a flat surface, arranging them until you like how they match up. Alternate the direction of the annular rings to keep the table from cupping.

Splining the tabletop

To help keep the boards aligned during glue-up, you can slot the board

Hefty tabletop is attached to base with screws through top support.

Loose wedge in stretcher adds nifty detail, and allows table to be taken down in no time.

edges for splines. Make ¼-inch wide by ⅜-inch deep slots with a slot-cutting bit in a router. Cut with the router base resting on the top of each board to ensure that the boards will line up. I used ⅞-inch strips of Baltic birch plywood for the splines, but any ¼-inch plywood will do. The splines are ripped ⅛ inch narrower than the combined depth of the slots to allow for glue space, and they should slip in and out of the slots easily.

If you do not have a slot-cutter, make the slots on a table saw. In any event, be careful not to cut through the ends of the boards or the splines will show. You can glue the top with dowels instead, using a doweling jig for proper board alignment.

Gluing and clamping

I like the True Grip Clamp 'n Tool Guide for edge-clamping, but any pipe or bar clamp will do the job. Use at least seven clamps to glue the tabletop, alternating top and bottom clamps to get even clamping pressure.

After the glue sets, remove the clamps and belt-sand any ridges. Cut off the ends of the table with a circular saw run against a straightedge guide. Next, run a router with mortising bit against a guide to clean the saw marks from the ends. To avoid tearing the wood at the end of the cut, stop the router an inch from the edge and come in right-to-left (hold the router firmly as it will want to run when moved this way). Finish the width in the same fashion.

Use a ¾-inch radius router bit to round all the edges of the top—both top and bottom. If your table is less than 1¾ inches thick, use a smaller-radius bit.

Making the base ends

The base consists of the stretcher and two ends. Each end has a foot, a top support and a leg.

First plane the stock, then cut the parts to size. Rout the ¾- by ¾-inch mortise into the foot and top support, then round the edges and ends of the top of the foot, and the bottom of the support.

Next, cut the tenons in the legs. There are many ways to do this—I made the rough cuts on my band saw, then cleaned the cuts with a router and straightedge guide. Finally, rasp the tenor ends round to fit the mortise.

I cut the mortise in the leg with a ¼-inch hardboard template cut to guide my router. The template is clamped to the leg and a plunge

router with a straight mortising bit makes the cut. Bore several 1-inch-diameter holes in the center of the mortise area first to remove waste and make the routing job go faster.

The drawing gives a grid and pattern for shaping the legs, but if you wish to change the pattern, you can use the same method I used, shown in the step-by-step photos, below. After shaping each leg, round over the in- and outside edges of the leg, but leave its top and bottom square.

The stretcher

Begin making the stretcher by cutting it exactly to length (54 inches, including the tenons), and shaping it with a sabre saw or band saw. Round over the edges just as you did the end pieces.

Next, cut the tenons according to the dimensions shown in the drawing, shaping the ends and rounding the corners to fit through the leg mortise. The tenon has four shoulders to neatly cover the mortise.

Finally, cut the mortise for the wedge. The mortise should extend into the leg about ¼ inch so the wedge bears against the leg. The wedge itself should be slightly tapered (a gentle taper exerts more force than a sharp one) to match the angle of the mortise.

Sanding: Don't be shy

Use 80-grit sandpaper and a rasp to make sure all edges and corners are well rounded, and to remove any router bearing marks (they may be difficult to see, but can show up after finishing). Wipe the edges with a water-dampened cloth which simulates a finish and makes any unwanted marks visible. Use your hands to feel your progress—if it doesn't feel good it's not right. Move to 100-, 120-, then 220-grit paper.

Finally, sand the top and the visible surfaces with 320-, then 400-grit paper. I even sand up to 600-grit, although most woodworkers I've talked to stop sanding at 220-grit paper. But sandpaper leaves scratches and although my eye can't see scratches from 220-grit paper, they still reflect and diffuse light and may interfere with subtleties in the grain. The 600-grit makes scratches so fine that such interference is no longer a factor.

Leg assembly

Assemble the ends with glue and four pipe clamps—two on each side—and check that the top support and foot are square to the leg.

A TEMPLATE FOR CURVED LEGS

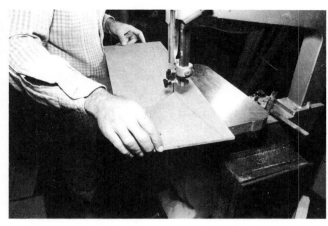

1. Working on kraft paper from a stationery store, bend a metal ruler to measured marks on the paper and proceed to mark the curve.

2. Trace shape onto ¼-inch hardboard template and cut on band saw. Template is 1½ inches shorter than the leg to allow for tenons.

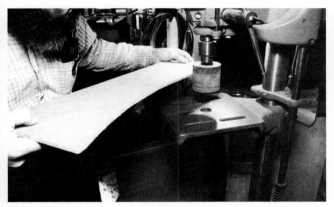

3. Use a drum sander to clean saw marks from the template and smooth the curve down to the pencil marks.

4. Clamp template to the leg, which has already been rough cut on a band saw. A backup board protects work table. Smooth the curve with a straight mortising bit and guide bushing which bears against template. Photo, right, shows the bit and bushing.

5. Closeup of work in progress shows what router does in a single pass. Saw marks can, of course, be cleaned with spokeshave.

Complete the base assembly by inserting the stretcher and tapping the wedges into place. (Note: The wedges should be checked, and tapped tight periodically.) Lay the tabletop upside-down on a clean, heavy pad and place the base assembly in position. Attach it to the top with brass screws in counterbored holes.

Finishing

Because this table is for a kitchen, I used a mixture of turpentine, tung oil and urethane varnish (one part of each). I brushed on three coats, wiping with fine (0000) steel wool between each coat.

When applying a finish, be sure to call anyone within earshot to watch

the magic—by Marty Kraft. Drawing by J. Dyck Fledderus.

Reprinted by express permission of WORKBENCH — the do-it-yourself magazine.

Materials Needed

- 72 board feet of 8 × 4 mahogany
- ¼ × 4 × 68-inch plywood (splines)
- ¾-inch radius-router rounding-over bit (or rasp and file)
- Wood glue
- Sandpaper: 80-, 120-, 220-, 320-grit (up to 600-grit if you wish)
- No. 10 × 2½-inch flathead wood screws
- Finishing materials: 1 quart each of tung oil, turpentine, urethane varnish; brush; 0000 steel wool

two easy-to-build storage dividers

2

1

Though designed for different lifestyles, these storage cabinets serve similar functions: They stow home entertainment gear. The hutch (above) also has display cubbyholes.

Divide and conquer awkward spaces in your house with these modular storage units. Although either style can be placed against a wall, both are designed to be freestanding to serve as room dividers. You can build as many modules as you need to create the partition you want—one, two, or three—and stand them side by side. For example:

● If your front door opens directly into the living room, create an entry area with a peninsula of two modules facing the living room.

● In a basement den, create a conversation area by marching two or three of these units across the floor with their backs to the playroom.

● In either case, one unit could become a refreshment bar. The blank back panels of the modules create a display wall for posters or a cluster of framed prints.

The panel-look modules stand 72 inches tall; the Maxi-Hutch is more than 90 inches high—so these are effective visual dividers. But they do more than merely redefine space: They provide generous storage for items that now clutter your home—entertainment and camera equip-

1

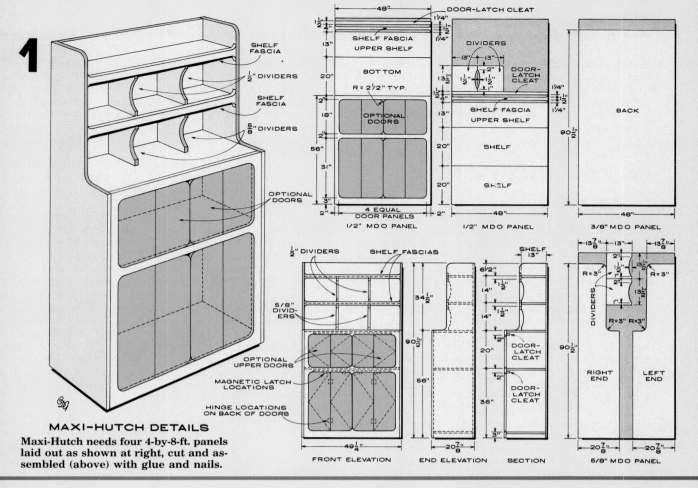

SHELF FASCIA

½" DIVIDERS

SHELF FASCIA

⅝" DIVIDERS

OPTIONAL DOORS

48"

SHELF FASCIA
UPPER SHELF

BOTTOM

R = 2½" TYP.

OPTIONAL DOORS

4 EQUAL DOOR PANELS

½" MDO PANEL

DOOR-LATCH CLEAT

DIVIDERS

DOOR-LATCH CLEAT

SHELF FASCIA
UPPER SHELF

SHELF

SHELF

½" MDO PANEL

BACK

90½"

48"

3/8" MDO PANEL

½" DIVIDERS   SHELF FASCIAS

5/8" DIVIDERS

OPTIONAL UPPER DOORS

MAGNETIC LATCH LOCATIONS

HINGE LOCATIONS ON BACK OF DOORS

49¼"

FRONT ELEVATION

SHELF 13"

34½"

90½"

56"

20⅞"

END ELEVATION

DOOR-LATCH CLEAT

DOOR-LATCH CLEAT

SECTION

DIVIDERS

R = 3"   R = 3"

R = 3" R = 3"

RIGHT END   LEFT END

90½"

20⅞"   20⅞"

5/8" MDO PANEL

MAXI-HUTCH DETAILS

Maxi-Hutch needs four 4-by-8-ft. panels laid out as shown at right, cut and assembled (above) with glue and nails.

2

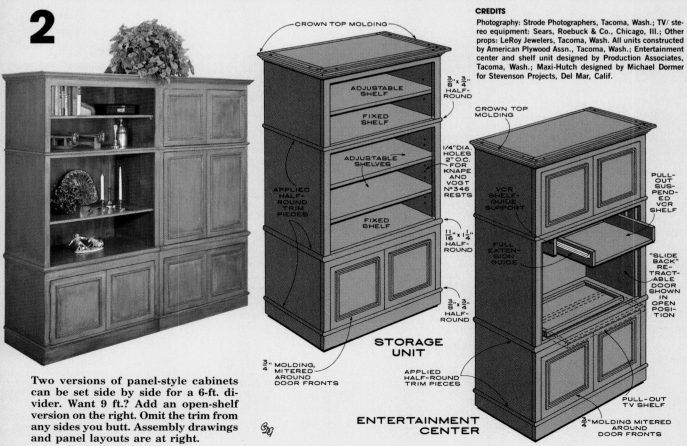

CREDITS

Photography: Strode Photographers, Tacoma, Wash.; TV/ stereo equipment: Sears, Roebuck & Co., Chicago, Ill.; Other props: LeRoy Jewelers, Tacoma, Wash. All units constructed by American Plywood Assn., Tacoma, Wash.; Entertainment center and shelf unit designed by Production Associates, Tacoma, Wash.; Maxi-Hutch designed by Michael Dormer for Stevenson Projects, Del Mar, Calif.

CROWN TOP MOLDING

ADJUSTABLE SHELF

FIXED SHELF

ADJUSTABLE SHELVES

APPLIED HALF-ROUND TRIM PIECES

FIXED SHELF

¾" MOLDING, MITERED AROUND DOOR FRONTS

STORAGE UNIT

3/8" x 3/4" HALF-ROUND

¼" DIA. HOLES 2" O.C. FOR KNAPE AND VOGT N° 346 RESTS

11/16" x 1¼" HALF-ROUND

3/8" x 3/4" HALF-ROUND

APPLIED HALF-ROUND TRIM PIECES

CROWN TOP MOLDING

VCR SHELF GUIDE SUPPORT

FULL EXTENSION GUIDE

PULL-OUT SUSPENDED VCR SHELF

"SLIDE BACK" RETRACTABLE DOOR SHOWN IN OPEN POSITION

PULL-OUT TV SHELF

¾" MOLDING MITERED AROUND DOOR FRONTS

ENTERTAINMENT CENTER

Two versions of panel-style cabinets can be set side by side for a 6-ft. divider. Want 9 ft.? Add an open-shelf version on the right. Omit the trim from any sides you butt. Assembly drawings and panel layouts are at right.

ment, games, video cassettes, books, knickknacks. And best of all, either style is easily built in a home shop. They're made of structural panels—plywood or waferboard—so you need no support frames.

Check out the color photos: You'll note that both designs seem to have a front frame of solid lumber. Now check the cutting diagrams: That effect is achieved by cutting doors and shelf openings from a solid four-by-eight-foot panel. For most-efficient use of these structural panels, interior cutouts were made by means of plunge cuts with a circular saw blade. With this method, the outer frame remains intact and the cutout panels can be hinged back into their openings as doors. If you use a thin plywood blade, its narrow kerf will give proper clearance.

If you've never tried a plunge cut with your portable circular saw, you'll want to clamp a straightedge across the panel, spaced to put the saw blade on the layout line for the first interior cut. Rest the saw on the toe of its base, with the blade guard temporarily tied up and the blade protruding only an inch or so, and move the base against your improvised fence. With care, start the saw and lower the blade into the panel. When you've pivoted the base flat against the surface, move it along the layout line until the kerf just nicks the limit line at right angles to it. Repeat this procedure, repositioning your fence for each new interior cut. You'll then only need to cut away the webs in each corner, using a keyhole or sabre saw.

These interior cuts for the Maxi-Hutch can, if you prefer, be made with a sabre saw. The rounded corners of the doors (intended as finger holes, so you could omit the handles shown on the prototype) create a waste area through which you can drill an entry hole for the saw blade. The

doors for the hutch are split and hinged in the middle for compactness when open. This is especially helpful when several of the units stand side by side. The doors close against magnetic catches. In the model shown, doors (with a pair of optional U-handles) were put on the lower compartment only. If you have more need for concealed storage, you can give the same door treatment to the smaller compartment above it.

Although the hutch could be built of textured panels such as waferboard or OSB (oriented-strand board—an upgraded version of waferboard), I'd recommend plywood for the panel-style units. If you choose MDO, no surface preparation is needed before finishing. But if you go with an A-C plywood, you'll need to fine-sand all surfaces.

If you want to duplicate the grained effect that the American Plywood Assn. and I chose, first apply the primer recommended for use with the top coat of your choice. We used a semigloss latex enamel (Fuller O'Brien's Mushroom H20H) and let it dry thoroughly. You just stroke on a graining stain (mine was Zar Satin Stain and Sealer, Teak Natural 120) with wadded-up cheesecloth.

If your first application doesn't give you as dark an effect as you'd like, just add more "graining" by stroking with the dipped cheesecloth again in the same direction. It takes a bit of practice, but if you goof you can always wipe off the stain with a solvent and start over—*by Al Lees. Drawings by Carl De Groote.*

LIST OF MANUFACTURERS

Photography: Strode Photographers, Tacoma, Wash.; TV/stereo equipment: Sears, Roebuck & Co., Chicago, Ill.; Other props: LeRoy Jewelers, Tacoma, Wash. All units constructed by American Plywood Assn., Tacoma, Wash.; Entertainment center and shelf unit designed by Production Associates, Tacoma, Wash.; Maxi-Hutch designed by Michael Dormer for Stevenson Projects, Del Mar, Calif.

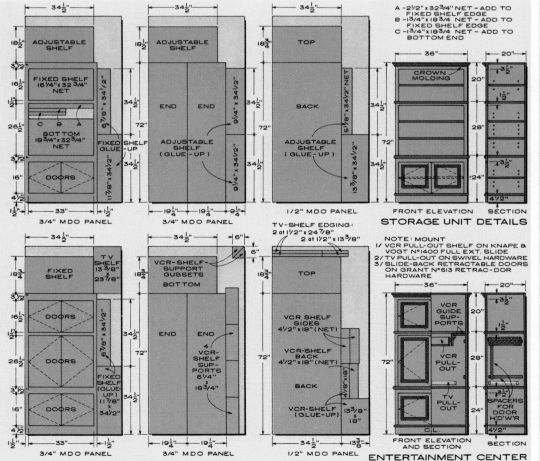

MATERIALS LIST

QUANTITY	DESCRIPTION

MAXI-HUTCH

Panels: MDO, overlaid both sides, or APA trademarked A-B or A-C; or non-veneer structural panels (waferboard or OSB)

1	5/8" × 4' × 8'
2	1/2" × 4' × 8'
1	3/8" × 4' × 8'

Other materials:

4 pr.*	2" brass door hinges
4*	Magnetic door catches
	Door pulls (optional)

*8 pr. hinges and 8 catches with optional doors

SHELF UNIT

Panels: MDO, overlaid both sides, or APA trademarked A-B or A-C

2	3/4" × 4' × 8'
1	1/2" × 4' × 8'

Other Materials:

14	3/8" × 3/4" half-round molding
7	11/16" × 1 1/4" half-round molding
10	3/4" decorative molding
7	Crown molding
2 pr.	2" cabinet door hinges
2	Door latches and pulls
16	K.V. #346 shelf rests

ENTERTAINMENT CENTER

Panels: same type as shelf unit

2	3/4" × 4' × 8'
1	1/2" × 4' × 8'

Other materials:

32	3/4" decorative molding
14	3/8" × 3/4" half-round trim
7	11/16" × 1 1/4" half-round trim
7	Crown molding
4 pr.	2" cabinet door hinges
3 pr.	Touch-latch door catches
1 set	Retractable door hardware
1 set	Swivel shelf TV hardware

built-ins with paneling

LIGHTED FOYER

Any picture that flashes in your mind when someone says "plywood paneling" is likely to be out of date. In the last couple of years, the range of patterns and colors available in prefinished panels has dramatically increased. You're no longer limited to a selection of wood grains, whether real veneers or photographic reproductions. Now you can choose panels with bold or subdued patterns, stripes, florals, and pictorials that remind you of wallpaper. The newest paneling products reproduce such surfaces as grass cloth, woven-reed matting—even marble. And some of the designs are embossed to provide textures for an even greater degree of realism.

Unlike wallpaper, however, these panels give you a tough, durable surface that not only can be scrubbed, but resists dents and tears as well. And if you tire of the look after a time, you can always resurface with paint or paper.

Today's broader choice in plywood paneling inspired me to seek out projects in which the material would be used structurally—not just to cover a flat wall. The home improvements shown here are the result—all but one of them designed by Michael Cannarozzi for the Plywood Paneling Council and shot by Photography House. The exception is the divider arch on the previous page, which was created by Georgia-Pacific Corp., featuring its Firelight Forum oak paneling as an accent in the study alcove of an upstairs apartment. The alcove was created by framing a partition and facing both sides with matching paneling. Note that both the arch and window treatment echo the under-roof slant of the ceiling, their open-

WINDOW BOX AND CORNICE

COUNTER AND LIGHT VALANCE

Some paneling projects to get you started show range of patterns now available in plywood paneling, from actual or reproduced wood grains to wallpaper-like designs—even a combination of the two, as shown above. Most panels are prefinished, so once you've applied them (with nails or adhesive), the job is done. For purchasing information on any panel shown in these photos, send a business-size self-addressed and stamped envelope to Plywood Paneling Council, 1633 Broadway, New York, NY 10019.

LAMBREQUIN

TV PEDESTAL

DIVIDER ARCH

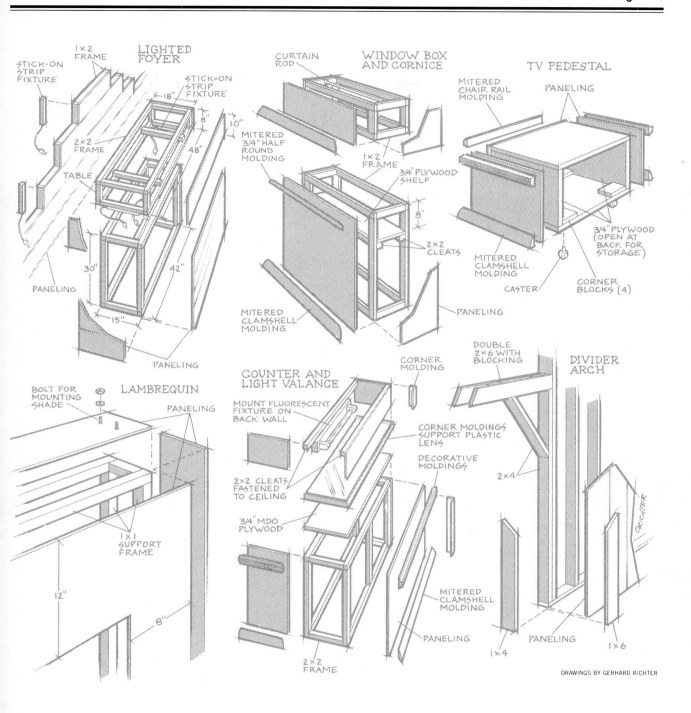

LIGHTED FOYER

STICK-ON STRIP FIXTURE

1×2 FRAME

STICK-ON STRIP FIXTURE

X→18"

8"

10"

2×2 FRAME

48"

TABLE

PANELING

30"

42"

15"

PANELING

PANELING

WINDOW BOX AND CORNICE

CURTAIN ROD

MITERED 3/4" HALF ROUND MOLDING

1×2 FRAME

3/4" PLYWOOD SHELF

8"

2×2 CLEATS

MITERED CLAMSHELL MOLDING

TV PEDESTAL

MITERED CHAIR RAIL MOLDING

PANELING

3/4" PLYWOOD (OPEN AT BACK FOR STORAGE)

MITERED CLAMSHELL MOLDING

CASTER

CORNER BLOCKS (4)

PANELING

LAMBREQUIN

BOLT FOR MOUNTING SHADE

PANELING

1×1 SUPPORT FRAME

12"

8"

COUNTER AND LIGHT VALANCE

MOUNT FLUORESCENT FIXTURE ON BACK WALL

2×2 CLEATS FASTENED TO CEILING

3/4" MDO PLYWOOD

2×2 FRAME

CORNER MOLDING

CORNER MOLDINGS SUPPORT PLASTIC LENS

DECORATIVE MOLDINGS

MITERED CLAMSHELL MOLDING

PANELING

DOUBLE 2×6 WITH BLOCKING

DIVIDER ARCH

2×4

1×4

PANELING

1×6

GRICHTER

DRAWINGS BY GERHARD RICHTER

ings outlined in pine trim boards finished with an oak stain.

Most of the other projects shown in the photos (and sketched above) are compact enough to be framed in 2 × 2 lumber. You can join the 2 × 2s with glue and flathead screws, or by bridging joints with metal plates on the inside. The paneling faces are then cut to cover the frame, and are applied with adhesive or colored nails—or a combination of both. Though usually only a little thicker than 1/8 inch, the paneling will stiffen the frame joints for a sturdy assembly. Most paneling comes in standard four-by-eight-foot sheets. For economical cutting, it's best to lay out (on graph paper) scale drawings of the pieces you'll need.

The lighted foyer achieves its dramatic recessed effect by means of a false wall framed and paneled six inches in front of the actual wall. The oak paneling has evenly spaced grooves (every eight inches) and is applied horizontally to both walls. Don't waste paneling on the lower part of the rear wall, because only the top will show. The "planks" of the front paneling are cut back in steps for a ziggurat effect, and a stick-on shelf light is mounted vertically behind every other step.

More concealed lighting is tucked under the paneling-faced top of the slab-on-cube table. The paneling here is real birch veneer finished with a transparent wipe-on stain—*by Al Lees. Photos courtesy Georgia-Pacific. Drawings by Gerhard Richter.*

the ultimate workbench

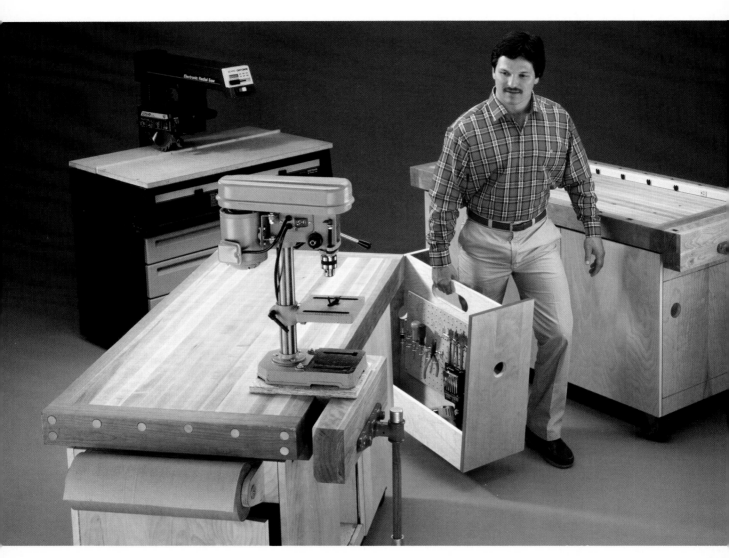

Though designed to flank a radial-arm or bench saw, the two bench units are on casters for easy repositioning. Unit at left has a center tool caddy that slides out for toting to jobs elsewhere in the house.

The search was for nothing less than the ultimate workbench—and what evolved was a two-bench system with 2⅓-by-5-foot laminated maple tops and the long list of practical features listed. Many of those features are shown in the photos on these pages. Less obvious is the full-access island concept of the benches that allows working from both sides. The benches also sport skirts for clamping, and other clamping provisions.

I had lots of input in tackling this assignment. Many *Popular Science* staff members and all of the magazine's home and shop contributors (like me) have home workshops—and firm convictions about what type of workbench is best.

Writer Tom Jones said, "The top must be designed for clamping access. Nothing screws up a project more than discovering you can't clamp it. And I want a bench with generous surface area." *PS* Art Director Dave Houser pushed for movable modules. Editor-in-Chief C. P. Gilmore was strong for making the modules the same height as a saw to provide a continuous, flat working surface. Tool-techniques expert "Cris" DeCristoforo wanted built-in electrical outlets, a metalworking vise, and a metal plate for "banging on." Home and shop consultant Rich Day seconded the metal vise need and wanted to make sure we had bench dogs for clamping boards on the bench top. Tool expert A. J. Hand proposed drawers that would open from either side, because, as he said, "I currently have this arrangement, and like it a lot." Home and Shop Editor Al Lees, who originated the assignment, put in a bid for a built-in tool caddy that could go to remote jobs, and for a

unit: the fir or pine and plywood structural base unit; and the lumber-core hardwood plywood panels, drawers, and doors.

Start planning your bench units by deciding if they are to work with a power tool so you can establish the height you'll want them to be. My benches stand 37¼ inches high to match my Sears radial saw. That's the maximum height you should go—most workbenches are from about 34½ to 36½ inches high. If you want to match a bench to a tool that stands higher than mine, don't. Find a way to reduce the height of the tool—unless you're very tall.

Build the top first. The 2-inch-thick top is laminated from 1¾-inch-wide maple strips. Maple is durable and is probably the most readily available hardwood for bench

21 great ideas to choose from

Movability (with locking casters)
Full-access island positioning
Splits in two to flank saw table
Portable tool caddy (large photo)
Slide-through accessory drawers
Storage cabinets for tools
Built-in shop vac (Photo 1 at left)
Butcher-paper dispenser (Photo 2)
Paper-towel dispenser (Photo 2)
Bench brush (Photo 2)
Front vise (Photo 2)
Tail vise (Photo 3)
Strip outlets for power tools (Photo 3)
Small-parts trough (Photo 3)
Switchable bench-top tools (Photo 4)
Laminated maple work top
Clamping skirt
Bench-dog holes
Studs for hold-down clamps
Add-on metalworking vise
Lockable security compartments

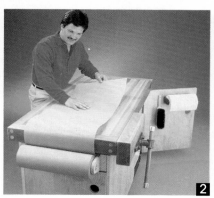

Other features listed are demonstrated in photos.

kraft paper roll for disposable bench-top protection.

This was just a sampling of the many ideas that flowed: There was general agreement that the bench must have a sturdy wood top, solid construction, and full accessibility. Also, most consultants wanted heavy locking casters. While the photos and drawings call for two benches built to work with a radial-arm saw, one, two, or more bench modules can be built to work alone or with a table saw instead.

The system is heavy and not inexpensive to build—the price of all the features we wanted. The tops, which are removable (and must be removed for transporting the benches), weigh over 100 pounds each. Figure on each bench unit costing $300 to $600, depending a lot on how much you pay for the materials and the features you select.

Because of variables including bench height, tolerance buildup in the laminations, and top thickness variation, some of the components are not dimensioned in the plans. Construction is in three parts: the skirted hardwood top

tops in the U.S. For contrast, we dressed up the project by making the top skirts and vise jaws of cherry. Using maple throughout would be standard because it's harder than cherry. Take your pick.

The *width* of the bench tops? I kept mine 28 inches so they'll roll through the door to my shop. That's wide enough so that when I place the two units back to back, they offer the firm support I need for laying out 4-by-8-foot plywood sheets.

Select flat, smoothly planed, one-edge-surfaced 1¾-inch -thick stock and carefully rip it 2¼ inches wide. Ten 56-inch-long strips are needed for the top with the tool trough, 13 for the full-width top. (The length's extra inch allows for trimming.) Lay out and drill tie-bolt holes in one of the strips and use it for a jig to transfer the holes to all the other strips. Note that holes in the rear strip for the trough top are counterbored for washers and nuts, and that this strip is also rabbeted on the bottom edge to accept the trough's bottom panel.

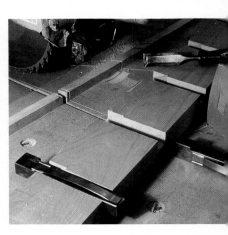

Maple strips for the laminated top are drilled, glued, and clamped in alignment for rods that pass through assembly.

Clamping versatility includes bench dogs for wide boards, bench skirt for C-clamps, stud holes, and vise grip.

Skirt for top that takes bench dogs has slots cut at 2-degree angle before adding inner strip. Chisel-cut head notches.

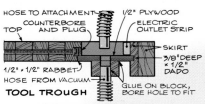

TOOL TROUGH

HOSE TO ATTACHMENT
COUNTERBORE AND PLUG
TOP
1/2" PLYWOOD
ELECTRIC OUTLET STRIP
SKIRT
3/8" DEEP × 1/2" DADO
1/2" × 1/2" RABBET
HOSE FROM VACUUM
GLUE ON BLOCK, BORE HOLE TO FIT

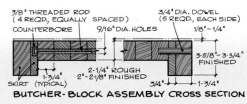

BUTCHER-BLOCK ASSEMBLY CROSS SECTION

3/8" THREADED ROD (4 REQD, EQUALLY SPACED)
COUNTERBORE
9/16" DIA. HOLES
3/4" DIA. DOWEL (6 REQD, EACH SIDE)
1/8"–1/4"
3-5/8"–3-3/4" FINISHED
2-1/4" ROUGH 2"–2-1/8" FINISHED
SKIRT (TYPICAL)
1-3/4"
3/4"
1-3/4"

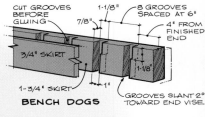

BENCH DOGS

CUT GROOVES BEFORE GLUING
1-1/8"
7/8"
8 GROOVES SPACED AT 6"
4" FROM FINISHED END
3/4" SKIRT
1-1/8"
1-3/4" SKIRT
1"
GROOVES SLANT 2° TOWARD END VISE

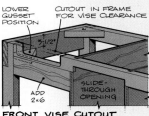

ALTERNATIVE TIE-DOWN
(TO GUSSETS IN MAIN DRAWING)

SKIRT
CUT OFF
LAG SCREWS
3-1/2" CORNER BRACE
TOP
FOR REAR CORNERS OF TOOL-TROUGH TOP AND FRONT-VISE CORNER
BASE FRAME
PANEL

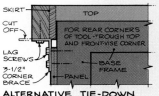

FRONT VISE CUTOUT

LOWER GUSSET POSITION
CUTOUT IN FRAME FOR VISE CLEARANCE
3-1/2"
ADD 2×6
SLIDE-THROUGH OPENING

RAIL DETAIL 1

CUT NOTCH 1/8" HIGHER THAN PANELS
3/4" × 3/4" DADOES
TOOL CADDY OR DRAWER WIDTH PLUS 1/8"

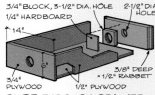

SLIDE-THROUGH DRAWER

3/4" BLOCK, 3-1/2" DIA. HOLE
1/4" HARDBOARD
2-1/2" DIA. HOLE
14"
6"
3/4" PLYWOOD
1/2" PLYWOOD
3/8" DEEP × 1/2" RABBET

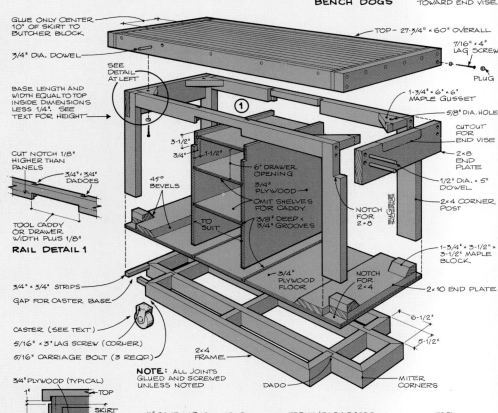

GLUE ONLY CENTER 10" OF SKIRT TO BUTCHER BLOCK
3/4" DIA. DOWEL
SEE DETAIL AT LEFT
BASE LENGTH AND WIDTH EQUAL TO TOP INSIDE DIMENSIONS LESS 1/4". SEE TEXT FOR HEIGHT
TOP - 27-3/4" × 60" OVERALL
7/16" × 4" LAG SCREW
PLUG
1-3/4" × 6" × 6" MAPLE GUSSET
5/8" DIA. HOLE
CUTOUT FOR END VISE
2×8 END PLATE
1/2" DIA. × 5" DOWEL
2×4 CORNER POST
1-3/4" × 3-1/2" 3-1/2" MAPLE BLOCK
2×10 END PLATE
6-1/2"
5-1/2"
3-1/2"
3/4"
1-1/2"
6" DRAWER OPENING
3/4" PLYWOOD
OMIT SHELVES FOR CADDY
3/8" DEEP × 3/4" GROOVES
NOTCH FOR 2×8
NOTCH FOR 2×4
45° BEVELS
TO SUIT
3/4" PLYWOOD FLOOR
3/4" × 3/4" STRIPS
GAP FOR CASTER BASE
CASTER (SEE TEXT)
5/16" × 3" LAG SCREW (CORNER)
5/16" CARRIAGE BOLT (3 REQD.)
2×4 FRAME
DADO
MITER CORNERS
①

NOTE: ALL JOINTS GLUED AND SCREWED UNLESS NOTED

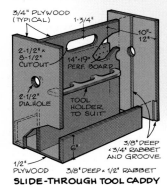

SLIDE-THROUGH TOOL CADDY

3/4" PLYWOOD (TYPICAL)
1-3/4"
10"–12"
2-1/2" × 8-1/2" CUTOUT
14"×19" PERF. BOARD
2-1/2" DIA. HOLE
TOOL HOLDER TO SUIT
6"
1/2" PLYWOOD
3/8" DEEP × 1/2" RABBET
3/8" DEEP RABBET AND GROOVE

DOOR/PANEL DETAIL

3/4" PLYWOOD (TYPICAL)
1"
TOP
SKIRT
FRONT/BACK DOOR OR SOLID PANEL HEIGHT
END DOOR
SKIRT
FLUSH WITH 3/4" STRIPS
FLOOR

BENCH ARRANGEMENT - FRONT VISE

1/2" CONTINUOUS HINGE (TYPICAL)
SOLID PANEL
FRONT/BACK DOORS
END DOOR
SLIDE-THROUGH TOOL CADDY
SOLID END PANELS
FRONT VISE

BENCH ARRANGEMENT - END VISE

TOOL TROUGH
SLIDE-THROUGH DRAWER
END VISE
END DOOR
DOOR UNDER DRAWER (BOTH SIDES)

To cut 2-degree slanted slots in vise jaws for bench dogs, put shim under the edge of the jaw block.

Position the vise base on blocks against the edge of the skirt. Here, the vise block is drilled but not yet glued.

Make a cardboard template that clears the vise mechanism; mark area where the top of bench frame must be cut out.

Lay the strips on a flat surface and check that the edges fit flush, the bolt holes are in alignment, and everything is ready for gluing. Gluing must be done quickly. There will not be time to correct mistakes after you start, so get help for the gluing process.

Glue up the 4-inch-wide material for the skirts—a 1¾-inch strip glued to a ¾-inch strip. Note that the skirt for the rear of the trough top is dadoed to take the trough's bottom strip. Also note that the bench-dog slots must be cut in both the front and rear 1¾-inch strips prior to gluing on the ¾-inch strips. Counterbore the inside of the skirt face to clear the cross tie nuts. For the top with the trough, glue on only the front skirt. For the plain top, glue both front and rear skirt pieces to the top. Dowel the skirts to the top edges, and sand the dowel ends flush with the faces of the skirts. Very carefully cut the ends of the tops to a 55-inch length. Support the work well, and get help handling these heavy units.

Recognizing that the strip tops will expand and contract (more in some climates than others), I took steps to minimize the problem: The end skirts are designed so they can move. The tops are lagged—not glued—to the base through oversize holes for mobility. For the same reason, the skirt has clearance as it sits on the base.

Cut the skirt end pieces about 1/16 inch over length for finish-sanding flush. Drill ½-inch holes and counterbore with a one-inch bit for 7/16-inch lag bolts. Carefully transfer the hole locations to the ends of the top and drill pilot holes. Then glue only the center 10 inches of the skirt to the end of the top and bolt in place. The center gluing plus the oversize lug body holes should allow for some movement of the wood. For the top with the trough, plug and sand the counterbores for the bolts on the rear edge. Cut a stopped dado at the rear of the skirt end strips. Glue and position the trough bottom strip, and assemble the rear skirt and the end pieces.

Take the tops to a cabinetmaker with a 36-inch power feed belt or drum-sanding machine and have him sand the tops to finish for you. It cost me $40 to have both tops sanded flat and smooth. After final touch-up sanding and edge breaking, I finished the top with three coats of tung-oil-based penetrating finish, steel-wooling between coats.

Base assembly

Select high-quality flat, straight, dry 2×4s and ¾-inch plywood for the base materials. To allow for assembly clearance and for growth and shrinkage of the top, make the base ¼ inch narrower and shorter than the dimensions inside the skirt.

Start the work by cutting the base floor to those dimensions from ¾-inch plywood. Make the dado cuts in the top floor face for the plywood panels that form the ends of the center slide-through for the drawer or caddy.

On a flat surface, assemble the 2×4 reinforcing and the ¾-by-¾-inch strips to the bottom side of the base floor, gluing and screwing all joints.

Carefully notch the 2×10 end plates to accept the vertical 2×4 corner posts. Glue and screw the end plates to the base floor. Glue on the 1¾-by-3½-by-3½-inch maple blocks in alignment with the notch-outs.

The length of the 2×4 corner posts establishes the height of the bench. To determine what the overall finished bench height is to be, calculate the finished thickness of the top by subtracting from the height of the skirt the dimension from the bottom of the skirt to the bottom surface of the laminated top. Then determine the exact height of the casters by setting a caster, bracket down, on a flat surface and measuring the wheel height. I ordered the 5-inch-diameter, 2-inch-wide roller-and-ball-bearing caster sets—two locking and two plain—from Kennedy Manufacturing Co. (Box 151, Van Wert, Ohio 45891-0151; they're No. 80837 heavy-duty casters for Kennedy's tool chests). Add the thickness of the top less the skirt, ¾ inch for the base floor, plus the caster height. Subtract this from the desired overall bench height. The difference should be the length the 2×4 corner posts should be cut.

Subassemble the corner posts to the 2×8 end plates. Subassemble the center drawer or tool-caddy frame by making sure the corners are square, and glue in place in dados on the base floor. Glue and screw the end subassemblies to the base floor. Add the top rails, gluing, screwing, and doweling in place. Glue and screw the corner gussets in place. Using the vise template you made, cut the vise clearance on either the rail (for the front vise) or the top end plate (for the end vise). Note that extra material must be added to the frame in the front vise area before making the cutout.

Check to make sure the top fits. Drill for and fit the top corner tie-down lags. Trim or shim under the top or on top rails for a solid fit. Note that the rear of the trough top and the corner of the top adjacent to the front vise are fastened with corner brackets instead of through the gusset into the top.

Make up the tool caddy, drawer, and doors using lumber-core hardwood plywood (I chose birch). The slide-through drawer and caddy must be made about 1/16 inch under the size of the opening to slide freely. Glue and screw fixed panels to the bench frame and mount the doors with piano hinges. Magnetic or detent latches can be used. For security, install locks on the doors. I applied veneer tape to all exposed edges, then finished the panels with the same tung-oil-based finish used on the tops. The three-prong outlet strip shown in the photo is Wiremold's PM-45—*by Phil McCafferty. Drawings by Eugene Thompson.*

build your own custom carport

Whether your carport is attached to your house, or built as a freestanding unit (above, right), this elegant yet practical addition can greatly increase the value of your home.

Thinking about building a carport? It's a wise investment. Besides protecting you and your car from the weather, there are many other advantages.

Under the shelter of a carport roof, the car stays cleaner. And it's shaded from direct sunlight, so the paint won't fade as readily. Remove the car from the carport, and the structure doubles as a patio cover or a picnic shelter for cookouts and get-togethers. As home-improvement projects go, a carport is inexpensive and relatively easy to put up, and it can be an interim step in a more ambitious project. Later on, you can put siding on a carport to create a garage or workshop, or put up screening to make a screened-in porch.

Planning your custom carport

There are few plans available for carports, and for a good reason: Most carports have to be custom-designed for the house they will be attached to or stand beside. The first step in building a carport is drawing up a plan that will work with your home.

There are several questions you need to answer as you begin making your plan. How big should your carport be? Do you want a freestanding carport, or will you attach it to the house? If you intend to make an attached carport, how will you attach it to the house? What sort of foundation will your carport have? What sort of roof will it have—simple rafters or trussed?

Once you've answered those questions, read through the following suggestions and draw up a plan *before* you begin construction. Many of the challenges this project presents can be worked out first on paper, without wasting time and materials. Besides, you'll find a plan is essential for another reason: This project is probably big enough to require a building permit, and your local Building Inspector will require a set of working drawings along with your application for a permit.

Standard car spaces. As a norm, most one-car garages and carports are 12 feet wide by 20 to 22 feet long. A 1½-car space is 18 feet wide, while a two-car space is 22 feet wide.

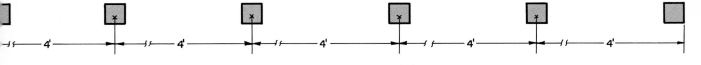

POST LAYOUT

1. Space the posts to support the top plate at the proper intervals. A 4 × 4 top plate must be supported every 4′.

2. Lay out the foundation of the carport (right) with stakes and string. Measure diagonally from corner to corner. *AD* must equal *BC.*

Maximum spans. The maximum safe span for a 4 × 4 is 4 feet. Since we show a 4 × 4 beam for the top plate in our drawings, we've supported it with posts every 4 feet (Fig. 1). If you use a 4 × 6 top plate, you need to support it every 6 feet. A 4 × 8 must be supported every 8 feet. As for rafters, the maximum safe span for 2 × 6s in this application (24 inches on center, holding up a light roof) is 12 feet. If you want to span 18 feet, use 2 × 8 rafters. Beyond 18 feet, we suggest you build trusses, or support the rafters in the middle.

Putting down a solid foundation

Since the purpose of the foundation is to support the posts, you must locate these posts when you lay out the foundation. Stretch string between stakes to form a rectangle, as shown in figure 2. (If you're building an attached carport, one side of this rectangle should be your house.) To make sure the rectangle is perfectly square, measure diagonally between the corners. Both diagonals should be the same.

Mark the locations of the posts by measuring along the string. Put a piece of tape on the string where you want to locate a post, then use a plumb bob to find the location on the ground (Fig. 3). Mark each ground location with a spike and a piece of paper. You'll need just one line of posts for an attached carport, and two parallel lines for a freestanding structure.

There are three types of foundations common to carports: pad, pier, and pole.

Concrete pad. This is the most involved of the three, and you'll probably want to contract out most of the work, especially pouring and smoothing the concrete. But you can save a good deal of money by putting up the forms and digging the footer trenches yourself. Make these trenches

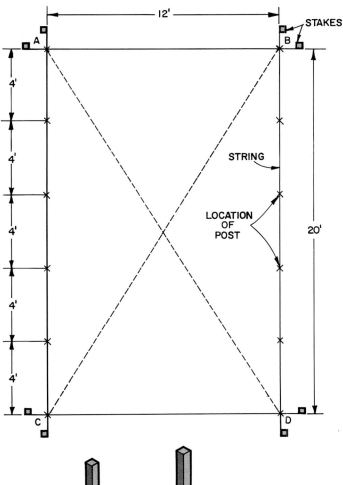

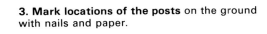

3. Mark locations of the posts on the ground with nails and paper.

12 to 16 inches wide and 18 to 24 inches deep all around the perimeter of the foundation. Put up the forms, as shown in figure 4, bracing them every 18 inches with stakes. Throw some gravel in the bottom of the trenches and over the pad area for drainage, then roll out 6 inches wire reinforcing mesh over the entire pad area to strengthen the pad once it's poured. Prop this mesh up on stones so the concrete flows over *and* under the wires. When poured, your pad should be at least 6 inches thick

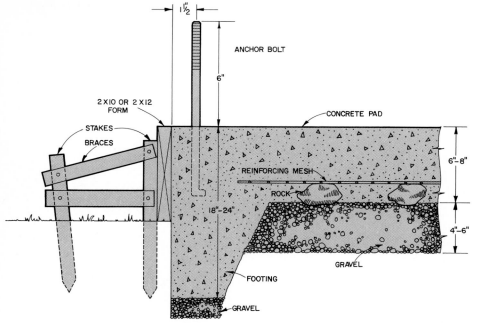

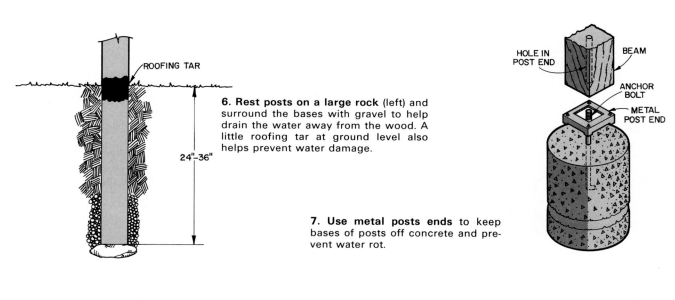

5. Set concrete piers at least 24 inches in the ground (above), or below the frost-line.

4. Proper concrete pad requires a footer around the perimeter and steel reinforcing mesh to keep it from cracking. Brace the forms to keep them from bowing. Set anchor bolts just as the concrete begins to stiffen.

6. Rest posts on a large rock (left) and surround the bases with gravel to help drain the water away from the wood. A little roofing tar at ground level also helps prevent water damage.

7. Use metal posts ends to keep bases of posts off concrete and prevent water rot.

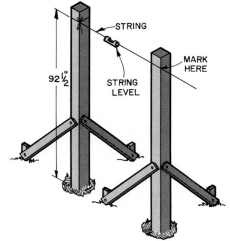

8. Use string and a string level (left) to find the tops of the posts.

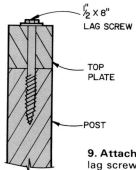

9. Attach the top plate to the posts with lag screws.

for compact and mid-sized cars, and 8 inches thick for larger cars. Set anchor bolts in the concrete where you want to place the posts.

Concrete piers. These are a good deal easier—and less expensive—to pour than a pad, and they provide just as much support for the posts. Dig a hole 8 inches in diameter, 24 inches deep or below the frost line for your area. Cut a 4-inch length of 8-inch stovepipe, and use this as form for the pier above the ground. Pour the concrete, and set an anchor bolt in the center of the pier (Fig. 5). When the concrete sets up, remove the stovepipe form.

Pole foundations. A pole foundation is actually no foundation at all. The posts, made from pressure-treated lumber and rated for ground contact, are set directly in the ground. Dig each post hole 8 inches wide, 24 inches deep or below the frost line. Place a large rock at the bottom of the hole to keep the post from settling. Put the post in the hole, and brace it plumb. Coat the sides of the post, 3 inches above and below ground level, with roofing tar—this will keep the rain water from soaking it. Throw a few shovelfuls of gravel into the hole for drainage, then fill the rest of the hole with dirt and tamp it down (Fig. 6).

All three of these foundations are suitable for attached carports, but the pole foundation works best for freestanding structures. By burying the posts in the ground, you add rigidity to the uncovered walls. If you want to use a pad or a pier foundation for a freestanding carport, consider casting the posts in the concrete.

Building a freestanding wall

If you've poured a pad or pier foundation, the next step is to set the posts. (If you opted for a pole foundation, the posts are already set.) Set metal post ends over the anchor bolts. These will keep the posts from contacting the concrete and absorbing moisture. Drill holes in the bottom ends of the posts, then set them over the anchor bolts as shown in figure 7.

Brace the posts plumb, and mark the height of one post above the ground. Normally, you want the lowest part of your carport to be 8 feet high, so mark the post 92½ inches above the ground. The width of the top plate will bring the height of the wall to an even 96 inches, or 8 feet. Using this mark as a reference, mark the tops of the other posts with a string and a string level as shown in figure 8. Cut the posts off to the proper height with a handsaw.

Cut the top plate to the proper length, and attach it to the tops of the posts with lag screws (Fig. 9). If you need to join two or more beams to make the top plate, lap them.

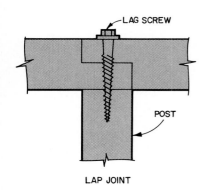

LAP JOINT

10. If you can't buy 4 × 4s long enough for the top plates, lap to shorter beams.

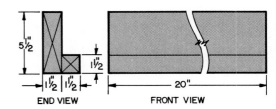

END VIEW   FRONT VIEW

LEDGER STRIP

12. Make a ledger strip (above) to support the upper end of the rafters.

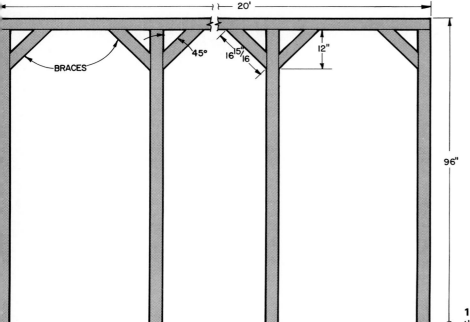

BRACES

WALL FRAME – SIDE VIEW

11. Brace posts to the top plate to keep the structure square.

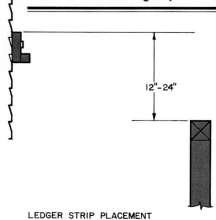

LEDGER STRIP PLACEMENT

13. Position ledger strip 12 to 24 inches above the top plate (left). The more precipitation you have, the steeper the roof should be.

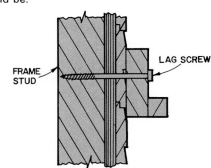

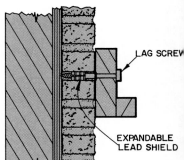

14. Secure the ledger strip to your house with lag screws. If you are attaching the strip to a masonry wall, drill the mortar and insert expansive lead anchors.

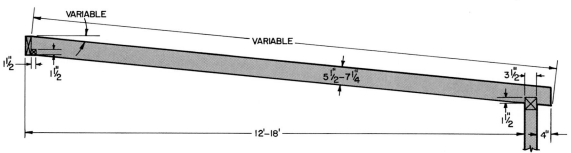

RAFTER LAYOUT

15. Cut a notch in the upper ends of the rafters (above) to fit over the ledger, then cut a "bird's mouth" near the lower end to fit over the top plate.

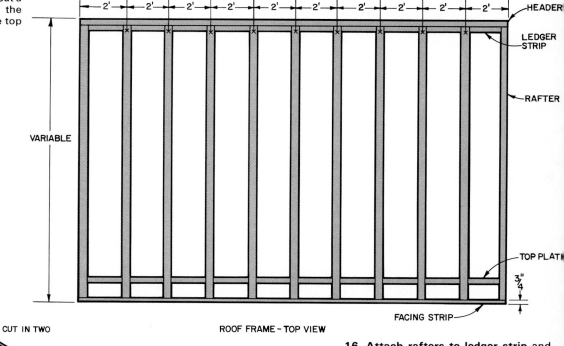

ROOF FRAME – TOP VIEW

CUT IN TWO

16. Attach rafters to ledger strip and top plate, 24 inches on center as shown above.

17. To bend a corner with drip edge, first cut it in two. Snip out a square from one of the bottom flanges. Instead of removing the square on the second piece, bend it back at 90 degrees.

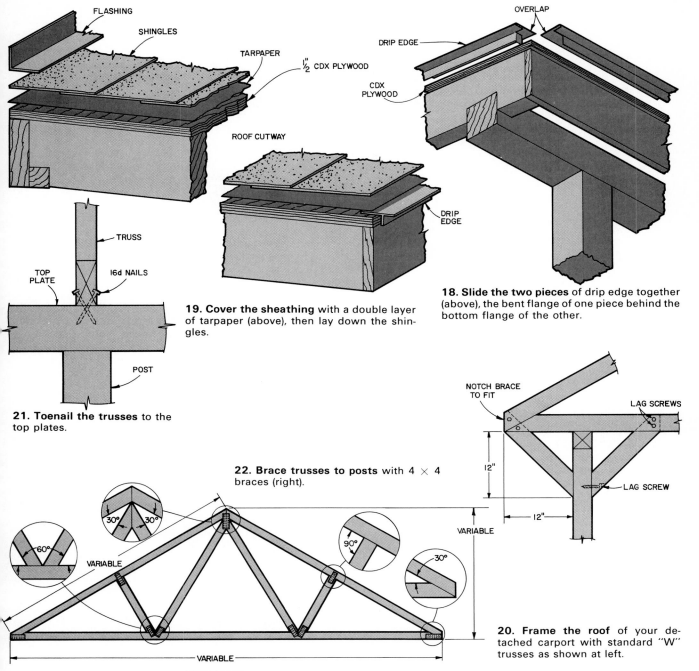

FLASHING
SHINGLES
TARPAPER
½" CDX PLYWOOD

ROOF CUTWAY

19. Cover the sheathing with a double layer of tarpaper (above), then lay down the shingles.

OVERLAP
DRIP EDGE
CDX PLYWOOD
DRIP EDGE

18. Slide the two pieces of drip edge together (above), the bent flange of one piece behind the bottom flange of the other.

TRUSS
TOP PLATE
16d NAILS
POST

21. Toenail the trusses to the top plates.

22. Brace trusses to posts with 4 × 4 braces (right).

NOTCH BRACE TO FIT
LAG SCREWS
12"
VARIABLE
LAG SCREW
12"

30° **30°**
90°
60°
30°
VARIABLE
VARIABLE
VARIABLE

TRUSS LAYOUT

20. Frame the roof of your detached carport with standard "W" trusses as shown at left.

Plan this lap joint so that it occurs over a post, as shown in figure 10.

Brace the posts to the top plate to keep these parts square to one another. Cut the braces from 4 × 4 stock, and secure them in place with lag screws (Fig. 11). Leave the other, temporary braces on the posts to help keep the wall straight up and down while you put up the roof.

Putting up an attached roof

The upper edge of an attached roof is anchored to the house with a "ledger strip". This strip consists of a *header,* a board the same size and thickness as your rafters that is mounted to the house, and a *ledger,* a 2 × 2 nailed flush with the bottom edge of the header to create a ledge on which to mount the rafters (Fig. 12).

Where you mount the ledger strip to the house determines the pitch of your roof. Generally, the more precipitation you have in your area, the steeper the pitch should be. In most cases, for a one-car carport, mount the ledger strip 12 inches above the top plate if you need a shallow pitch, and up to 24 inches above the top plate for steeper pitches (Fig. 13).

Attach the ledger strip to your house with lag screws. If you have a frame home, simply drive the lag screws into the side of the house so that they bite into the frame studs. If your home is masonry or concrete, drill the wall with a concrete drill bit and insert expansive lead anchors where you want to attach the ledger strip. Screw the lag screws into these anchors (Fig. 14), spaced every 2 to 4 feet along the header.

Using a framing square, lay out a single rafter. Miter the ends, then notch the upper end to fit over the ledge. Cut a "bird's mouth" near the lower end to fit over the top plate as shown in figure 15. Put this rafter in place to see if it fits properly. Then use it as a template for cutting the rest of the rafters. Nail the rafters in place, 24 inches on center. Complete the roof frame by nailing a facing strip to the lower end of the rafters (Fig. 16).

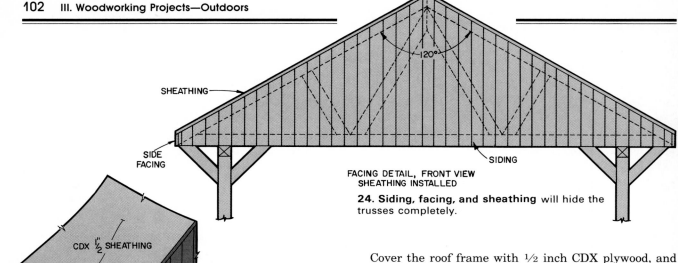

FACING DETAIL, FRONT VIEW
SHEATHING INSTALLED

24. Siding, facing, and sheathing will hide the trusses completely.

23. Cover end trusses with siding, and overhangs with facing strips. Then cover the entire roof with sheathing.

25. Make drip edge follow the peak by snipping the bottom flange and bending it to the proper angle.

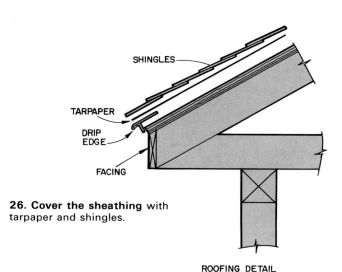

26. Cover the sheathing with tarpaper and shingles.

ROOFING DETAIL

Cover the roof frame with ½ inch CDX plywood, and remove the temporary braces from the posts. Install a metal drip edge all around the perimeter of the roof with roofing nails, to keep water from seeping under the roofing materials. Where you need to turn a corner, cut the drip edge in two, then snip out a small square from one of the bottom flanges. Start to snip the second piece in a the same manner, but instead of removing the square, bend it back at 90 degrees. Slide the two pieces of drip edge together on the roof, with the bent flange of one piece behind the bottom flange of the other as shown in figures 17 and 18.)

Finally, install the roofing materials. Put down a double layer of tarpaper, sealing the edge of the roof with roofing cement where the tarpaper meets the drip edge. Lay the shingles or the roofing felt over the tarpaper, then seal the seam between the roof and the house with aluminum flashing (Fig. 19).

Putting up a freestanding roof

The roof of a freestanding carport should be trussed, to make the structure more rigid. From 2 × 4s, build standard "W" trusses nailed together with metal truss plates (Fig. 20). Put these truss plates on *both* sides of the trusses. If you wish, install siding on the two end trusses while the trusses are still on the ground.

With a helper or two, set the finished trusses so that they span the top plates. Space them every 24 inches on center, and toenail the trusses to the top plates as shown in figure 21. Temporarily brace the trusses upright with long scraps of wood.

If your posts are 4 feet on center, every other truss should be positioned over a post. Where this occurs, brace the trusses to the posts the same way you braced the posts to the top plate. Cut the braces from 4 × 4 stock, and notch the upper end to lap the trusses. Secure the braces in place with lag screws (Fig. 22).

Install siding to the end trusses, if you haven't already. Nail facing strips along the overhangs, tying the trusses together. Then cover the trusses with ½-inch CDX sheathing, removing the temporary truss braces as you put the plywood in place (Fig. 23). When you've completed this step, the roof frame should be covered with siding, facing, or sheathing, completely hiding the trusses as shown in figure 24.

Nail the drip edge to the sheathing, all around the perimeter of the roof. Turn the corners with the drip edge as was shown in figures 17 and 18. When you come to the gables, snip the bottom flange of the drip edge, then bend the upper flange to fit the peak (Fig. 25). Install the roofing materials, "double wrapping" the shingles at the peak to form a ridge cap as shown in figure 26—*by Nick Engler.*

two custom decks

shaded "patio-deck"

Perimeters of deck complex are defined by built-in benches and planter boxes. Plants and wind socks add color accents.

Before the Heckers built their deck system, their outdoor living space was confined to a tiny, 11-by-14-foot concrete patio. But the Brookfield, Wisconsin, family needed more room, since their summer parties often included more than forty guests. They also wanted to create an interesting focal point for the extensive landscaping they were planning.

To meet their needs, the old patio was floored-over with 2-by-6-inch redwood and new angled decks were built to the south and west, providing 430 square feet of outdoor living area.

The new decks are elevated eight inches off the ground and rest on a substructure of 4-by-6-inch beams, 2-by-6-inch joists and 4-by-4-inch posts embedded 42 inches into the ground; all are of economical pressure-treated Southern yellow pine. The exposed decking is 2-by-6 construction heart redwood, angled to visually divide the open conversation deck from the trellised dining area.

The unusual angled trellis provides some shade and a lot of eye-appeal to the dining deck. Built of 2-by-6-inch redwood, each grid is 24 inches

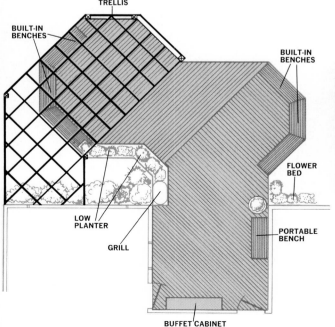

TRELLIS

BUILT-IN BENCHES

BUILT-IN BENCHES

FLOWER BED

LOW PLANTER

PORTABLE BENCH

GRILL

BUFFET CABINET

Grid-work trellis creates interesting shadows over dining section of deck. Post at far right is imbedded four feet in the ground, about three feet from the deck edge. Its distant placement allows the massive structure to be supported by just five posts.

Decking between two wings of home is over the old patio. Doors lead to sun room and a hallway to the kitchen.

square. Rising about eight feet above the deck, the trellis is anchored to a house eave and supported by five 4-by-4 posts. Four posts are anchored to the deck substructure, and the other is embedded 48 inches into the ground about three feet from the edge of the deck. This cuts down on the number of posts needed to support the grid, which helps preserve a broad, open view of the backyard. (The Heckers plan additional landscaping to fill the area between the post and deck.)

Built-in benches and planters line the edges of the deck and enhance its angles. One of the planters is cleverly designed to conceal the base of a gas grill and its LP gas tank. Planters are sided with three horizontal redwood 2 × 6s and capped with a 2 × 4.

Bench legs are 4 × 4s, toe-nailed to decking; seats are made of 2 × 4s, on edge, spaced ½ inch apart.

Another built-in convenience, a buffet cabinet, is located against the house (see illustration). The buffet wasn't in the original plan; the idea for it grew out of conversations between Carol Hecker and deck designer Bonnie Brocker-Beaudry. After construction had already begun, both remarked that it was a shame not to utilize the empty space. Made of 1 × 6 cedar, with a redwood countertop, the 34-inch-high unit comes in handy as a bar, a place to store dishes and tableware and to do last-minute meal preparation.

The deck complex cost $6,435 to build, including trellis and built-ins, an investment that has been more than recovered in pleasure for the Heckers and their friends—*by George Lyons. Designed by Bonnie Brocker-Beaudry.*

Low, clean-lined deck doesn't interfere with the Heckers' lovely wooded view.

spacious storage deck

Any way you look at it, this is one handsome deck complex, but the huge amount of storage underneath is what makes this design extra useful. The wooden doors of the storage area hide the deck's pressure-treated fir and hemlock substructure and keep it from having the "stilted" appearance so common in elevated decks. And the doors are finished to match the siding, further strengthening the unified house-deck connection.

The Nicholson family lived in their lake-view house for about three years before deciding to add the deck. The house has no basement or garage; the only storage area they had for bulky items like garden tools, barbecue gear and boating equipment was beneath an existing 10-by-25-foot deck. They

Redwood steps and railing (above) join midlevel deck to upper level. Galvanized common and finishing nails were used for the whole job.

Living and dining rooms look out onto spacious upper deck (left). Large trees shade this dining/entertainment area.

asked landscape architect John Herbst Jr. of Lake Oswego, Oregon, for a design that would give them a maximum amount of storage and more room for entertaining, plus give them an even better vantage point for viewing the lake.

Except for some help pouring concrete and framing the structure, Nicholson did all of the work himself. The old cedar deck was reinforced and covered over. All new levels are built of redwood; the facing is of 2 × 4s, decking consists of 2 × 2s and the rail caps are 2 × 6s. The 16-by-32-foot main deck adjoins the living and dining rooms and tops the storage area. It's an ideal area for entertaining and for children's play. The open railing doesn't interfere with the lake view.

A few steps lead down to a 9½-by-12-foot deck, used mainly for sunbathing. Two more steps go down to a small, decklike landing that serves as a transitional area between the garden and the house. The smaller sun deck and ground-level step-deck parallel the upper deck and frame attractive, mature landscaping.

Building the steps and railings was the part of the job Nicholson enjoyed the most. Working on the project nights and weekends, he crafted the railings out of 2 × 4 posts flanked by 1 × 2 stringers, with three vertical 1 × 1 lath pieces per section. The edges of the 2 × 6 cap are beveled at a 45-degree angle and the 1 × 1 lath wraparound is stained darker for contrast. Like the redwood decking, the stair treads are redwood 2 × 2s with 2 × 4 facing. The whole structure was sanded and sealed with a wood preservative before Nicholson finished it with a semitransparent stain.

The below-deck storage area is completely weatherproof. It has a concrete floor, 6-foot high ceiling, electric wiring, some built-in shelves and two hinged double doors for access. The Nicholsons also use the area for a wine cellar.

Nicholson said he didn't have much building experience—"just a little remodeling,"—before taking on the deck project. "These things always take a lot longer than you expect," he said. "But I'm glad I did it. We enjoy the deck all year round. During the mild weather, I eat breakfast out there almost every day, looking out over the lake"—*by Cathy Howard. Photos by Karlis Grants. Landscape architechture by John Herbst, Jr.*

Reprinted by permission of THE HOMEOWNER magazine.

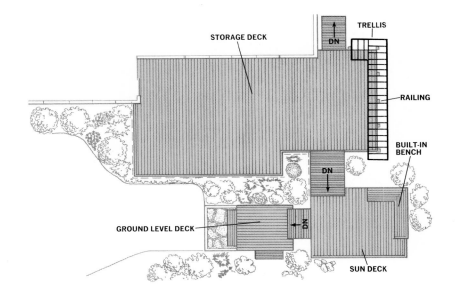

Substructure of elevated deck is enclosed for good looks and to provide storage space. Double doors swing open for easy access to yard equipment. Lower deck is positioned away from the trees and is used primarily for sunning. Plan (below) shows how decks are tied together.

three decks for impossible sites

DECK A

What good is a backyard you can't enjoy? Whether a yard is steeply sloped, overgrown with vegetation, or just too ugly to be inviting, it's useless space. It increases your property tax without contributing anything at all to your lifestyle.

But summon Cary Recker, a muscular deck-building specialist from Atlanta, Georgia, and your useless backyard can be transformed into the focal point of your house. Recker designs and constructs "impossible" decks on what might be considered hopeless sites.

Take deck A, for example. Here, Recker confronted a backyard 26 feet below the house's main living area. To make matters worse, the site was buried in primitive forest. A carpenter with guts was needed—one who was both acrobat and jungle fighter.

In the case of deck B, the backyard was a steep slope terraced with more than 500 railroad ties for $20,000 worth of landscaping. Obviously, the deck job called for more than superior building skills. Fine decorative taste was required, too.

For deck C, a concrete patio had outlived its usefulness. A once-small family had grown, with in-laws and grandchildren visiting each summer. Space was needed for outdoor entertaining, but the slab was edged with low brick walls that prevented any extension. This job called for a demolition expert.

Though widely varied, the assignments all drew on Recker's basic belief that a deck should make an architectural statement. "Most people who build decks just hang a rectangle on the back of the house," he says. "I've yet to build a square deck. All my decks are custom-shaped to their site. And the design may be adapted as I build."

Deck A was originally intended to extend 8 feet from one corner of the house at a 45-degree angle. As Recker dug his footings, however, he uncovered an underground stream. To bridge it, he extended the deck another four feet at a 60-degree angle.

Deck B stands a foot high where it takes off from a ledger attached to the house. But by the time it extends 26 feet, it's over 12 feet off the ground.

"It was designed like an observa-

DECK B

DECK C

These two decks cover special problems: one stands on a steep site (left) and the other over a grim patio slab (right).

tion deck on the side of a mountain," Recker says. "With the yard's dramatic slope, the bow shape—like the front of a ship—gives an ideal vantage point for viewing the yard."

To add visual interest to deck C, built over a nondescript patio tucked into an L-shaped ranch, Recker built it on two levels, notching out one corner for a large tree. "The idea here was to create a natural addition to the house," he says. "That's why most of the deck lacks a railing, and the benches are low enough to sit on facing either in or out."

Recker also has strong opinions when it comes to construction techniques. "Even though a deck is your eyeball on the world," he says, "it should be built for safety first and the best view second." For Recker, safety means taking no chances on structural integrity. "When in doubt, overbuild," he says, "especially when your deck is going to be more than a couple of feet high."

Some of Recker's construction methods are "above and beyond the call of duty." For instance, he obtains maximum anchorage for posts by setting them directly into wet concrete.

Recker favors plywood boxes for footing forms, and he sets them at least a foot deep—below local frost lines. The posts for deck A were set directly on bedrock, a granite vein five feet down. To keep posts elevated and level as the concrete in the forms sets, Recker tacks a 2 × 4 brace to each

DECK A

"I wanted this one to float above the jungle as if hung from a helicopter," says Recker of the deck at left. (1) Plywood boxes are forms for concrete footings, located by laying out shape of deck with twine. (2) Bulked-up wooden posts are set into concrete piers. (3) In corner of house, ledgers meet atop a post lag-bolted to the foundation block. (4) Joist pattern is similar on both levels; 3/4-inch ply is loose-laid on lower level as a work platform. (5) Skewed right side adds design interest. (6) Knee braces to posts firm up the 26-foot-high upper deck securely, as shown here.

1

side of the post, with stakes driven into the ground to anchor the opposite ends.

Recker shuns the notion of setting posts after the deck is built. "Temporary posts tend to warp the deck," he claims, "and posts can sink further into the ground, causing a deck to separate from the house." His footings will set at least a week before Recker knocks the braces down.

For even greater safety on a tall deck, Recker may also attach posts to

Terraced backyard fell steeply from the side of the house, so the deck had to be custom-fitted to the terrain. (1) Support structure was tied together with lattice; large underdeck area can be used for storage. Two panels can be hinged for access. (2) Lower panels were cut to follow ground contour; steps were provided next to the house. (3) Outer half-hex railing doubles as a backrest for a built-in bench of 2 × 6s nailed over a support frame of 2 × 4s.

2

3

1 2

The problem here was an uninviting slab edged with a low brick wall. (1) Recker floats a 4-by-4-foot grid over the slab, resting on concrete bricks under the joints. (2) Brawn takes care of restricting walls so the deck can extend past the existing slab. (3) Raised deck section is framed out from a diagonal beam supported (where Recker stands) on a post and pier. (4) Framing scheme permits lively pattern in deck planks; note angled steps between two levels.

3

4

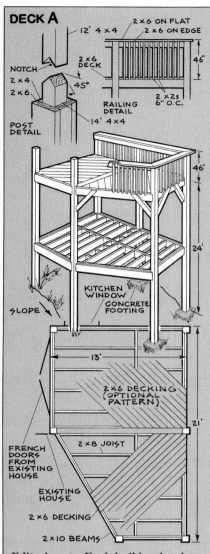

DECK A

12' 4×4
2×6 ON FLAT
2×6 ON EDGE
2×6 DECK
46"
NOTCH
2×4
2×6
45°
RAILING DETAIL
POST DETAIL
2×2s 6" O.C.
14' 4×4
46"
24'
KITCHEN WINDOW
CONCRETE FOOTING
SLOPE
13'
2×6 DECKING (OPTIONAL PATTERN)
21'
FRENCH DOORS FROM EXISTING HOUSE
2×8 JOIST
EXISTING HOUSE
2×6 DECKING
2×10 BEAMS

Editor's note: Each builder develops an individual approach to construction—and some prejudices. Recker's reservations concerning joist hangers are not confirmed by the experience of PS editors. But Koppers Corp. (major franchiser of pressure treatments) recommends using a water repellent on Wolmanized lumber after 6 mos., as Recker does.

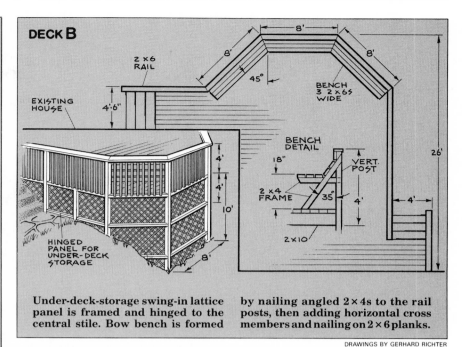

DECK B

2×6 RAIL
EXISTING HOUSE
4'6"
8'
8'
45°
8'
BENCH 3 2×6s WIDE
8'
26'
BENCH DETAIL
18"
VERT. POST
2×4 FRAME
35
4'
4'
2×10
HINGED PANEL FOR UNDER-DECK STORAGE
4'
4'
10'
8'

Under-deck-storage swing-in lattice panel is framed and hinged to the central stile. Bow bench is formed by nailing angled 2×4s to the rail posts, then adding horizontal cross members and nailing on 2×6 planks.

DRAWINGS BY GERHARD RICHTER

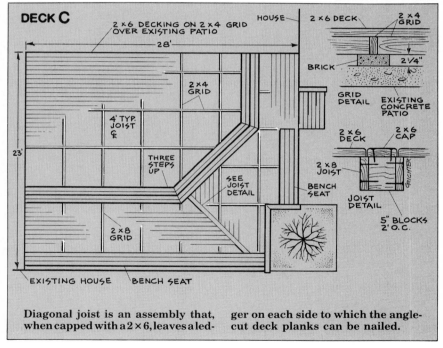

DECK C

2×6 DECKING ON 2×4 GRID OVER EXISTING PATIO
HOUSE
2×6 DECK
2×4 GRID
28'
2×4 GRID
4' TYP. JOIST ℄
BRICK
2¼"
GRID DETAIL
EXISTING CONCRETE PATIO
2×6 DECK
2×6 CAP
23'
THREE STEPS UP
SEE JOIST DETAIL
2×8 JOIST
RICHTER
BENCH SEAT
2×8 GRID
JOIST DETAIL
5" BLOCKS 2' O.C.
EXISTING HOUSE
BENCH SEAT

Diagonal joist is an assembly that, when capped with a 2×6, leaves a ledger on each side to which the angle-cut deck planks can be nailed.

the wall of the existing house, as shown in the photos for deck A. For beams and ledgers, Recker prefers 2 × 8s, 2 × 10s, or even 2 × 12s—and he doubles the thickness when the deck height is more than four feet. When possible, he face-nails beams into posts with 20-penny nails; to secure ledgers he drives 3½-inch anchor bolts into lead anchors spaced 1½ feet apart. For deck A, he wrapped the 4 × 4 posts with 2 × 6s and 2 × 4s on opposing sides, face-

nailed right up beneath the beams.

Even more unorthodox is Recker's refusal to use joist hangers without reinforcing them. "Joist hangers are good for keeping joists flush with the top of beams," he says. "Structurally, you should come in with face nails. A strip of wood—at least a two-by-two running under the joists as a ledger—is still more insurance."

For best drainage, Recker nails his deck planks so the grain rings at the ends cup down. He also checks both

ends of a board to be sure that the grain cups the same way. If it doesn't, the board was cut diagonally from the log, which may lead to warping.

Even though he always uses pressure-treated lumber, Recker recommends that decks receive some sort of treatment after six months. "After all," he says, "I expect them to last longer than the houses they're attached to"—*by Douglas Traub. Photos by the author and Ann Recker. Drawings by Gerhard Richter.*

all-seasons sun porch

Winter or summer, cars slow down when they pass the home of Anthony J. Wydra in the western New York town of Grand Island. The sun porch Wydra notched into the front of his house is an eye-catcher.

An eggcrate grid of redwood 2 × 4s soars out over an airy, handsomely framed structure. In summer the broad "windows" are filled with screen panels. Suspended from the projecting rafters are flower baskets and drop-lights for evening illumination. For winter the screens are stored and the openings are shuttered with ³/₈-inch plywood. The porch still has ample illumination through glazed strip windows tucked under the eaves and through the translucent roof panels of fiberglass-reinforced plastic (FRP).

In the summer mode the porch is an ideal breezeway for breakfast and lunch (photo inset, opposite page). In winter it can be used to store outdoor gear or can serve as a party room. The winter porch also doubles as an airlock entry, a buffer against chill winds when you use the house's front entry.

And this is no small consideration in Grand Island, where winds can howl up to 70 mph and January can dump six feet of snow on the roof. Snow load was one of Wydra's main design concerns, and his interlocking eggcrate grid of 2 × 4s provides sturdy support for the Filon panels. (Filon is a quality brand of FRP, available in attractive "awning" stripes on a squared-off corrugation. Your Filon dealer can supply the various closure strips that are called for on the construction drawing.) Wydra decided to get Cool Rib Cinnamon in 26-by-144-

PHOTOS BY GREG SHARKO

inch sheets, and bought 12 of the closure strips.

Wydra's intricate design for the support structure calls for facing the 4 × 4 posts and most beams with one-by lumber. This not only added architectural detail, but permitted Wydra to erect the frame without using a single nail; the interlocking notches created by this "skinning" process make for solid joints. You can simplify construction by using redwood or pressure-treated lumber throughout, bolting members together in a conventional way.

It's all erected on a 12-foot-square concrete slab, poured without any pitch (it must be perfectly level). Wydra first dug a perimeter trench nearly a foot wide and down to frost line. After leveling six inches of gravel over the surface and erecting a perimeter form, he placed rigid insulation, as shown in the dimensioned drawing, and brought in a ready-mix truck for a continuous pour.

The FRP panels were attached to the frame with screws that have rubber gaskets under their heads (you get them where you buy Filon).

Some interior 1 × 3 facing planks are attached with screws so as to be removable. This lets you take out the screen frames and insert the shutters. Not all of the 1 × 3s must be detached, though: Just take off one side and the top and bottom so panels can be swung out or in. You only do this twice a year, and it takes less than an hour.

"One of the nicest features," Wydra says, "is that thirty-inch overhang. It keeps the screens and floor dry and lets you enjoy a summer thundershower outdoors"—*by Al Lees. Drawings by Eugene Thompson and Carl De Groote. Photos by Greg Sharko.*

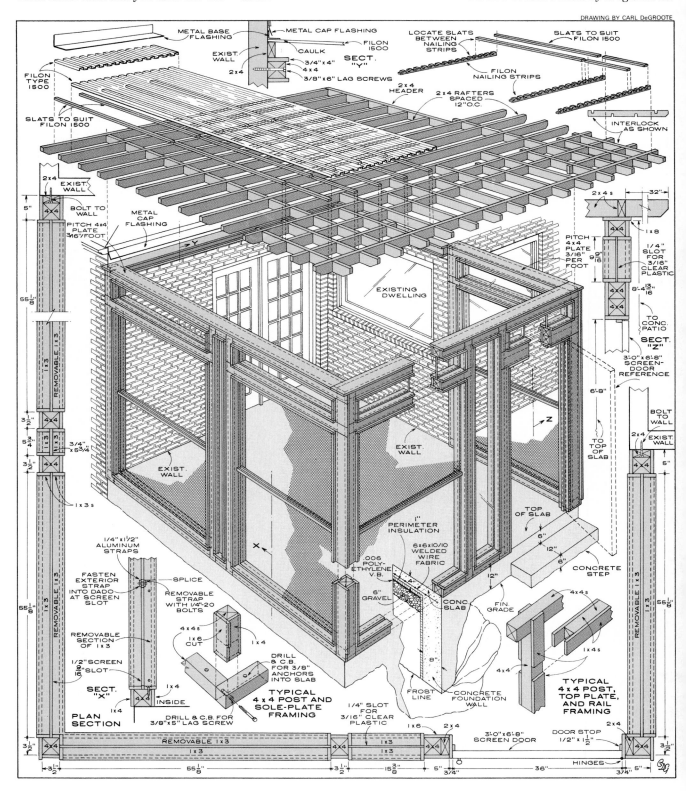

DRAWING BY CARL DeGROOTE

entry-level upgrade

First impressions count, and the first impression most people get from your home will probably come from the entry. If that's so, my entry never had very much to say. Oh, the door itself was fine. But the trim around it? Simple five-quarter pine, $3\frac{1}{2}$ inches wide. Flat, plain, and boring, with absolutely no personality at all. Chances are your front door trim is pretty much the same. If you'd like to change it, and the first impression people get of your home, do what I did. Cover it up with an upgraded trim package that adds some personality to your home.

The techniques I used make the job simple. By covering up the old trim, I eliminated the work of removing it. I also eliminated the work of cutting back the surrounding siding to make room for new wider trim, as well as the risks of damaging the surrounding siding in the process. Leaving the old trim in place also provides a solid base on which to build, so things go fast. The whole job shouldn't take you more than a few hours, once you get your design worked out to your liking.

Design ideas

You can copy my design to the letter if you like, but you'll probably be happier if you use it as a source of ideas on which to build your own design. That lets you create a trim package that fits both the style of your house and the specific dimensional constraints of the construction around your front door.

In my case, for example, I needed a fairly simple design—one that would add a bit of visual interest to the front door without overpowering the rest of the house. I also had to design the *head,* or top part of the trim package, to fit within specific limits. Eight inches above my door is a soffit that hangs out $3\frac{1}{2}$ inches. It seemed logical to design the head so it fits up under that soffit and visually supports it. Thus the dimensions of my head were prede-

Inset shot shows plain flat door trim, which adds nothing to author's front entryway. New trim package fits up beneath the soffit and seems to support it, tying the trim into the rest of the house.

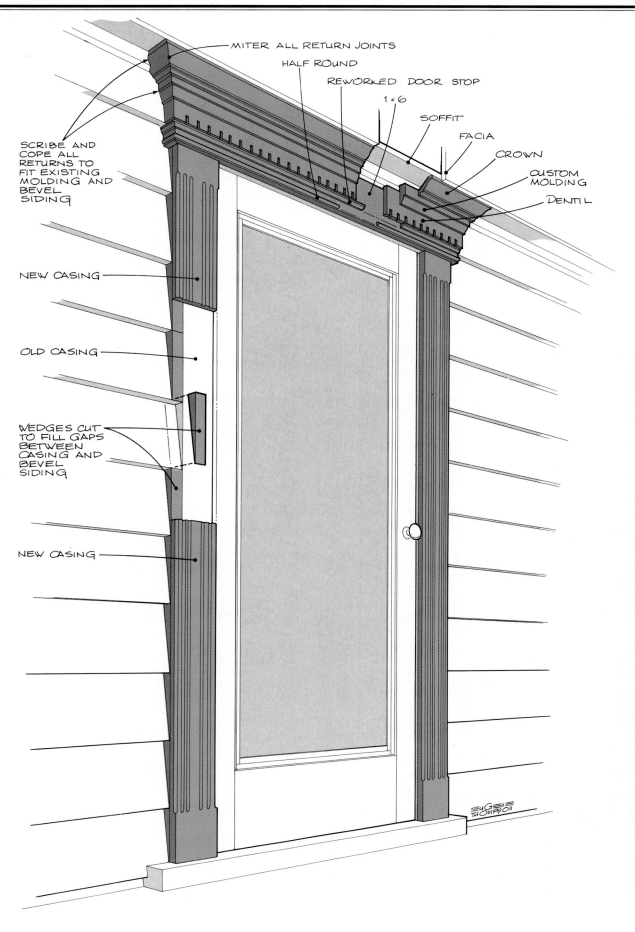

MITER ALL RETURN JOINTS

HALF ROUND

REWORKED DOOR STOP

1 × 6

SOFFIT

FACIA

CROWN

CUSTOM MOLDING

DENTIL

SCRIBE AND COPE ALL RETURNS TO FIT EXISTING MOLDING AND BEVEL SIDING

NEW CASING

OLD CASING

WEDGES CUT TO FILL GAPS BETWEEN CASING AND BEVEL SIDING

NEW CASING

termined. It had to be 8 inches high, and no deeper front to back than the 3½-inch overhang of the soffit.

Sitting down to design your own casing cold turkey can be intimidating at first, but here are a few tricks that can make it easy and even fun:

1. Look at other designs first. As you drive around town, check out the trim around other front doors. If you'd like to familiarize yourself with different trim styles, such as Federal, Georgian, or Greek Revival, try doing a little detective work at your local library or book store.

2. Experiment on paper. Take a photo of your front door and have it printed up 8 × 10 or larger. Now you can use tracing paper over the print and draw on various design ideas until you find one you like. If you don't want the delay or expense of producing the photo, make up a scale drawing and work with tracing paper over that.

3. Try working with actual moldings. Your new casing will consist of three basic parts. There will be two *pilasters* (the vertical sides or columns that flank the door) and a horizontal crosspiece at the top called the head. Making the pilasters is relatively simple. These will probably be made up of a single board. But the head is normally built up from several different moldings, stacked one above the other, and this makes it difficult to visualize your design.

The solution? Go to a good lumberyard and check out the selection of stock moldings sold there. There should be a dozen or so that you think have possibilities. The larger crowns, coves, beds, battens, stops, and half- and quarter-rounds are all worth looking at. Ask the yard if you can have a couple inches cut off the end of each molding you think you might like to use. If not, buy the shortest possible length of each. This will cost you a few bucks, but will be worth the expense.

When you get home, cut a couple inches off the end of each molding. Now you can lay these short lengths down on end and play with them like blocks, building up actual full-size cross-sections of various molding configurations

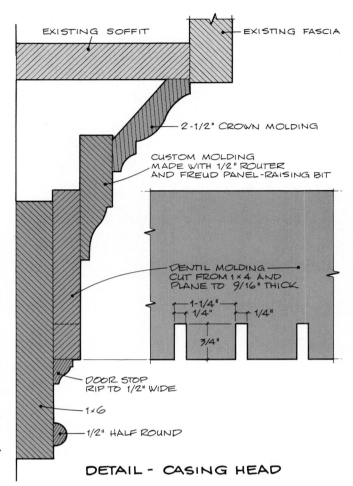

EXISTING SOFFIT

EXISTING FASCIA

2-1/2" CROWN MOLDING

CUSTOM MOLDING MADE WITH 1/2" ROUTER AND FREUD PANEL-RAISING BIT

DENTIL MOLDING CUT FROM 1 × 4 AND PLANE TO 9/16" THICK

1-1/4"
1/4"   1/4"
3/4"

DOOR STOP RIP TO 1/2" WIDE

1 × 6

1/2" HALF ROUND

DETAIL - CASING HEAD

Old rotting sill was removed by making two cuts across each end and chiseling out the sections that ran beneath the door jambs.

New sill was scribed and cut to slip in place, then fastened down with screws driven into the floor joists. Author counterbored the screws and plugged over them with oak plugs.

until you get an idea that appeals to you. Then you can trace around each molding to make up full-scale working drawings. As you work with these moldings, you may decide the design needs a shape you can't buy at your local yard. In that case, consider making your own.

Construction and installation

Since my threshold was rotting out, I started my upgrade by removing it and replacing it with a new one. Stock oak from the lumberyard did the trick, although I had to re-shape it a bit to make it work.

Actual trim work started with the pilasters. These are nothing more than half-inch clear pine 5½ inches wide. To give them a look suggesting Ionic columns, I routed flutes into them with a core box bit and then chamfered the edges. I stopped these flutes and chamfers about 5 inches from the bottom of the pilaster and about 3 inches from the top. This furthers the column look by creating a *plinth* or base at the bottom and a *capital* at the top.

The preceding technique quickly creates a simple but effective pilaster. You can add more detail if you like. You could, for example, run small half-rounds across the pilasters to further delineate the capitals and plinths. Or you could add half-rounds running vertically between the flutes to add more depth to the design.

Once the pilasters are complete, nail or screw them in place over the old casings, flush with the inside of the existing door opening. If your new pilasters are wider than the old casings as mine were, they will overlap onto the bevel siding, creating little triangular pockets that must be filled. To fill them, cut wedges from pine, slip them into the gaps as shown in the photo, then nail them in place.

Making the head

After the pilasters were in, I built the head in place ever them. Once the design is worked out, this goes quite easily.

Just start at the bottom, nailing on one layer at a time. The first layer to go on for me was a piece of clear pine ¾-inch thick. I let the ends of this hang out about an inch past the pilasters, but you could cut it flush if you like. The ends of this and all other moldings in the head are mitered at 45 degrees. After you install each piece across the head, miter and install *returns*—short sections of the same molding, which turn back at 90 degrees and butt into the house. These returns are the smallest pieces in the head, but they will probably require the most time and attention. Reason? The miters must fit snugly, and the ends that butt up against the house will have to be scribed and cut to fit the angle of the bevel siding. If you have problems with fit, however, you can always fill minor gaps with caulk.

Making the dentil molding

My next major molding is a dentil molding, so called because it resembles a row of teeth. I couldn't find a dentil I liked so I made my own on the table saw. To do the same, screw a wooden face a couple feet long and about 6 inches high to your miter gauge. Then slip a dado blade on your saw arbor. Set it to the width of the gap you want between the teeth on your molding. I set mine to ¼ inch.

Next, raise the blade to the desired height of your teeth. This will be somewhere around an inch. Turn on the saw and slide your miter gauge past the blade to cut a slot through the wooden face. Next, cut a 2-inch strip of wood

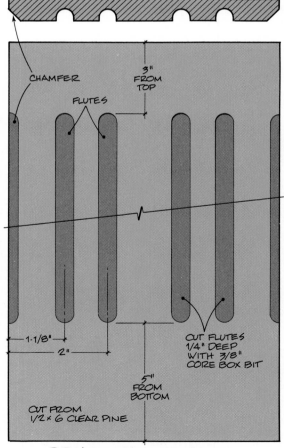

CHAMFER

3" FROM TOP

FLUTES

1-1/8"

2"

CUT FLUTES 1/4" DEEP WITH 3/8" CORE BOX BIT

5" FROM BOTTOM

CUT FROM 1/2 x 6 CLEAR PINE

DETAIL—CASING COLUMN

so it's a snug fit in this slot and glue it in place so that it sticks out the far side of the face. This creates a stop peg that will space the teeth perfectly and automatically.

Decide on your tooth width. Unscrew the face from the miter gauge and slide it to the right so your stop is the desired tooth width to the right of the blade. Screw the face back onto the gauge in this position and you are ready to cut your molding.

Stand your stock on edge against the miter-gauge face, slide it to the right until its end hits the stop, and make a cut. Slip this cut over the stop and make another cut. Slip that cut over the stop and make another cut. Keep this up all the way across the board.

Over the dentil molding I fastened another custom molding, made with a big Freud panel-raising cutter in a half-inch router. Over that I put a 2½-inch crown molding as the next step.

Once all those moldings were in, I decided my design

Gaps created where pilasters overlap the bevel siding must be filled with weges cut from pine. These can be nailed in place and, when caulked and painted, look like part of the pilasters.

All moldings in the head have *returns,* or short sections at the ends that are mitered to turn back and butt into the house. Cut these and nail them in place, filling any gaps with caulk.

still looked a bit incomplete. So I went back and added the half-round, as well as a doorstop directly below the dentil. The doorstop looked too wide as it came from the lumberyard, so I ripped it down a bit.

After filling all nail holes, I caulked all joints, primed the wood with a good alkyd primer, and followed up with two coats of latex trim paint.

Working from kits

If you don't want to design your own trim package, you can achieve the same rich effect for your doorway with trim kits all ready to cut and install. Any good lumberyard should have catalogs of millwork from major makers such as Morgan. You might also investigate some of the new molded-plastic millwork kits such as those offered by Fypon, Inc., 22 W. Pennsylvania Ave., Stewartstown, PA 17363—*by A. J. Hand. Drawings by Eugene Thompson.*

Pilasters go on right over the old casing. These were cut from half-inch clear pine and fluted with a core box bit in a router. If you don't have a router, you can simulate flutes by nailing on half-rounds running up and down the pilasters.

truck topper in wood

Handsome truck topper combines the beauty of natural wood with the strength and durability of epoxy. At 23 inches high, wood topper is streamlined for maximum mpg while cruising.

Even before we bought our new Dodge 4 × 4, we began shopping for a topper to fit over its bed. We wanted a small, streamlined topper that would be lightweight for easy placement and removal. It had to have a low profile that would not affect gas mileage, yet be well insulated for comfortable camping during Montana winters. We also wanted something that had more appeal than aluminum or fiberglass production models, yet was also maintenance free for long periods. Add to that list our specific ideas about ventilation hatches, windows, and doors, and you can see why we had no luck trying to buy the topper we wanted. That's when we decided to *build* it.

The wood-epoxy construction we used for this project is the same technique used in state-of-the-art boatbuilding.

Basically, it involves laminating together thin stock with epoxy to form a structure that's much lighter than a single thick piece of wood, yet stronger. And because the structure is encased in epoxy, it is impervious to the dry-rot, warping, and peeling that eventually befall conventional wood structures.

We designed the shell similar to an upside-down boat using an internal frame system of spruce and rounded plywood gussets to form the taper and rounded shape of the top. Hardwood plywood sealed with epoxy offered the beauty of wood and by far the best strength-to-weight ratios. By using a large radius curve on the top corners we could provide good looks and strength while taking advantage of the principles of small-boat design.

Building our own shell also allowed us to place the top hatches and side windows where we wanted them, as well as a rear door to suit our special needs. We wanted to be able to load and unload a 4-foot-wide sheet of plywood, which determined the actual size of the door. The wide flat top is ideal for installing one or more adjustable hatches for light and ventilation. You can also fit a large sunroof fitted between the roof racks. The top racks, like many other features, are optional and may be designed and installed to meet particular hauling needs such as small boats, bicycles, sailboards, or skis.

Choosing your wood

We used mahogany plywood for the skin of the topper because hardwood ply takes epoxy well and, unlike domestic grades of softwood plywood, does not require sheathing with fiberglass cloth. Hardwood ply is also available in a wide variety of standard and metric-size thicknesses expressly for laminating.

The large 12-inch radius rounds on the top edges of the shell were achieved with two epoxy-glued laminations of 4-millimeter mahogany plywood, while the single-sheet top and sides of the shell were done with 9-mm thickness to provide a close match in thickness. The two laminations of 4-mm stock, plus the epoxy glue line, finish out acceptably close to 9 mm. Substitutions of plywood thicknesses are

entirely possible, but 1/8-inch thickness is close to the maximum limit for achieving the radius shown in the photos and further detailed in the building plans. Tighter radius shapes will obviously require thinner plywood. Domestic softwood plywood may of course be used, if it is of high quality such as AA marine or the equivalent, and so long as it will make the required bend. As noted before, softwood plywood will usually require sheathing with lightweight fiberglass cloth saturated with epoxy to ensure long term waterproofing. Premium grades of hardwood plywood are more stable and usually do not require sheathing unless unusual abrasion is expected.

All flat sections of the truck topper are single-thickness plywood, epoxy-glued to sitka spruce ribs. The large radius rounds on the top of the shell are laminated of two thicknesses of thinner plywood epoxy glued over rounded plywood gussets. Top rounds are laminated in place first to provide the best access to edges and ends for clamping, while simpler flat sections, sides, and top, are fitted last.

The top rounds are done in two stages. First the inside lamination is rolled with epoxy resin and clamped exactly in place over the round plywood gussets. Clamps are applied wherever they will reach and the inside surface is then visually inspected to ensure that all surfaces are mated. Deep-throat clamps or staples may be used if additional clamping pressure is needed in specific areas. Once the epoxy cures, clamps are removed and the exterior lamination of the round is prepared for gluing by applying a generous coating of epoxy resin to both mating surfaces.

After each surface is wet with resin, a mixture of epoxy thickened with microballoons and silica is also applied to the mating surfaces. Then the final lamination is clamped in place with pads under the clamp heads to prevent marking the exterior surface. A few deep-throat clamps are useful to reach to the center of the lamination, or staples can again be used to apply pressure to spots that need extra pressure. After the epoxy cures and the clamps are removed the round will be very strong, and the longitudinal grain will make the round self-fairing all along its length.

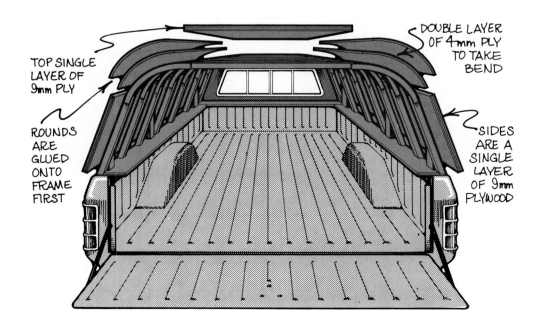

TOP SINGLE LAYER OF 9mm PLY

ROUNDS ARE GLUED ONTO FRAME FIRST

DOUBLE LAYER OF 4mm PLY TO TAKE BEND

SIDES ARE A SINGLE LAYER OF 9mm PLYWOOD

Some notes on epoxy

The Epoxy resin and catlyst you'll be using require precise mixing in the correct proportion, which is done with *metering pumps.* These pumps—and there are various types from very simple to complex large-volume pumps—dispense the required amounts of resin and catlyst into a mixing cup. After thorough mixing, the resin is applied by roller to large surfaces that require a uniform coating; brushes are used for applying the resin to small specific locations. If a thickened mixture is required for filling voids, uneven surfaces, or to change consistency, *microballoons* and/or *collodial silica,* among other more specific types, are added to the mixed resin until the proper consistency is achieved. Microballoons are a relatively low-density, low-strength filler used primarily as a fairing compound because it is easy to sand, while silica is a high-strength filler used where great strength is required.

These two fillers may be mixed in varying proportion with epoxy resin according to your needs.

Using epoxy eliminates the need for metal fastenings of any kind in the shell, except perhaps for attaching hardware for doors, hatches, and windows. Sitka spruce is unexcelled in strength-to-weight ratio, and it kept the weight of the bare shell before doors, windows, and insulation to approximately 75 pounds. This is on a standard size truck with 8-foot bed; a similar topper would obviously weigh less for a 6-foot bed or one on a mini truck. Even with insulation and all accessories the topper is easy for two people to lift on and off the truck.

Final alignment and reinstallation after removal is made extremely simple by the short tapered studs that slip into the holes in the truck bed. To remove the shell requires lifting it about 4 inches and then sliding it to the rear. Two people can accomplish this easily by sliding a

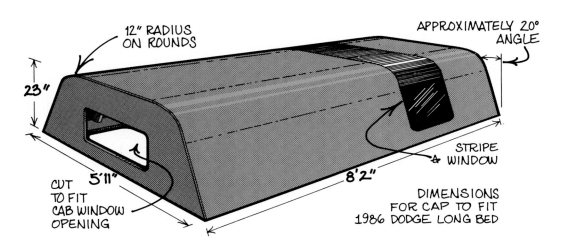

12" RADIUS ON ROUNDS

APPROXIMATELY 20° ANGLE

23"

5'11"

CUT TO FIT CAB WINDOW OPENING

8'2"

STRIPE & WINDOW

DIMENSIONS FOR CAP TO FIT 1986 DODGE LONG BED

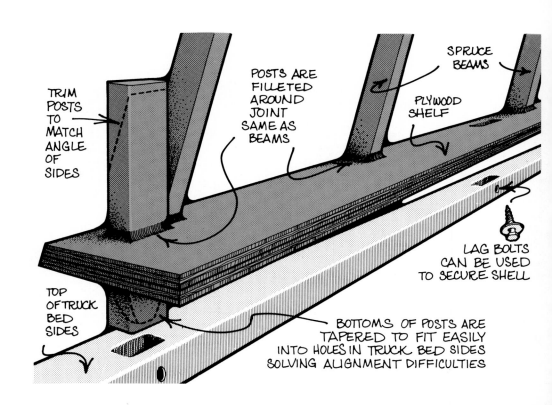

TRIM POSTS TO MATCH ANGLE OF SIDES

POSTS ARE FILLETED AROUND JOINT SAME AS BEAMS

SPRUCE BEAMS

PLYWOOD SHELF

LAG BOLTS CAN BE USED TO SECURE SHELL

TOP OF TRUCK BED SIDES

BOTTOMS OF POSTS ARE TAPERED TO FIT EASILY INTO HOLES IN TRUCK BED SIDES SOLVING ALIGNMENT DIFFICULTIES

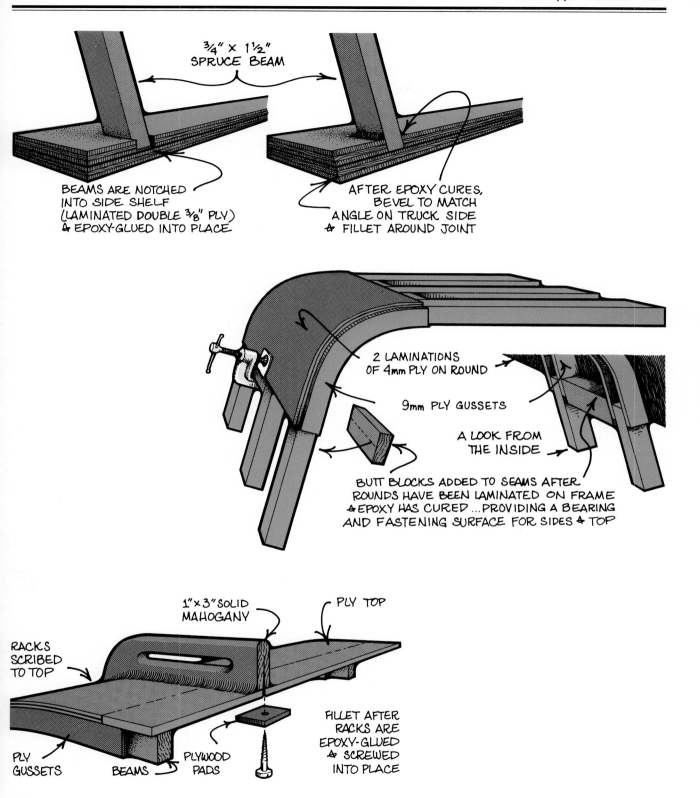

¾" × 1½" SPRUCE BEAM

BEAMS ARE NOTCHED INTO SIDE SHELF (LAMINATED DOUBLE ⅜" PLY) & EPOXY-GLUED INTO PLACE

AFTER EPOXY CURES, BEVEL TO MATCH ANGLE ON TRUCK SIDE & FILLET AROUND JOINT

2 LAMINATIONS OF 4mm PLY ON ROUND

9mm PLY GUSSETS

A LOOK FROM THE INSIDE

BUTT BLOCKS ADDED TO SEAMS AFTER ROUNDS HAVE BEEN LAMINATED ON FRAME & EPOXY HAS CURED ...PROVIDING A BEARING AND FASTENING SURFACE FOR SIDES & TOP

1"× 3" SOLID MAHOGANY

PLY TOP

RACKS SCRIBED TO TOP

FILLET AFTER RACKS ARE EPOXY-GLUED & SCREWED INTO PLACE

PLY GUSSETS

BEAMS

PLYWOOD PADS

pair of 2 × 4s under the topper and simply walking it off the bed of the truck. The short mounting studs also provide an alternative to bolting the shell in place by drilling bolt holes through the bed of the truck. Simply equip the alignment studs with lag screws and large washers to anchor the shell in place. You can also use the studs as an additional safety hold-down, if you'd like.

Aside from these basic construction techniques, our design is adaptable to any size pickup truck. The truck topper can also be made taller by simply deepening the sides. Options such as doors, windows, and cab openings are left to the builder's preference.

Rear doors

Rear doors are hollow with a perimeter plywood molding, and are filled with the same 1½-inch-thick polystyrene foam insulation used inside the walls of the shell. Although the doors may extend to the rear of the truck bed or even beyond, our doors are designed to fit inside the tailgate when closed. The tailgate could be removed or left in place to be used as a seat or table for picnics. A single door would be slightly easier to build than the double doors we used, but, again, that is entirely a matter of builder preference.

Cab access hole

We ordered a sliding rear cab window on our truck and then cut an access hole in the front of the topper to match. The opening is sealed and padded with two black pneumatic boots, one inside and one outside, from Universal Allied Products, Ltd. The opening is just large enough for an adult to crawl through, and perfect for kids and for communicating between truck cab and camper. The insulated shell heats easily and quickly from the truck cab even in the coldest weather, and stays almost as warm as the cab when traveling.

Windows

Windows and doors may be screened sliding RV units, which are easily installed, or acrylic non-opening ports designed by the builder. Our acrylic windows are smoked for privacy inside the topper and held in place with matching black flathead screws driven into wood moldings glued to the inside of the topper. The perimeter is sealed with a tiny bead of silicone placed between the window and the wood. As shown in the photos the actual window is 12 inches square, complemented by a painted black stripe that extends over the top of the shell.

Racks

Mahogany racks atop the shell are built to act as reinforcement as well as a carrier. The racks are designed according to the needs of the builder and intended usage. If heavy loads are planned, you can attach three or more racks atop the shell to support extra weight and for safety. The racks are laminated of mahogany, screwed and glued to the top and filleted for an extra measure of stiffness. Attached like this, they become an important structural addition to the shell, as well as a convenience.

Interior

If, when camping, you choose not to sleep on the bottom of the truck bed, you can fit a comfortable bunk across the inside of the topper using sections of ¾- or 1-inch plywood. This platform on the truck-bed sides, and also provides extra storage space beneath. The interior of our shell is insulated with 1½-inch thick polystyrene foam fitted between the spruce ribs. Since the ribs are 1½ inch wide, the foam fits perfectly and makes for a smooth surface over which we have fitted a fabric covering. Aside from acoustic benefits, the fabric is much easier to apply and usually less expensive than other interior treatments. Paneling is another choice but fabric is best for sound deadening, especially when driving. Our four-year-old daughter plays in the topper while we're traveling, such is its warmth and quiet.

Insulation is obviously not mandatory, but makes the shell warm in winter and cool in summer. If a lot of hot-weather use is planned, you might paint the shell white or some other heat-reflective color. To make the shell even more comfortable we also insulated the bottom of the truck bed and sides with 1-inch polystyrene foam, which is glued onto ⅛-inch-thick mahogany plywood in easily removable sections.

Maintenance

With all exterior wood surfaces properly sealed with three coats of epoxy, or sheathing if applicable, all that remains is to provide an efficient sunscreen. Paint is the best sunscreen, and a pigmented finish over an epoxy-sealed surface will protect the wood for many years without maintenance of any kind. If you want the beauty of wood, however, the choices are sunscreen varnish or two-part urethane paint. Under normal conditions varnish will protect the surface for about a year at a time until a touchup is needed. Two-part clear polyurethane paint will protect the epoxy finish for four or five years without a touchup, but it is much more expensive and more difficult to apply than varnish.

After using the truck topper for a fall and a winter, we have found it an unqualified success. It has proven very comfortable during a number of long trips and also for short runs to town. It holds more camping gear than a family should ever need and will also take a number of bicycles carried inside and safe from the elements. We have yet to install the large opening hatch we bought for the top, which fits between the racks, and it will be necessary for ventilation when the weather turns hot this summer. Otherwise there is nothing we would change or build differently. To order detailed building plans for this project, send $25 to The Butlers, Box 1513, Hamilton, NT 59840-1513—*by Paul and Marya Butler. Drawings by Marya Butler.*

Suppliers' addresses: **Epoxy, Fillers, and Accessories** available from Gougeon Brothers, Inc., Box X908, Bay City, MI 48707; **Rubber Boots** supplied by Universal Allied Products Ltd., Box 58044, Seattle, WA 98188; **Veneer, Spruce** from Hudson Marine Plywood, Box 1184, Elkhart, IN 46515.

Inside, the truck topper is quiet—and warm in winter—thanks to generous 1½-inch-thick polystyrene foam insulation fitted between the spruce ribs.

sliding-seat dory

This handsome wood-and-epoxy boat is fast, easy to build—and it may last forever!

There is a thrill in moving fast through the water under your own power, the bow of the single-seat boat slicing the surface with a hissing sound on a quiet early morning when you're the only person on the lake. There's only one hitch: You can't share that special experience with a passenger.

We've designed a simple-to-build multipurpose dory that combines some of the features of a fast rowing shell with the qualities of a family weekend boat. Although not as stable as a wider and heavier boat, it is more comfortable and safer than a sensitive rowing shell. And though designed primarily as a one-person boat, it can carry passengers fore and aft—as long as they sit on the bottom of the craft to maintain a low center of gravity.

With its light weight and smallish size, the boat is not intended as the supreme rough-water craft, but it will nevertheless handle wind chop and moderate waves that would swamp a rowing shell. And it is still small enough to be car-topped to the bay or lake for an early morning row. Because the dory is built from thin hardwood plywood that is bonded and sealed with epoxy, it is light and strong and will resist the traditional boat problems of rot, delamination, and water soak. In fact, a builder who is concerned with keeping weight to a minimum can build a hull for this dory that will tip the scales at less than 60 pounds—even with the two large fore and aft flotation compartments.

Light weight means the boat is faster through the water, and it's easy to load and unload from atop a vehicle. Be-

cause the sliding-seat mechanism is easily removable as a unit, it can be hauled separately and refitted when the boat is unloaded.

Although the dory can be fitted with traditional thwart seats, most builders are likely to choose a commercial sliding-seat mechanism. Such a seat takes a bit of practice to get used to, but it provides by far the best rowing performance, as well as a good upper- and lower-body workout for the rower.

The complete sliding-seat mechanism and its associated hardware are available from Martin Marine Co. (Box 251, Kittery Point, ME 03905). To make the setup work best, you also need a balanced pair of nine-foot, six-inch spruce spoon oars (Martin Marine stocks these, too). When the dory is used for fishing in rough water or for carrying gear and passengers, the sliding seat is best replaced by a detachable wood thwart; a pair of eight-foot spruce oars will make the dory much more manageable in these situations. The shorter oars are also the best choice for beginners as well as children.

The boat contains two sealed flotation compartments, which are made watertight with epoxy fillets (see drawing); once bonded to the hull, they become primary structural members. Even when the boat is full of water, the wood hull and flotation compartments will support one person with shoulders out of the water. The compartments may also be fitted with screw-in access hatches that convert them to dry storage compartments.

A natural finish shows off the attractive grain of the dory's hardwood plywood hull (top and above). The sliding-seat mechanism helps you sprint across lakes—double the fun of an indoor rowing machine.

Using the wood-epoxy building method eliminates much time-consuming fitting from the construction process. The boat is built without metal fasteners of any kind; the plywood pieces are joined with a simple butt joint reinforced by an interior butt block. The chine—where the sides and bottom meet—is filleted on the inside and wrapped on the outside with fiberglass tape saturated with epoxy resin. The dory's bottom is coated with black graphite powder added to the resin to produce a hard low-friction surface.

The wood-epoxy dory—we christened ours *The Osprey*— is built upside down using a simple temporary-frame system. It does not require exacting lofting or previous boat-building experience, and is entirely within the capability of most home woodworkers. Detailed building plans, including an instruction manual and sources for all materials, are available for $25 from Butlers (Box 1513, Hamilton, MT 59840-1513)—*by Paul and Marya Butler. Photos by Paul Butler. Drawings by Marya Butler.*

Wood-epoxy dory construction

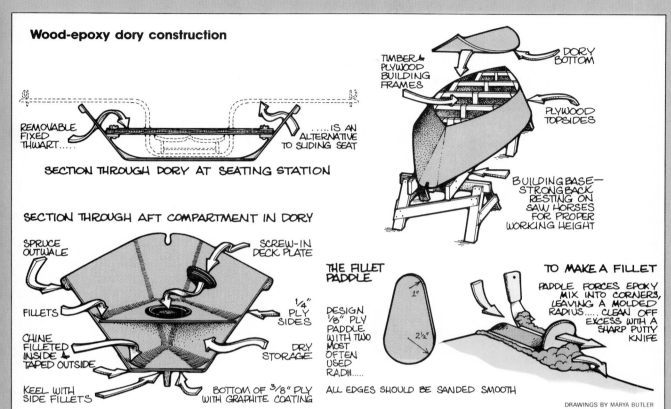

SECTION THROUGH DORY AT SEATING STATION

REMOVABLE FIXED THWART.....

.....IS AN ALTERNATIVE TO SLIDING SEAT

TIMBER & PLYWOOD BUILDING FRAMES

DORY BOTTOM

PLYWOOD TOPSIDES

BUILDING BASE— STRONG BACK RESTING ON SAW HORSES FOR PROPER WORKING HEIGHT

SECTION THROUGH AFT COMPARTMENT IN DORY

SPRUCE OUTWALE

SCREW-IN DECK PLATE

FILLETS

CHINE FILLETED INSIDE & TAPED OUTSIDE

KEEL WITH SIDE FILLETS

1/4" PLY SIDES

DRY STORAGE

BOTTOM OF 3/8" PLY WITH GRAPHITE COATING

THE FILLET PADDLE

DESIGN 1/8" PLY PADDLE WITH TWO MOST OFTEN USED RADII.....

1"

2 1/2"

ALL EDGES SHOULD BE SANDED SMOOTH

TO MAKE A FILLET

PADDLE FORCES EPOXY MIX INTO CORNERS, LEAVING A MOLDED RADIUS..... CLEAN OFF EXCESS WITH A SHARP PUTTY KNIFE

DRAWINGS BY MARYA BUTLER

The detail at top left shows construction of the optional plywood thwart that replaces the sliding seat. The sides of the dory (above) are made of quality 1/4-in. hardwood plywood that is butt-joined to the 3/8-in. plywood bottom. (Flounder Bay Lumber, Third and O Sts., Anacortes, Wash. 98221, will ship anywhere.) Epoxy fillets reinforce and seal the inside of the joint, while the outside is wrapped with epoxy-soaked fiberglass tape. Temporary assembly frames (top right) made from scraps of plywood and lumber hold the hull pieces in place until the epoxy cures. Before assembly, all parts are finished with three rolled-on coats of West System epoxy (available from Gougeon Brothers, Inc., Box X908, Bay City, Mich. 48707), followed by a coat of clear linear polyurethane paint. If you choose to use domestic AA-grade marine fir ply, you must sheathe the hull with 4-oz. fiberglass cloth to prevent hairline cracks. This will result in a heavier but more abrasion-resistant hull. Filleting detail is shown at center right. The diagrams at right suggest plywood cutting patterns.

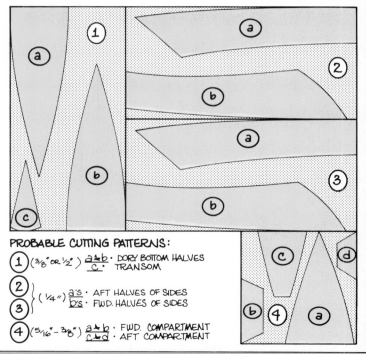

PROBABLE CUTTING PATTERNS:

1 (3/8" OR 1/2") a & b · DORY BOTTOM HALVES
                   c · TRANSOM

2 (1/4") a's · AFT HALVES OF SIDES
3   b's · FWD. HALVES OF SIDES

4 (5/16" - 3/8") a & b · FWD. COMPARTMENT
                   c & d · AFT COMPARTMENT

band-saw basics

Shove over, table saw. Look out, jigsaw. Make room for one of the most useful tools in the workshop: the band saw.

A band saw? I questioned their value, too . . . until I tried one. It won't replace my jigsaw or table saw, but for lots of special woodworking jobs, I found that nothing beats a band saw in power, speed, and accuracy. For example:

● Heavy-duty work: Square off the end of a heavy beam or slice through it lengthwise.
● Delicate jobs: Carefully—but quickly—follow the intricate profiles of compound shapes on adjacent sides of heavy stock.
● Repetitive operations: Make identical components in a single pass by resawing a preshaped pattern.

The photos and drawings show you the details of how to make some of these special cuts and more. Then, after adding a master jig (I'll tell you how to make one later), you'll wonder how you got along without a band saw for so long. Here are the basics:

Tricks of the blade

If you think a band saw is a large, cumbersome piece of equipment, you're right. The heavy-duty professional models take up lots of space and will likely require some planning before you fit one into your workshop.

DRAWINGS BY ADOLPH BROTMAN

General band-saw techniques

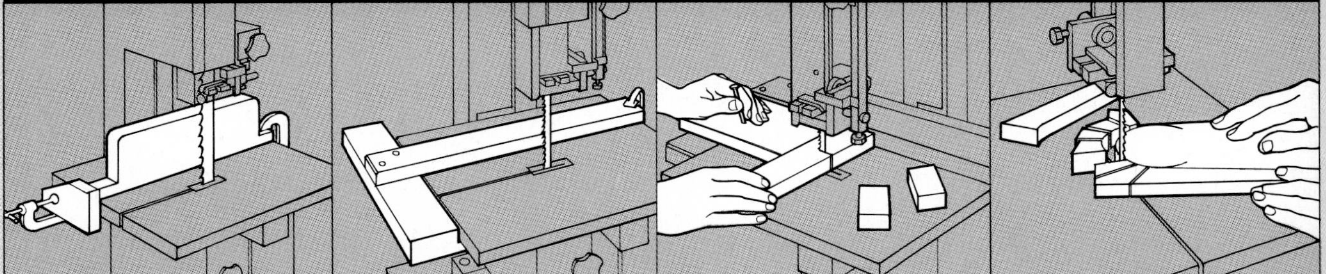

1 An extra-high fence keeps large work upright. A shim keeps the kerf open. **2** Use a T-square fence on either side of the blade if the saw lacks a fence. **3** The fence can be used as a stop for making similar pieces. A pusher gets the stock past the blade; a 16d nail becomes a convenient handgrip. **4** Get a wide blade around a small curve by making radial cuts. **5** To make a cutout with square corners, cut the two sides first, back out of the second cut, and lead into the third. **6** Make a cutout with rounded corners by drilling corner holes. **7** Compound sawing is done by drawing the piece's profile on adjacent sides of the stock. After cutting first side, tape waste pieces back in place, then saw through the second side. **8** A pre-shaped block can be sliced into components that are exactly alike.

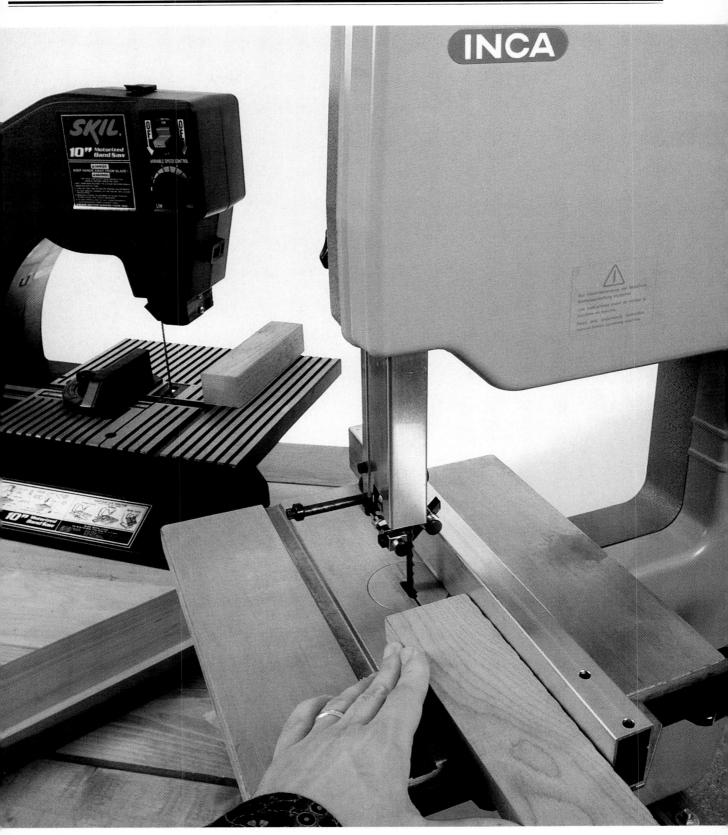

(The cords are short, so you should be prepared to add a high-on-the-wall AC outlet, as well.)

For lighter work, there are new compact band saws. These have less horsepower than the pro models and are limited to a cut depth of about four inches (pro models can cut up to 12 inches), but they're relatively inexpensive (about $200 compared with $300 and higher for pro models) and can do the same types of work. Many

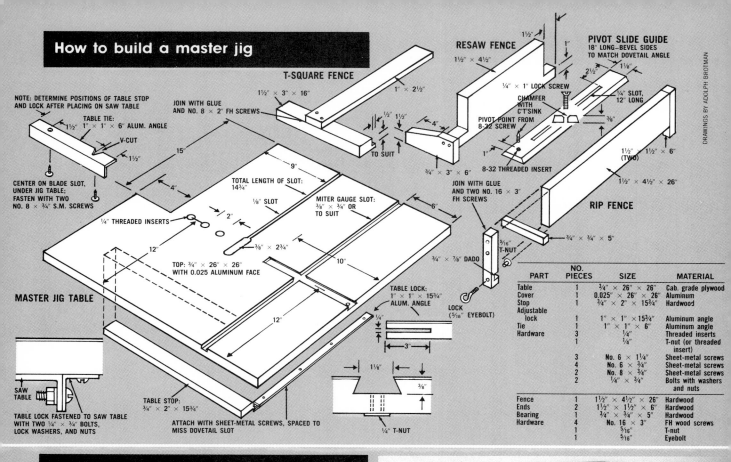

NOTE: DETERMINE POSITIONS OF TABLE STOP AND LOCK AFTER PLACING ON SAW TABLE

TABLE TIE:
1½" 1" × 1" × 6" ALUM. ANGLE

V-CUT

1½"

CENTER ON BLADE SLOT, UNDER JIG TABLE; FASTEN WITH TWO NO. 8 × ¾" S.M. SCREWS

¼" THREADED INSERTS

2"

12"

MASTER JIG TABLE

T-SQUARE FENCE

1½" × 3" × 16"

JOIN WITH GLUE AND NO. 8 × 2" FH SCREWS

1" × 2½"

15"

4"

9"

TOTAL LENGTH OF SLOT: 14¾"

⅛" SLOT

MITER GAUGE SLOT: ⅜" × ¾" OR TO SUIT

½" 1½"

4"

TO SUIT

¾" × 3" × 6"

6"

10"

TOP: ¾" × 26" × 26" WITH 0.025 ALUMINUM FACE

⅜" × 2¾"

12"

¾" × ⅞" DADO

5/16" T-NUT

TABLE LOCK

SAW TABLE

TABLE LOCK FASTENED TO SAW TABLE WITH TWO ¼" × ¾" BOLTS, LOCK WASHERS, AND NUTS

TABLE STOP: ¾" × 2" × 15¾"

TABLE LOCK: 1" × 1" × 15¾" ALUM. ANGLE

LOCK (5/16" EYEBOLT)

¼"

3"

ATTACH WITH SHEET-METAL SCREWS, SPACED TO MISS DOVETAIL SLOT

1⅛"

⅜"

¼" T-NUT

RESAW FENCE

1½"

1½" × 4½"

1"

¼" × 1" LOCK SCREW

CHAMFER WITH C'T'SINK

PIVOT POINT FROM 8-32 SCREW

4"

1"

8-32 THREADED INSERT

JOIN WITH GLUE AND TWO NO. 16 × 3" FH SCREWS

PIVOT SLIDE GUIDE
18" LONG—BEVEL SIDES TO MATCH DOVETAIL ANGLE

2½"

1⅛"

¼" SLOT, 12" LONG

⅜"

1½" (TWO)

1½" × 6"

1½" × 4½" × 26"

RIP FENCE

¾" × ¾" × 5"

DRAWINGS BY ADOLPH BROTMAN

PART	NO. PIECES	SIZE	MATERIAL
Table	1	¾" × 26" × 26"	Cab. grade plywood
Cover	1	0.025" × 26" × 26"	Aluminum
Stop	1	¾" × 2" × 15¾"	Hardwood
Adjustable lock	1	1" × 1" × 15¾"	Aluminum angle
Tie	1	1" × 1" × 6"	Aluminum angle
Hardware	3	¼"	Threaded inserts
	1	¼"	T-nut (or threaded insert)
	3	No. 6 × 1¼"	Sheet-metal screws
	4	No. 6 × ¾"	Sheet-metal screws
	2	No. 8 × ¾"	Sheet-metal screws
	2	¼" × ¾"	Bolts with washers and nuts
Fence	1	1½" × 4½" × 26"	Hardwood
Ends	2	1½" × 1½" × 6"	Hardwood
Bearing	1	¾" × ¾" × 5"	Hardwood
Hardware	4	No. 16 × 3"	FH wood screws
	1	5/16"	T-nut
	1	5/16"	Eyebolt

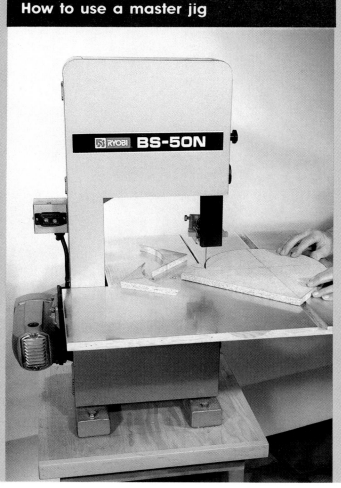

RYOBI **BS-50N**

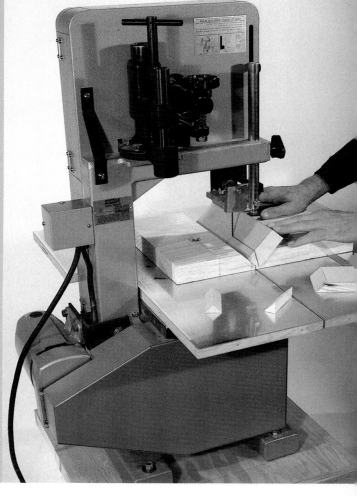

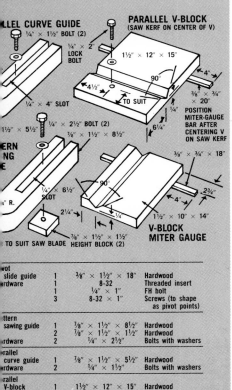

LLEL CURVE GUIDE
1/4" × 1 1/2" BOLT (2)
1/4" × 2" LOCK BOLT
1/4" × 4" SLOT
1/2" × 5 1/2"
1/4" × 2 1/2" BOLT (2)

PARALLEL V-BLOCK (SAW KERF ON CENTER OF V)
1 1/2" × 12" × 15"
90°
4"
4 1/2"
TO SUIT
3/4" × 3/4" × 20"
POSITION MITER-GAUGE BAR AFTER CENTERING V ON SAW KERF
6 1/4"
3/8" × 1 1/2" × 8 1/2"
3/8" × 3/4" × 18"

ERN NG E
90°
1/4" × 6 1/2" SLOT
4" R.
2 1/4"
2 3/4"
4"
1 1/2" × 10" × 14"

V-BLOCK MITER GAUGE
TO SUIT SAW BLADE
7/8" × 1 1/2" × 1 1/2" HEIGHT BLOCK (2)

...vot			
slide guide	1	3/8" × 1 1/2" × 18"	Hardwood
rdware	1	8-32	Threaded insert
	1	1/4" × 1"	FH bolt
	3	8-32 × 1"	Screws (to shape as pivot points)
ttern			
sawing guide	1	1/8" × 1 1/2" × 8 1/2"	Hardwood
	2	7/8" × 1 1/2" × 1 1/2"	Hardwood
rdware	2	1/4" × 2 1/2"	Bolts with washers
rallel			
curve guide	1	1/8" × 1 1/2" × 5 1/2"	Hardwood
rdware	2	1/4" × 1 1/2"	Bolts with washers
rallel			
V-block	1	1 1/2" × 12" × 15"	Hardwood
	1	3/8" × 3/4" × 20"	Hardwood
rdware	1	1/4" × 2"	Bolt with washer
block			
miter gauge	1	1 1/2" × 10" × 14"	Hardwood
	1	3/8" × 3/4" × 18"	Hardwood

compacts have built-in speed controls. With variable speed—and the correct blade—they can be used to cut metal, too.

All band saws use a flexible continuous-loop blade that moves in a clockwise direction. The blades are available in a variety of widths from 1/8 to 3/4 inch. The one you use depends on the job.

For example, unlike a table or radial-arm saw, band saws aren't limited to just a few inches of depth when resawing or ripping. And for these jobs wide blades are used. (A narrow blade could bow and produce a curved surface instead of a flat one.)

However, the wider the blade, the fewer the number of teeth per inch—and the rougher the cut. How do you cut big stock and get a smooth cut, too? My trick: Aside from using the smallest blade that will do the job, I lightly hone—dull—both sides of the blade. Honing lowers the cutting speed but because it reduces the set of the teeth, the cut is smoother.

Narrow blades are used for intricate work. For instance, when I made cabriole legs for furniture, only the steady blade of the band saw would do. The usually versatile jigsaw was useless.

The narrower the blade, the tighter the turn it can make. A one-inch circle can be cut by using a 1/8-inch blade. A 3/4-inch blade can't do better than a six-inch circle. But it's not always necessary to change blades for one cut. I start with relief cuts (see drawings) so waste falls away to leave more room for the blade to turn.

Even though the band saw uses a continuous blade, don't discount the tool for inside cuts. For example, I wanted to cut a center section out of a large stock of wood—too large for the jigsaw—without making a lead-in cut. To do it, I first drilled a hole in the wood the width of the blade. Then I cut the blade, routed it through the hole, and welded it back together.

After I made the cut, I broke the blade again and removed the finished stock. Sound extreme? Not really. Blade-welding units are available for this purpose, and blade stock can be bought in hundred-foot coils so you can assemble blades as needed.

Master jig

A master jig increases the table surface and has accessories that allow controlled procedures for most band-saw operations. My jig (see drawings) is made for a nine-inch saw with a 15 3/4-inch-square table. Unless your saw is radically different, you needn't make extreme changes in the design.

Cut the table to size, and attach the aluminum cover (with contact cement) before checking to see what changes might be required. A relief area for the column of the machine is needed so the table can be tilted. Mine is L-shaped because my saw has rear-mounted tension and tracking mechanisms. Otherwise, the relief area can be U-shaped.

When complete, sand all surfaces and apply several coats of sanding sealer, lightly sanding after each coat. Finally, apply paste wax rubbed to a polish on all bearing areas, including the cover, miter-gauge slot, and pivot-guide slot. The result is an accessory that will last a lifetime— *by R. J. DeCristoforo. Lead photo by Greg Sharko. Drawings by Adolph Brotman.*

BAND-SAW MANUFACTURERS

Inca AG (Switzerland), distributed by Garrett Wade Co., 161 Ave. of the Americas, New York, NY 10013; **Ryobi America Corp.**, 1158 Tower Lane, Bensenville, IL 60106; **Skil Corp.**, 4801 W. Paterson Ave., Chicago, IL 60646

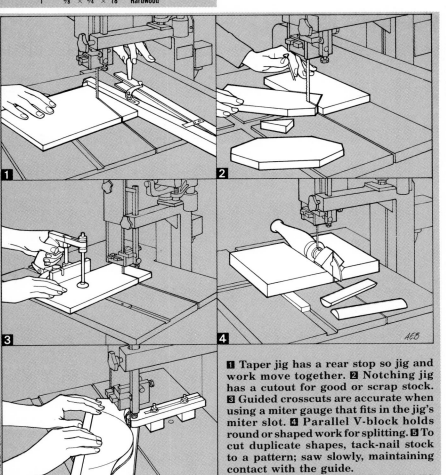

DRAWINGS BY ADOLPH BROTMAN

1 Taper jig has a rear stop so jig and work move together. **2** Notching jig has a cutout for good or scrap stock. **3** Guided crosscuts are accurate when using a miter gauge that fits in the jig's miter slot. **4** Parallel V-block holds round or shaped work for splitting. **5** To cut duplicate shapes, tack-nail stock to a pattern; saw slowly, maintaining contact with the guide. NOTE: FOR ALL WORK ALWAYS KEEP THE BLADE GUARD AS LOW AS POSSIBLE.

two new approaches to finger joints

a machine you can build

Finger joints are stronger than most router-cut dovetails, and they make elegant, professional-looking wooden box corners and hinges. But the joints entail painstaking labor because tiny imprecisions in the fit of pins to slots can undermine both strength and appearance.

I disliked making finger joints until I designed a simple machine that does the job for me. I spent two days and less than $50 (excluding the price of a motor) building my saw table. With it, I can cut the slots for all four sides of a box or drawer in less than seven minutes.

To power the machine (see drawings), you'll need a ½-horsepower 3,450-rpm capacitor motor. With a four-inch sheave on the motor and a three-inch sheave on the arbor, your spindle will turn at approximately 4,600 rpm—about right for a set of carbon-steel dado cutters six inches in diameter.

A word of caution: Most saw arbors have left-hand threads so the nut will tend to tighten with clockwise spindle rotation, and that's the way my machine is laid out. If your spindle has a right-hand thread, you will have to reverse the layout and motor rotation.

Use sound and dry materials for your machine. Hard maple is your best choice for the carrier guide bar; red oak and mahogany are excellent for other parts, with dry fir for the feet and legs. To avoid sticking in humid weather and looseness in dry conditions, use plywood for the slide's dovetail. Two coats of penetrating oil will seal it, and the plies will absorb oils from the paste wax which is used as a lubricant.

Place the fixed gib parallel to the left side of the back plate, and secure it with wood screws. Wax the dovetail and put it in place. Now position the adjustable gib snugly against the dovetail and drill five ¼-inch holes through it and the back plate. Remove the gib and open its holes to ⅜ inch, then reinstall the gib over two-inch carriage bolts. The enlarged holes let you tighten or loosen the slide.

Add the motor and spindle mounting plates, made from ¾-inch plywood, with their left sides flush with the left edge of the fixed gib. Fasten them to the dovetail with 1¼-inch wood screws. Set the motor and arbor in place, line them up, and mark hole positions. Use carriage bolts that are a little smaller than the holes in your mounting plates, and counterbore the back of the dovetail for the bolt heads. Attach the cable arm.

Operated by a treadle, the cutters "climb" through four pieces of stock clamped in a carrier. All are cut at once.

Make finger joints for box decorations, chisel tray recesses, drawer corners, kerfs for bending wood, or doweled hinges.

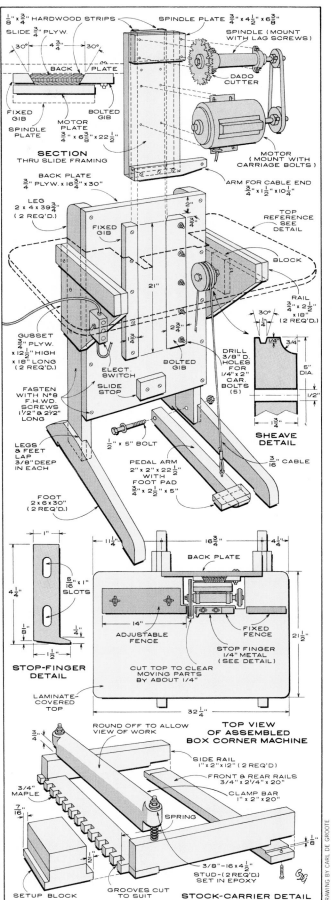

Add the leg assemblies, gussets, and top support rails. Then position the cable sheave above the back plate so the cable will pull in a line parallel with the plate.

Clamp a straightedge across the rails, and make sure the spindle is the same distance below it at both ends. When you are sure the blades and slide will be at right angles to the table top, tighten the nuts holding down the spindle. Align the belt and adjust the tension.

Don't forget to attach a stop block below the slide. Then set the machine upright on the floor and hook up a 3/16- to 1/4-inch-thick cable. Lift the slide assembly, and put a 6-inch-long block on top of the stop block to hold up the slide. Now adjust the cable until the pedal touches the floor with the cable taut.

Lay the table top on the rails, and center the cutters. Make clearance cuts with your sabre saw, and fasten the top to the rails with wood screws.

I band-sawed my stop finger from an aluminum plate. Steel works just as well, as does plastic. The left-hand fence, made of 1/4-inch plywood, is adjustable because I use this machine for other jobs.

For cutting box corners, I usually set my adjustable fence to provide a 3/8-inch-deep slot. If I want to cut longer or shorter pins, I use a setup block when I clamp the pieces into the carrier (see drawing). After you've made a satisfactory test cut, lay a straightedge across the adjustable fence and install the two fixed fences.

Now set the stop for the width of pin you want, and make more test cuts to check the fit of pins to slots. Moving the stop toward the cutter loosens the fit; moving away from the cutter tightens it.

When you build the carrier, take special care to keep the sides square with the front of the guide bar. The accuracy you build into the guide bar will be duplicated in each box side you make.

After you assemble the carrier, you can begin crafting professional-looking boxes and drawers. And instead of tucking it away, leave it ready to go all the time; you'll be surprised by the number of uses for it—*by Cy Wedlake*.

a nifty new jig

If you don't need a dedicated machine to make finger joints—or you don't have time to build one—you can buy a finger-joint jig that works with your table saw and a dado blade. Compared with the time-consuming trial-and-error process I once used, cutting finger joints with the Accujoint jig is effortless. Now I make strong corner joints in minutes. Here's how you set up the fixture:

First, make a reusable miter-gauge extension of 3/4-by-3-by-26-inch hardwood. Drill mounting holes in the hardwood carefully. Use bolts to attach the extension through the notches in your miter gauge. Then cut a slot in the extension with your blade. Use a stacking dado blade, not a wobble blade. If your blade width is accurate, your slots will be the right size.

Now clamp your first workpiece in the jig. With the saw off, position the jig on the miter extension with the stock against the blade. Clamp the stock and jig to the extension, and drill a hole—centered in the top side of the extension—through the first slot in the aluminum jig. Insert the steel indexing pin.

To cut a finger joint with 1/8-inch pins, move the indexing pin from one jig slot to the next, taking out a bite at each stop. To make the mating piece—its pins are offset by one pin width—insert a 1/8-inch drill shank in the endmost of the Accujoint's four aligning holes—one for each pin size. Reposition the stock with its edge against the drill shank, and saw the slots.

If you want to create a joint with wider fingers—1/4, 3/8, or 1/2 inch—snap the appropriate red plastic template onto the jig. The template covers the superfluous indexing slots and aligning holes.

Even if you make a long row of pins, Accujoint doesn't suffer from a problem I call "joint creep." In normal finger-joint setups, each slot position is determined by the preceding slot, and minute errors can be compounded into noticeable joint mismatches. An initial 1/64-inch gap, for example, can result in a 1/8-inch misalignment in pins at the far edge of a 10-inch-wide board.

Accujoint claims to keep the slot positions from varying by more than 0.002 inch. I was a bit skeptical about this until I talked with John Morse, the inventor. He told me that the 1/8-inch indexing slots are punched one at a time on 1/4-inch centers by a computer-controlled punch press.

The jig can't hold stock wider than 11 1/2 inches, and it's difficult to clamp a piece that's less than one inch wide. The maximum thickness is listed as 3/4, but you can squeeze 13/16-inch wood into the jig. With the three-inch-high miter-gauge extension, stock should be at least 3 3/4 inches tall.

If you hold down stock with an L-shaped board clamped in the jig, you can slice kerfs on the stock's face. Use adhesive transfer tape or double-faced tape to secure the work.

The Accujoint fixture is sold by Woodcraft Supply Corp., Box 4000, Woburn, MA 01888, for $39.95. It's also available from Trend-lines, Box 6447, Chelsea, MA 02150, for $39.95 plus shipping costs—*by Thomas H. Jones. Photos by Jim Wedlake and Greg Sharko. Drawing by Carl De Groote.*

PHOTO BY THOMAS H. JONES

Add a C-clamp for a firm grip on stock narrower than 10 inches. The jig's red snap-on templates come in four slot widths.

clever carpentry connectors

Strong joints are critical to any building project. But wood-to-wood joints often must be either toenailed—which is difficult for even a professional carpenter to do well—or nailed into inherently weak end grain.

Metal carpentry connectors—which range from simple plates to crazily convoluted forms—can free you from both of those sources of trouble. The connectors span the joint in two or three dimensions, and provide guide holes for nails, screws, or bolts. The fasteners are driven, in most cases, into the cross grain of dimensioned lumber, and are oriented so they will be in shear (at right angles to the stresses). In addition, some connectors hold the pieces together while

you drive the fasteners. Finally, they reinforce the resulting joint.

Carpentry connectors are made from steel—formed, punched, and in some cases welded to provide the configuration and strength required. Most are galvanized, although you'll find some that are painted.

For just about any joint on almost any project (short of fine cabinetry), there is a suitable carpentry connector. Use them to build a hexagonal gazebo, fence, deck, addition, partition, storage building, or even casual furniture. Some are designed to join wood at angles other than 90 degrees. And some can be bent in different ways to do different jobs.

Indeed, the variety of connectors available is almost overwhelming.

One maker's catalog lists nearly 100 different types, each available in a variety of sizes. Most connectors are for dimensioned lumber—from 2 × 4s on up. Some are available for one-inch boards. Simple connectors cost just a few pennies; big, complicated ones cost several dollars.

"Originally, connectors were marketed to professionals—architects, engineers, builders, and carpenters," says Teco's Dave Norcross. Now Teco and others sell them through consumer channels as well. Check the selection at your hardware store or home center. Some savvy retailers have bins of connectors with drawings on the display that show how to use them. A store may also have handout booklets and plans that show suggested uses.

The drawings above illustrate some typical connectors and the joints they form. Here are some others to consider when you plan your next project:

● Crawford and Teco sell kits containing all the connectors you need to build decks in 14 different sizes.

● Starplate connectors for making hex-shaped buildings also come in kits. The hardware forms all the odd-angle joints. You just cut, drill, and bolt.

● Mud-sill anchors connect a wooden sill plate to a concrete foundation, eliminating anchor bolts and drilling.

● Wall braces made as flat or formed metal strips are used to diagonally brace a stud wall. They replace traditional 1 × 4 bracing, which requires cutting notches.

● Staircase angles let you make steps without figuring angles and cutting notches.

● Nail plates are multipurpose connectors used for splicing, framing, and mending. Some have self-nails; others have nail holes.

● L-angles and T-straps attach to posts and beams for added strength at butt joints.

● Drywall stops are clever little clips that attach to framing wherever you need a stop for drywall. They can eliminate double framing at corners.

● Stud shoes and nail safety plates

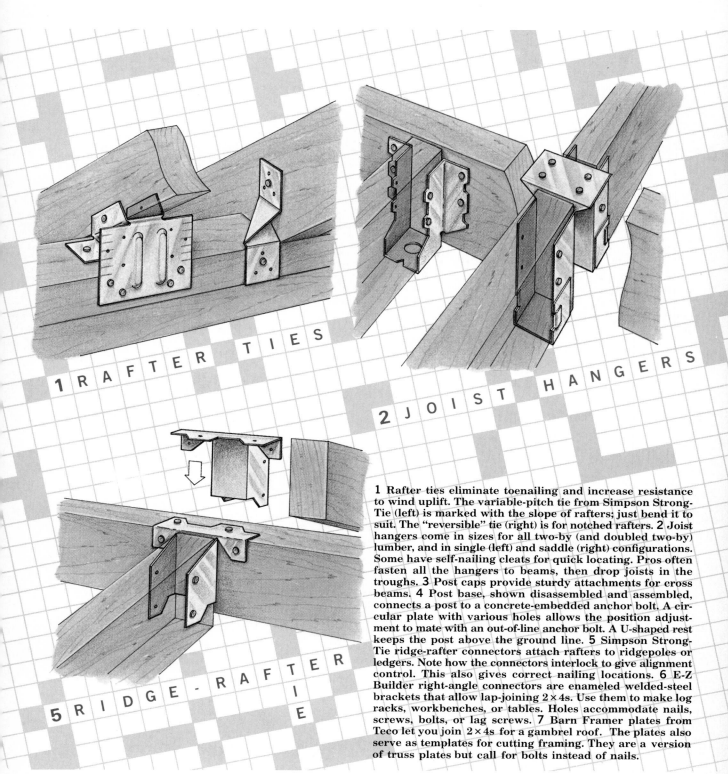

1 RAFTER TIES

2 JOIST HANGERS

5 RIDGE-RAFTER TIE

1 Rafter ties eliminate toenailing and increase resistance to wind uplift. The variable-pitch tie from Simpson Strong-Tie (left) is marked with the slope of rafters; just bend it to suit. The "reversible" tie (right) is for notched rafters. 2 Joist hangers come in sizes for all two-by (and doubled two-by) lumber, and in single (left) and saddle (right) configurations. Some have self-nailing cleats for quick locating. Pros often fasten all the hangers to beams, then drop joists in the troughs. 3 Post caps provide sturdy attachments for cross beams. 4 Post base, shown disassembled and assembled, connects a post to a concrete-embedded anchor bolt. A circular plate with various holes allows the position adjustment to mate with an out-of-line anchor bolt. A U-shaped rest keeps the post above the ground line. 5 Simpson Strong-Tie ridge-rafter connectors attach rafters to ridgepoles or ledgers. Note how the connectors interlock to give alignment control. This also gives correct nailing locations. 6 E-Z Builder right-angle connectors are enameled welded-steel brackets that allow lap-joining 2×4s. Use them to make log racks, workbenches, or tables. Holes accommodate nails, screws, bolts, or lag screws. 7 Barn Framer plates from Teco let you join 2×4s for a gambrel roof. The plates also serve as templates for cutting framing. They are a version of truss plates but call for bolts instead of nails.

protect and support through-the-stud piping and wiring.
● Between-joist metal bridges can prevent or cure squeaky floors.
● Hurricane and seismic anchors strengthen trusses and rafters against wind uplift and earthquake damage. They also can be used as ties where one member crosses another.
● Framing clips are used for fast, accurate perpendicular joining of 2 × 4, 2 × 6, and 2 × 8 framing without toe-nailing. They are also ideal for fence construction.

● Fence brackets are nailed to fence posts, then rails are dropped into their U-shaped channels. Rails can be nailed or screwed to the brackets or left free for easy removal.

Follow the makers' specifications for maximum load limits on all car-

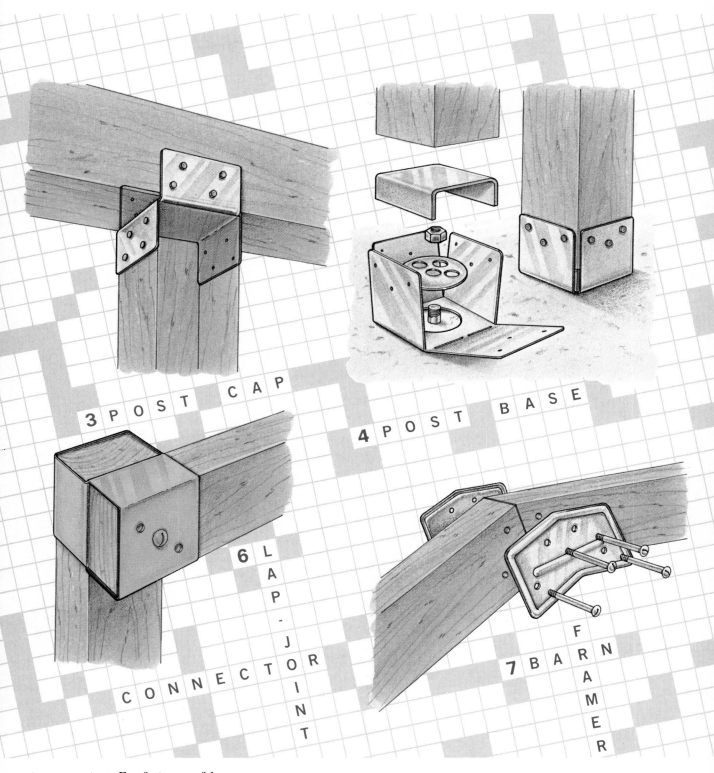

3 POST CAP

4 POST BASE

6 LAP-JOINT CONNECTOR

7 BARN FRAMER

pentry connectors. For fasteners, follow the specs or use the largest-diameter nail, screw, or bolt that the holes will take—*by Phil McCafferty. Drawings by David Dann.*

SOME MAKERS OF CARPENTRY CONNECTORS
Atlas Engineered Products, 10611 E. 59th St., In-dianapolis, IN 46236; **Cleveland Steel Specialty Co.,** 14400 S. Industrial Ave., Cleveland, OH 44137; **Crawford Products,** 301 Winter St., West Hanover, MA 02339; **Fulton Corp.,** 303 Eighth Ave., Fulton, IL 61252 (E-Z Builder); **KC Metal Products,** 1960 Har-tog Dr., San Jose, CA 95131; **Panel Clip Co.,** Box 423, Farmington, MI 48024; **The Billy Penn Corp.,** 1831 N. Fifth St., Philadelphia, PA 19122; **N. H. Rudeen Co.,** 2721 Nevada Ave. N., Minneapolis, MN 55427; **Silver Metal Products,** 2150 Kitty Hawk Rd., Livermore, CA 94550-9611; **Simpson Strong-Tie Co.,** Box 1568, San Leandro, CA 94577; **Steel and Wire Products Co.,** Box 207, Baltimore, MD 21203; **Teco,** 5530 Wis-consin Ave., Chevy Chase, MD 20815; **United Steel Products,** Hickory at Fourth St. N.E., Montgomery, MN 56069 (Kant-Sag and Starplate)

turn your router into a shaper

Versatile and inexpensive—that's how I'd describe a router. This often-overlooked tool can perform a score of unexpected chores, everything from precision joinery to adding decorative flourishes. Now you can expand that repertoire even further by building a freestanding table that lets a router double as a stationary shaper.

With an $80 router and this easy-to-build table, you can handle any shaping chore. And you can save the $450 you'd need to purchase a conventional stationary shaper. Secure the router in place and fit it with the appropriate bits, and you can make any number of classic molding forms such as Roman and reverse ogees, cove and bead, quarter round, and ovolo. You can also cut wedge-type tongue-and-groove joints and special joints for drawers. And you can do freehand shaping, just as you would on a regular shaper.

Of course, you can use a router as a shaper without the table. But there's often a gain in precision when you bring the project to the tool rather than the other way around.

I designed the shaper stand to include the best features of a standard shaping table (except for a switch that lets a regular shaper run in reverse): fences, guards, a fulcrum pin for freehand shaping of curved edges, and miter-gauge capability for working with narrow boards.

And unlike some commercial tables, this one is designed to accommodate any router. The only part of the stand that needs to be customized is the recess on the underside of the table, which has to be cut to fit the router's base. I chose to build in two drawers, which left me an easy-to-reach shelf for temporary storage. You may want to enclose that space, depending on your storage needs and work habits.

I've also included a convenient slot

Anything a regular shaper can do, a router attached to this shaping stand can match. Attach the router to the underside of the stand's top (right) by driving screws from the top through counterbored holes. The recess, formed with the router, holds the tool's base. For some router models, you may have to cut a special groove, as shown, to accommodate the D-shaped handle. A miter gauge enables you to make end cuts on narrow stock that can't be safely held by hand (above). Note the large, near-flush drawer pulls.

for an on-off switch. It's there because it's a good practice to keep the router running only when you're cutting. There's no reason to keep the machine's ball bearings going at 25,000 rpm unnecessarily.

A tip on maintenance: Because the router is inverted under a table top, it

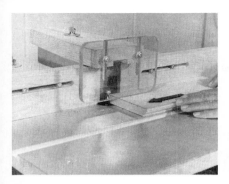

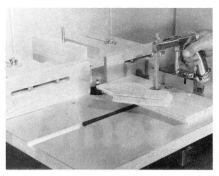

Keep both fences in line for a partial cut (left). When cutting off a stock's edge, slide the outfeed fence forward to support the wood after the cut. Always feed from right to left and try to cut with the grain. The guard keeps sawdust from kicking up. Set the fences to minimize the opening around the bit. Use a miter gauge (center) to move the work for an end cut. Do end cuts first when a piece requires four shaped edges. For freehand shaping (right), use a ball-bearing piloted bit. Brace the work against the fulcrum pin, and advance it slowly to make contact with the bit. To shape narrow, curved pieces, do the work on wide stock and then simply saw off the part you need.

will probably catch more sawdust than it would under normal use. Check the router occasionally, and remove any waste with a blower or small brush.

Building the table is easy. I used fir for the members (see materials list), but you can substitute any hardwood, such as maple or birch. Stick with pine for the drawers, however. Keep in mind that the door pull should be almost flush with the door face. The reason for this is simple: While you're using the shaper, you'll be moving around the table, with your eyes on the table top and workpiece, and you don't want to snag your leg on protruding pieces. I used a ready-made glued-up pine slab for the table top and covered it with Wilsonart's decorative aluminum. You can use any kind of aluminum, however—*by R. J. De Cristoforo. Drawing by Gerhard Richter.*

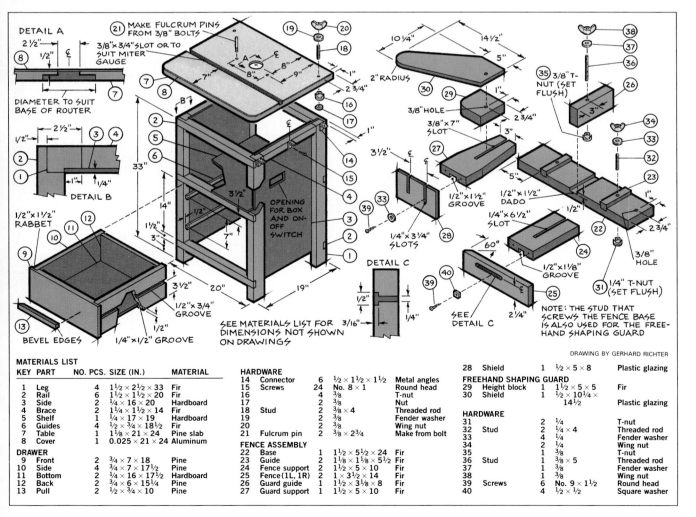

DRAWING BY GERHARD RICHTER

MATERIALS LIST

KEY	PART	NO. PCS.	SIZE (IN.)	MATERIAL
1	Leg	4	$1\frac{1}{2} \times 2\frac{1}{2} \times 33$	Fir
2	Rail	6	$1\frac{1}{2} \times 1\frac{1}{2} \times 20$	Fir
3	Side	2	$\frac{1}{4} \times 16 \times 20$	Hardboard
4	Brace	2	$1\frac{1}{4} \times 1\frac{1}{2} \times 14$	Fir
5	Shelf	1	$\frac{1}{4} \times 17 \times 19$	Hardboard
6	Guides	4	$\frac{1}{2} \times \frac{3}{4} \times 18\frac{1}{2}$	Fir
7	Table	1	$1\frac{1}{8} \times 21 \times 24$	Pine slab
8	Cover	1	$0.025 \times 21 \times 24$	Aluminum
DRAWER				
9	Front	2	$\frac{3}{4} \times 7 \times 18$	Pine
10	Side	4	$\frac{3}{4} \times 7 \times 17\frac{1}{2}$	Pine
11	Bottom	2	$\frac{1}{4} \times 16 \times 17\frac{1}{2}$	Hardboard
12	Back	2	$\frac{3}{4} \times 6 \times 15\frac{1}{4}$	Pine
13	Pull	2	$\frac{1}{2} \times \frac{3}{4} \times 10$	Pine

HARDWARE				
14	Connector	6	$\frac{1}{2} \times 1\frac{1}{2} \times 1\frac{1}{2}$	Metal angles
15	Screws	24	No. 8×1	Round head
16		4	$\frac{3}{8}$	T-nut
17		2	$\frac{3}{8}$	Nut
18	Stud	2	$\frac{3}{8} \times 4$	Threaded rod
19		2	$\frac{3}{8}$	Fender washer
20		2	$\frac{3}{8}$	Wing nut
21	Fulcrum pin	2	$\frac{3}{8} \times 2\frac{3}{4}$	Make from bolt
FENCE ASSEMBLY				
22	Base	1	$1\frac{1}{2} \times 5\frac{1}{2} \times 24$	Fir
23	Guide	2	$1\frac{1}{8} \times 1\frac{1}{8} \times 5\frac{1}{2}$	Fir
24	Fence support	2	$1\frac{1}{2} \times 5 \times 10$	Fir
25	Fence(1L, 1R)	2	$1 \times 3\frac{1}{2} \times 14$	Fir
26	Guard guide	1	$1\frac{1}{2} \times 3\frac{1}{8} \times 8$	Fir
27	Guard support	1	$1\frac{1}{2} \times 5 \times 10$	Fir

28	Shield	1	$\frac{1}{2} \times 5 \times 8$	Plastic glazing
FREEHAND SHAPING GUARD				
29	Height block	1	$1\frac{1}{2} \times 5 \times 5$	Fir
30	Shield	1	$\frac{1}{2} \times 10\frac{1}{4} \times 14\frac{1}{2}$	Plastic glazing
HARDWARE				
31		2	$\frac{1}{4}$	T-nut
32	Stud	2	$\frac{1}{4} \times 4$	Threaded rod
33		4	$\frac{1}{4}$	Fender washer
34		2	$\frac{1}{4}$	Wing nut
35		1	$\frac{3}{8}$	T-nut
36	Stud	1	$\frac{3}{8} \times 5$	Threaded rod
37		1	$\frac{3}{8}$	Fender washer
38		1	$\frac{3}{8}$	Wing nut
39	Screws	6	No. $9 \times 1\frac{1}{2}$	Round head
40		4	$\frac{1}{2} \times \frac{1}{2}$	Square washer

cop-in-a-box home sentry

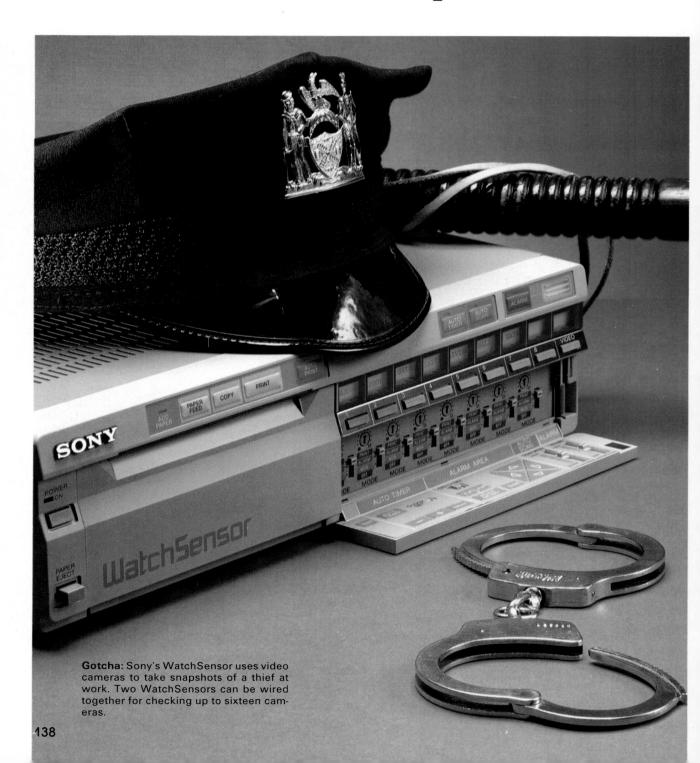

Gotcha: Sony's WatchSensor uses video cameras to take snapshots of a thief at work. Two WatchSensors can be wired together for checking up to sixteen cameras.

I reached out to touch what looked like a wall-mounted TV set. As I did, its screen suddenly burst to life, and I snapped my arm back to my side as a piercing alarm reached my ears. "There's an intruder," said Tom Riley, president of Unity Systems, as he pointed to the rapidly changing display in front of me.

A floor plan of the house appeared on the screen. Then one area—an upstairs bedroom window—began flashing. "The thief entered the bedroom," said Riley. "He's going through the house." As the intruder moved, the screen showed his progress down hallways and into other rooms. All the while, his actions were being recorded on a floppy disk by the system's computer. If this had been a burglary instead of a demonstration, the police would have been on the way.

The system I was watching—the Home Manager, developed by Unity Systems—typifies home security products that use advanced technology to beat the thief. Experts predict that all new models will use state-of-the-art electronics to spur another era in home security.

What techniques are being used in this new generation of security products? How will future systems improve on the current crop? To find out, I spoke with engineers, product planners, and experts in the security field. I learned that only in the last year has digital chip technology made its full impact felt in home security. The result has been a quantum leap in system ability, ease of use, and overall reliability.

Have it your way

My first step took me to Unity Systems' headquarters, in Redwood City, California, where Tom Riley unveiled his firm's new Home Manager system. "The screen is touch-sensitive," Riley told me, tapping the display with his finger tip.

As I touched the screen, the customized floor plans identified each security sensor and its status: armed, off, or malfunctioning. Home Manager is zoned, so I could arm individual room sensors or areas.

At up to $10,000 each, Home Manager is far from the primitive key-operated security boxes of a few years ago. Elaborate systems like this require professionals to string wires through walls to connect sensors to the control panel, which sounds the alarm.

However, new do-it-yourself systems are simpler to install: There are no wires. Instead, room sensors trig-

Touch the video screen to control the Home Manager. Multiple levels of security can be selected; if a sensor fails, the system isolates it automatically.

Schlage's kit of transmitters, control box, and battery backup is made for do-it-yourself installation. Automatic dialer (not shown) is an option.

ger tiny battery-powered transmitters that communicate with the control system via short-range radio broadcasts. Early wireless systems had re-

liability problems—caused by stray signals from CB radios or garage-door openers—but more recent digital designs have gone a long way toward changing that tarnished image.

"Our Keepsaver system uses an eight-bit digitally coded signal," says Greg Markes, consumer electronic products manager for Schlage Lock Co. "And the code has to be received by the control unit four times in less than a second to be acknowledged." That severely lessens the odds of a false alarm.

Keepsaver uses digital circuits for communications, too. When an alarm sounds, an optional dialer seizes the phone line and automatically calls a computer at Schlage's offices. "The dialer identifies itself by using a digital code and indicates the type of alarm— police, medical, or fire," says Markes. "The computer matches the identification number and alarm code with information stored in its data base. It then tells a human operator what to do and whom to call."

At $179 for a starter system and $99 for the dialer, Keepsaver is one of the lowest-cost wireless systems available. But it's not the only one.

For example, AT&T's Security System 8000 includes a smoke alarm, and there's a personal transmitter that you take with you. Press its button for help if you hear a prowler or if there's a medical emergency. Tandy Corp.'s Safehouse and Universal Security Instruments' Perim-A-Tron work similarly to Schlage's system, but they have an automatic battery test. These units sound a special alarm if a transmitter should fail due to low power.

Black & Decker's system, now being test-marketed (price not set, but about $500), is wireless, too, but it doesn't use over-the-air transmissions. "If a sensor detects a break-in," says product manager, Lon Mears, "it emits an audible sound. The sound is digitally coded and intended to be heard by a microphone inside the controller box."

Once the controller hears the electronic yell for help, it sounds the general alarm by sending a signal via the house wiring to remote modules. "The modules blink the house lights and activate the sirens," says Mears.

If a sensor is too far from the controller to be heard, another module, called a relay, is plugged into a wall outlet. The relay picks up the sound in the room and alerts the controller via house wiring.

Smile

"It's an electronic peephole," says Bill Yen, Sony's marketing director.

I'm looking at a new video surveillance camera. Because it uses a tiny solid-state charge-coupled device to see an image, the entire package fits in the palm of my hand.

This is just one of several security cameras made for residential use. For example, both Sony and Panasonic have models made for the front door. When someone rings the doorbell, you turn on a special TV—which is safely *inside* the house—to find out who's *outside*.

The $620 Sony system, called WatchCam, comes with an adapter to let the camera replace a conventional door peephole. But according to Yen, the camera is finding other "security" uses, too. "You can mount the camera over the baby's crib," he says, "or use one to watch the backyard pool."

An upgraded version of WatchCam is Sony's WatchSensor. This $3,300 system monitors up to eight cameras, and each can be programmed to watch specific areas in its field of view. If a thief enters the protected areas, WatchSensor can sound an alarm, call the police, and take up to 200 snapshots of the intruder using its built-in video printer. The printer makes a picture in about seven seconds, and up to four pictures can be stored in WatchSensor's memory. So the system can capture information from several cameras—all at the same time.

What happens if *you* walk past the window on your way to a late-night snack? You become a statistic.

"The largest single source of false alarms is caused by the homeowner," says John C. Johansen, marketing director for residential systems at ADT in New York. "Someone in the house violates the system and doesn't know how to go about disarming it before the signal goes out."

To deal with the problem, ADT's $995 system includes a code word. If the alarm is tripped and the system calls one of the company's monitoring stations, the first thing the operator does is call you back. "If you say the code word," says Johansen, "the operator cancels the alarm." If not, the police are at your door.

While call-back schemes such as this handle human errors, technology is at work to lessen the chance of electronic blunders. The newest thief detectors use dual-motion sensors. These combine two different sensor technologies into a single small device, and both must agree there's an

intruder before the alarm sounds.

"A passive infrared sensor can be fooled if it's mounted opposite a window and the sun suddenly strikes it," explains Robert Bergener, a leading expert on security systems and president of Bergener and Associates, of Rockville, Maryland. "And an ultrasonic detector can be fooled if a circulating fan turns on and moves the air in the room." But in a dual-detector system, both need to be tricked at the same time to cause a false alarm.

"That usually won't happen," says Bergener, "because the ultrasonic sensor ignores the sun and the infrared detector ignores the fan. The system goes off only when the detectors find something warm and moving."

Warm and moving? Could that include pets, wildlife, and non-security-minded children? Yes, and to security designers, all three pose recognition problems that will take years to overcome. But plans are already underway.

According to the experts, future home security systems will change dramatically because of two relatively new technologies: digital image analysis and voice recognition.

Image analysis uses a special computer technique to determine what— or who—a camera is seeing. Voice recognition allows the computer-controlled security system to understand your orders. Though both technologies are in limited use today, it will be some time before they are perfected to a level that allows your house to recognize the smile on your son's face.

But tomorrow's vision systems are already in the minds of today's visionaries. Says ADT's Johansen: "One day you'll walk up to your front door and say 'Hello'—and it will swing open for you"—*by G. Berton Latamore. Lead photo by Greg Sharko.*

SELECTED SECURITY-SYSTEM MANUFACTURERS

ADT Systems, One World Trade Center, New York, NY 10048; **AT&T Consumer Products Div.,** 5 Wood Hollow Rd., Parsippany, NJ 07054; **Black & Decker,** 10 N. Park Dr., Hunt Valley, MD 21030; **Panasonic Co.,** 1 Panasonic Way, Secaucus, NJ 07094; **Schlage Lock Co.,** Box 3324, San Francisco, CA 94119; **Sony Security Systems Co.,** 15 Essex Rd., Paramus, NJ 07652; **Tandy Corp.,** 1700 One Tandy Center, Fort Worth, TX 76102; **Unity Systems,** 2606 Spring St., Redwood City, CA 94063; **Universal Security Instruments,** 10324 S. Dolfield Rd., Owings Mills, MD 21117

optical fire spotter

Where there's smoke, there's fire. The old adage still holds true, but sometimes the wait to detect smoke or other products of combustion—as photoelectric and ionization-type fire alarms must do—means a delay that could endanger lives. That's why Fire Sentry Corp. has developed the Room Sentry line of early-warning fire sensors, which sound an alarm within a second of detecting a ¼-square-foot flame in a room up to 30 feet square.

The Room Sentry's sensor and alarm circuitry is enclosed in a high-impact ABS plastic box the size of a home wall thermostat. The alarm provides the same detection capabilities as industrial units costing five to ten times more. The sensors are designed to operate in single-room environments in houses (there's a special kitchen model), hotel rooms, offices, recreational vehicles, boats, and even in airplanes.

After I received the basic $374 Room Sentry and connected the battery, I left the unit on the stairs for a moment while I checked my fireplace insert. No sooner had I opened the insert door than the Room Sentry emitted a pulsing (85 decibels at 10 feet) blast from its piezoelectric sounder. The sensor had detected the electromagnetic emissions of the flame from 18 feet away.

As I moved the Room Sentry around the house to test it in different circumstances, it never failed to speak up in the presence of an open flame. One night in the kitchen, the sensor reported a flare-up of some pork chops on the grill (from 20 feet away) before my wife or I had even heard the sizzle (the exhaust fan was on at the time).

The bulblike device on the front of the basic unit, the business end of the sensor, is tuned to the ultraviolet spectrum. Other more expensive models employ the visible or the infrared spectra as well as the UV to verify the presence of flames in special conditions, such as bright sunlight, so as to reduce false alarms.

Room Sentries have several power options: a nine-volt alkaline battery, a long-life lithium battery, external power (10 to 39 volts DC) with an optional lithium standby battery. They also have two output modes: the built-in alarm and a simultaneous relay that connects to a home alarm panel or remote siren.

The Room Sentry is *no* substitute for a smoke detector, as the literature from Fire Sentry (39 Brookhollow Dr., Santa Ana, CA 92705) emphasizes: Both should be used for complete fire protection—*by David Petraglia. Photo by Jim Richards*

home wiring with pvc conduit

Flex-Plus ENT is flexible and easily bent by hand for quick installation, as shown in top photo. When using 1/2-inch tubing, drill 1-inch holes at the center of each 2 × 4 stud. For long runs, two pieces of tubing can be joined with a quick-connect coupler (center). Include a separate grounding conductor in each run to an outlet (bottom). The wire connects to the green hex-head terminal on grounding-type receptacles.

The National Electric Code (NEC) permits a number of kinds of wiring to be used in a home electrical system. Some are simpler than others; some protect the wires better than others. Now two wiring systems rate just about tops on both scores: They are easy to install, *plus* they give the conductors plenty of tough cover. Either can make new home wiring an easy job. Neither requires special tools, nor the touch of a pro. These systems are designed for the do-it-yourselfer.

Carlon's Flex-Plus Blue polyvinyl chloride (PVC) plastic electrical non-metallic tubing (ENT) is easier to use than thin-wall conduit. It installs in one-third the time, can be cut with a knife, and can be easily bent by hand and manipulated through framing.

Ready/Clad's type MC cable protects the conductors better than does armored cable. Its internal wires are encased in a seamless extruded-aluminum sheath. This outer tube is flexible, can be cut with a knife, and is as easy to install as the usual nonmetallic cable.

How do ENT and MC systems work? How do you use them? First,

the standard precaution applies: Be careful whenever you work with electricity you'll find safety tips at the end of this chapter.

ENT

The blue ENT tubing, outlet boxes, and fittings are made of touch PVC. The ENT tubes come in ½-, ¾-, and 1-inch diameters in 6- and 10-foot lengths. (The most commonly used ½-inch-diameter ENT sells for about $1.50 per 10-foot length.)

Plastic ENT provides no ground continuity, so a same-gauge bare or green-insulated equipment-grounding conductor must be included with the wires you feed through your runs. The ground conductor must be connected to every receptacle, switch, light fixture, and appliance. (Appliance grounding must conform to Article 250 in the NEC.)

Because all current-carrying conductors contribute heat, design temperature of the conductors you select must be no more than the 194°F rating of the ENT system. If you choose from among the conductors shown in NEC table 310-16, the system will meet the code. Both of the widely sold types TW and THHN conductors are usable. As with any raceway, the number and size of conductors contained in ENT must not exceed a total of 40 percent of its volume. Box fill is the same as for metal boxes of the same size.

Flex-Plus ENT is ruled out for lighting circuits unless you use a metal box to hold the fixture. Reason: A plastic ENT box can't hold the weight of a fixture. Most metal boxes and panels accept ENT box terminators just fine. ENT won't work with threaded conduit pull-boxes or other tapped outlet boxes, such as weatherproof boxes. (Because a plastic box can't be grounded, never use plastic ENT boxes with metal conduit.)

Installing ENT is easy. The boxes mount to the framing with nails or screws. I like to use short drywall screws. They're mostly self-threading, and run in quickly because they have twin threads. Carlon's ENT boxes contain ½-, ¾-, or 1-inch knockouts, depending on which box you select. Most wiring can be done with ½-inch ENT, especially if you use slender, nylon-jacketed THHN conductors.

The two-by-three-inch switch-outlet boxes mount a convenient ½ inch out from the framing when the mounting straps are set flush (see photo). Thus, the boxes project through ½-inch wallboard to come through flush with the wall surface. The four-by-four-inch boxes mount even with the studs. This way, single or two-gang box covers can be used. Covers are available flat (for surface-mount use) or with projections of ½, ⅝, ¾, or 1 inch. This enables them to extend through practically any thickness of wall material. A blank cover is available for a junction box.

Once the boxes are mounted, drill

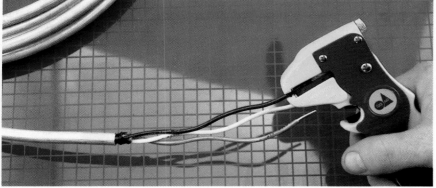

Ready/Clad can be pulled or pushed a reasonable distance into walls, floors, ceilings, ducts, and plenums (photo at right). Where the cable is exposed, it is secured with conventional conduit straps. Hidden behind walls, it need not be fastened. As with all cable wiring, splices must be made inside a box (above). To expose Ready/Clad's conductors (top), score its aluminum jacket with a knife and flex it. The aluminum sheath breaks easily at the score, and can be slid off. It takes only a few seconds, and there's little chance of slicing into the insulation. For convenience, expose at least 6 inches of the conductors.

WHERE AND HOW TO USE ENT CONDUIT AND TYPE MC CABLE IN THE HOME

ENT CONDUIT

Permitted
In one- to three-story houses inside walls, floors, and ceilings; also, most other dry and damp (partially protected) locations; OK for exposed work; boxes for walls only; maximum voltage: 600V

Not permitted
Hazardous locations or where exposed to weather; boxes not to be used to support fixtures; places that get hotter than 194° F; directly buried in ground or embedded in concrete or aggregates; where subject to physical damage

Supports
Maximum spacing 3' and within 3' of boxes; use nonmetallic clamps such as Carlon's E977 line

Bending
Bend by hand as needed; no radius less than 1/2" = 4", 3/4" = 5", and 1" = 6"

Other
Equipment grounding conductors must be provided within conduit runs where this is required by NEC Article 250; must also comply with applicable sections of NEC Article 300 on wiring methods

MC CABLE

Permitted
For services, feeders, and branch circuits; for appliance, motor, lighting, and receptacle circuits; indoors and out; exposed or concealed; direct buried (with PVC-coated conduit)

Not permitted
Where exposed to corrosive conditions, unless protected by a material suited to them; where subject to physical damage

Supports
At intervals not more than 6'; staples suited to nonmetallic cable may be used

Bending
Minimum radius of inner edge of bend is 10 times the cable's outside diameter

Other
Box connectors should be identified for use with Type MC cable; must be installed to comply with NEC Article 300

---

holes in the framing members for the ENT runs. The Code requires that when the edge of the hole is closer than 1¼ inches to the face of the framing member, 1/16-inch-thick steel straps are needed to protect the wiring from possible nail penetration. Therefore, ENT sizes larger than ½ inch, when run in 2 × 4 stud walls, need plate protection at each stud.

Bends are made by hand. They must not be so sharp as to damage the tubing or effectively reduce its inside size. As with all raceways, four 90-degree bends per run (a total of 360 degrees between boxes) is the maximum allowed. This represents the limit for good wire-pulling. If you cut ENT with a plastic pipe cutter, there are no burrs to remove. If you saw them, you must use a knife to remove the burrs inside and out.

At some point you may have to connect the ENT to a knockout in an existing box or panel. No problem. The box terminator fits into a same-sized knockout. Once the wires are in, all four-by-four-inch box covers may be installed using the furnished screws.

MC cable

The NEC refers to new Ready/Clad as type MC cable (Article 334). This pre-wired, aluminum-sheathed electrical cable can be used in exposed or concealed locations, and it's UL-listed for indoor and outdoor use. (Professional electricians use a similar material by another name: Signa/Clad.) If PVC-coated MC cable is used, the cable can be buried in the ground or cast within a concrete wall or slab.

The widely used 12/2 Ready/Clad cable costs slightly more than what's needed for a typical conduit system. But it's easier and faster to use: Unlike conduit, MC cable needs no joint every 10 feet. The runs are continuous between boxes. And the only tools you'll need are wire cutters, a knife, and a screwdriver—put away the hacksaw and pipe cutter.

The metal jacket of an MC cable serves as its equipment-grounding conductor. The sheath replaces an internal ground wire, but *metal* boxes and connectors must be used for good ground continuity. To ensure a sound electrical contact between connector and sheath, PVC-coated MC cable must have its outer coating removed wherever it enters box connectors.

Ready/Clad cable is slimmer than nonmetallic cable of the same current-carrying capacity. A cable containing two 12-gauge insulated conductors—a black and a white—is only about 3/8 inch in diameter. This is the size you'd use for wiring a 20-ampere household receptacle or lighting circuit. A cable containing three six-gauge conductors is about 1¼ inches O.D. This size might be used for wiring a branch circuit-breaker panel.

Ready/Clad cable is available from some hardware stores and home centers, and from electrical-supply dealers in three packaged lengths: 25, 50, and 100 feet. A supply of straps and dry-location box connectors comes with each package. You'll find that the 25-foot two-wire/12-gauge package costs about $25.

Safety tips

Use caution whenever you're working on your home's electrical system. Turn off the circuit by switching off its circuit breaker or unscrewing its fuse. (The main fuses or circuit breaker should be off when handling fuses.) Call your electric utility to cut off all power before you open a main panel.

Never touch a bare wire unless you are absolutely certain it is dead. (Test it with a voltage tester to be sure.) Because there could be more than one circuit inside a box, check to see that *all* of its circuits are off before continuing. Make sure your house wiring has the capacity to handle any add-ons that you make.

Check and adhere to all local electrical codes and to the NEC. Get a permit for your wiring, and have your work approved by an electrical inspector. A copy of the latest NEC can usually be found at the public library.

Finally, although home wiring is relatively easy, if you're not absolutely sure of your electrical-wiring capabilities, hire a pro—*by Richard Day. Drawing by Eliot Bergman.*

MANUFACTURERS OF PVC CONDUIT
Carlon Electrical Sciences (ENT), 25701 Science Park Dr., Cleveland, OH 44122; **Electrical Conductors** (Ready/Clad), 2500 Commonwealth Ave., North Chicago, IL 60064.

multi-switch wiring

There are bound to be areas in your home where it would be handy to control a ceiling fixture from two—or even three—different locations. The most obvious example: a long entry hall. One switch, just inside the door, turns on the light. To save having to retrace steps later to turn out the light, you have a second switch at the far end of the hall. And if the hall has a stairway, it would make sense to have a third switch at the top.

If such an area in your house lacks this convenience, would you know how to add it? Most home craftsmen find the job daunting—myself included. That's why I checked into a class taught (by Bill Dall) to California state park-maintenance crews.

The method is shown in the diagrams. You start by connecting all the bare or green-insulated grounding wires and the white- or gray-insulated "neutral" wires ahead of time. These wires aren't normally switched anyway, and this gets them out of the way as well as out of mind. You can now concentrate on black- and red-insulated "hot" wires (the lower portion of diagrams A, B, and C). Also, to simplify things, think about switching with the simplest circuit—one where the power source comes into the same outlet box with the first switch.

Naturally, before you tackle *any* rewiring, be certain the circuit you're working on is dead: Just remove the fuse or trip the circuit breaker. (If you do the latter, it's a good

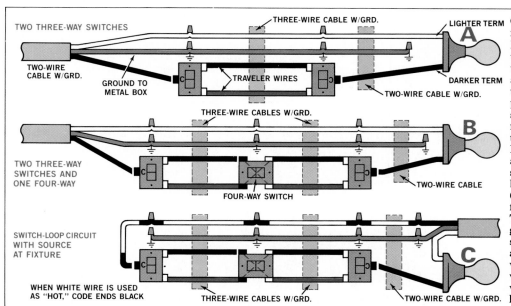

TWO THREE-WAY SWITCHES

THREE-WIRE CABLE W/GRD.

LIGHTER TERM

A

TWO-WIRE CABLE W/GRD.

GROUND TO METAL BOX

TRAVELER WIRES

DARKER TERM

TWO-WIRE CABLE W/GRD.

THREE-WIRE CABLES W/GRD.

B

TWO THREE-WAY SWITCHES AND ONE FOUR-WAY

TWO-WIRE CABLE

FOUR-WAY SWITCH

SWITCH-LOOP CIRCUIT WITH SOURCE AT FIXTURE

C

WHEN WHITE WIRE IS USED AS "HOT," CODE ENDS BLACK

THREE-WIRE CABLES W/GRD.

TWO-WIRE CABLE W/GRD.

Choose a diagram to match your situation. Diagram A gives you two switches between the source (power cable) and load (lamp or fixture). Need *three* control points? Diagram B shows how to wire a four-way switch between two three-ways. Pigtailed grounding and neutral wires are shown at each outlet box. Two-wire cable (with ground) serves the first switch and load. Three-wire cable (with ground) runs between switches to provide red and black traveler wires. Diagram C shows wiring for a circuit when the source and load share an outlet box.

idea to tape the breaker in its off position so no helpful person who happens to come along will decide to flick it back on while you're working.)

Three-way switches. When a light or appliance is controlled by only one switch, a single-pole type is used. You can't get more basic: It has two terminals, both the same color. Black (or red) wires go to these, and the switch makes or breaks the power to the load (lamp or appliance).

But to control a load from two locations, a pair of three-way switches is needed. They're single-pole double-throw switches, with three terminals. Three-way switches are always used in pairs. Never try to use one alone, and never use more than two in a switching circuit.

One terminal of each three-way switch is usually darker than the other two. The combinations may be aluminum and brass, brass and copper, or chrome and brass. One terminal may be marked "C" or "COM"—this lone terminal is the common. (For three same-color terminals without a marking, see the sidebar at the end of the chapter, Switch Terminals Aren't Coded?)

To wire a pair of three-way switches, start with the black or red hot wire from the 120-volt line, the power source. This *always* attaches to the common terminal of the first switch (see drawings). Similarly, the switched black or red hot wire to the load *always* takes off from the common terminal of the second three-way switch. These are the only wires you should ever connect to the common terminals, so take care to connect these next.

The other two switch terminals are for the "traveler," or "runner," wires. These are the wires that run between the pair of three-way switches. When you wire with cables, there's a black traveler wire and a red one. Connect the black to the light-colored terminals of the three-way switches at each end. (It doesn't matter which terminal, but it's best to be consistent.) Then connect the red wire to the remaining light-colored terminal at each end. Traveler wires are interchangeable. The switches will work whether you connect traveler wires top-to-top and bottom-to-bottom (as shown in the diagrams) or top-to-bottom and bottom-to-top.

In working with three-way switches, it helps to place

them with the two light-colored terminals facing each other, as shown in diagram A. (This assumes that the switches have both light-colored terminals on the same side—not all do.) To work this way, one switch will have to be inverted as shown, but that's OK. Unless they're mercury switches (where gravity's a factor), three-ways have no up or down. On mercury switches, the tops are indicated.

Four-way switches. To control a load from more than two places, one or more four-way switches can be used—but always between two three-way switches. (An example of this is a garage light switched from inside the front and back doors of the house as well as from inside the garage itself.) Four-way switches get their name from their four terminals. These terminals serve *only* traveler wires to adjoining three- or four-ways. You can use as many four-way switches as are needed, as long as all of them are between two three-way switches.

On most four-ways, two of the terminals at one end are colored darker than the two at the other end, to denote matched pairs. The darker-colored pair gets the red and black traveler wires (interchangeably) from an adjacent switch. The lighter-colored pair also gets the travelers interchangeably from the other adjacent switch. It's hard to go wrong.

Drawing B shows how a four-way switch fits between two three-ways. For clarity, the four-way is shown lying on its side, with the darker pair of terminals at one end and the lighter pair at the other. In actuality, each switch will be mounted vertically, not on its side.

If you mistakenly connect pairs of terminals with the same wire colors instead of connecting them to wires from adjoining switches, your switching system won't work, but no harm will be done. Make the corrections, and your switching will work fine.

Additional four-way switches, if used, go next to each other in the circuit. Theoretically, there is no limit to the number of four-way switches that can be used between a pair of three-ways.

About wiring. Because it's easy to work with, most DIY wiring is done using nonmetallic cable. Both the line

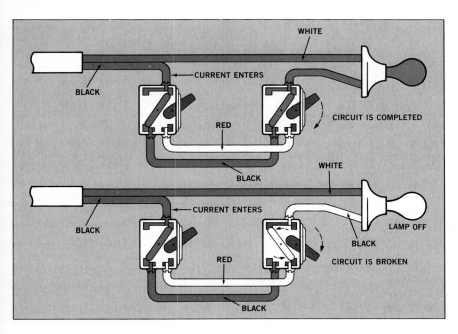

Three-way switches are single-pole, double-throw type (the pivot-handle, or toggle, version in these schematics is the most familiar); such switches must have three terminals, connected as shown. Because power flows between terminals as indicated in the cutaway sketches, the lamp will light when both toggles are up (top schematic), or when both are down—that's why there are no on/off markings on a three-way switch. But if the toggle of one switch is up and the other down (lower schematic), the circuit is broken. This lets you control the lamp from either switch location. (The modern rocker-type switch in the color photo is just another version of a toggle.) A four-way switch (with four terminals—not shown) lets you control the lamp from *three* locations. You connect it between two three-way switches as indicated in wiring diagrams B and C.

(power source) and load (light or appliance) side of multis-witch circuits are served by two-wire-with-ground cable. This contains a black hot wire, white neutral wire, and bare grounding wire. Cable for this purpose is identified as 14-2 G or 12-2 G, depending on its wire size. (Use No. 14 wire for a 15-ampere circuit, and No. 12 for a 20-amp circuit. Make sure circuits aren't overtaxed by new loads added to them.)

In wiring between a pair of three- or four-way switches, three-wire-with-ground cable is used. This will be identified as 14-3 G or 12-3 G. In addition to the necessary white and bare wires, this has both a black and red wire for use as travelers.

Bonding of switches to ground isn't normally needed, as it is in wiring receptacles. But if you're using switches with extra terminals marked GR, or having green-colored hex-head bonding screws, these should be grounded.

Follow local or National Electric Code requirements. When you're finished, test your work with the power on. Also use a neon tester to check from the neutral to a ground. No matter which way the switches are thrown, your tester should not light. (If you're not adept at home wiring, call in a pro.)

Switch-loop circuits. If the line enters the same outlet box with the load or enters one of the in-between switch boxes, the basic switch-wiring diagram stays the same. However, then the white wire in each cable is used as a hot wire, feeding current through the switch boxes all the way back to the first three-way switch. This is called a switch-loop circuit (diagram C). If you're using cable, the ends of the white wire at each box must be coded black—this is to avoid troubleshooting problems later. A black felt-tip marker is fine for this, or you can wrap the white ends with black electrical tape. (If you're wiring in conduit, the correct color of wires must be used.)

Once multi-switch wiring is written into your memory, you'll never again have to waste time doping out three- and four-way switch hookups—*by Richard Day. Photo by Greg Sharko. Drawings by Mitchell J. Albala.*

Switch terminals aren't coded?

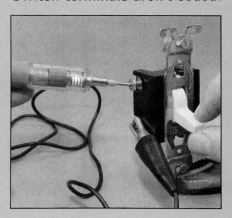

If terminals on three- or four-way switches aren't color-coded, you can tell them apart with a powered test light (continuity tester) or an ohmmeter. A VOM will do the job in its Rx1 function.

To check out a three-way switch, connect one test probe to any terminal and the other probe to each of the others in turn, as in the photo. You're looking for the terminal that shows continuity with *both* other terminals, one at a time, as the toggle is thrown. The common is the only terminal that acts that way. (Remember that a mercury switch only works with its top end up.)

On a four-way switch, you'll find paired-off terminals that, no matter which way the toggle is thrown, never show continuity. Mark one no-continuity pair darker than the other. It makes no difference which is which.

patching plastic pipe

The plastic pipe in your house won't corrode—but it will leak if you puncture it or if a fitting's joint wasn't properly welded. If you nail or drill into plastic pipe, you can patch the puncture. And you can replace an entire fitting assembly.

If the maker of your pipe offers slip couplings of the right size, they're ideal for patching. They're made without inner stops (shoulders), so they'll slide all the way onto a same-size pipe. If you can't find a slip coupling, you can make one from a regular coupling by grinding out the stop.

To make a repair, cut the pipe in two at the leak, spread the sections, slide on the coupling, and apply cleaner-primer and then solvent cement to both sides of the cut. Slide the coupling up, center it over the cut, and hold it while the cement sets.

Another way to patch is with a weld-on piece from a size-larger pipe. Generous coatings of solvent cement are needed on both the surface of the PVC pipe and the inside of the patch. Clamp the piece with mechanic's wire ties, as shown below, right—*by Richard Day. Photos by Greg Sharko and the author.*

The first two photos show a patch for a 1 ½-inch PVC venting stack. Slice through the puncture with a guillotine-type cutter; spread the pipes enough to add a slip coupling below the cut. To fix leaks at fittings (third photo), cut out the fitting, as well as some pipe (rear), and replace with the new assembly shown. For a weld-on patch, cut a piece from the next-larger-size pipe.

installing vinyl gutters

If you have ever tripped over a downspout extension, you know how quickly metal gutter parts can depreciate. One misstep can leave you with more than just a bleeding ankle—it can bend or dent the metal. And the first time you lean a ladder against a gutter, you may wreck your drainage system.

Metal is also vulnerable to its environment. It can corrode, and it must be repainted or replaced periodically. And unless you're careful, you may draw blood if you try to install a metal system yourself.

The alternative—vinyl gutters and downspouts—have become widely available in home centers in a greater variety of styles. The price has gone down in comparison to aluminum, too, so that vinyl is now likely to be lower in initial cost as well as in long-term maintenance. (The only possible problem with vinyl is exposure to extreme heat—see box, next page.) Best of all, vinyl gutters are simple to install. Cutting the segments and mounting them will be easy if you master these tips.

First, remove the old gutter system and all its hardware. Then you will be ready to mark your new gutter's position before attaching it to your roof. Mount the system below an imaginary line extending past the edge of the roof so that ice sheets will slide over the gutter instead of crashing into it.

The more gutters slope, the better they work. But gutters become the visual roof line of your house, so they *look* best when installed dead level.

Intense rainfall, as in the southern states, might require a slope of 1/4 inch for every 10-foot length of gutter. This is enough to direct the water flow toward the downspout. A slope of 1/2 inch gets things moving nicely but skews the gutter enough to make the roof line look "off."

Use a chalk line against the fascia to mark the gutter's alignment. Stretch the line level, then set whatever slope you need by moving one end down the desired amount at a drop-outlet location before you snap the line.

Gutter slope and the intensity of rainfall where you live govern the spacing of downspouts. Most systems are designed for a maximum of three gutter lengths—or 30 feet—between downspouts. If you install level gutters, plan to use a spout every 20 feet, especially in rainy regions.

One downspout will serve between 500 and 700 square feet of roof area. After you plan the spacing, make sure you have enough downspouts to drain the area above. An extra-wide house or one with a shed roof might need more downspouts.

There is one way to minimize the number of downspouts you install. A couple of manufacturers offer high-

Shingles should project at least ½ inch beyond the roof so that water will run off into the gutters. If necessary, push a vinyl drip edge up underneath the bottom shingles to extend the roof edge. Drip edges are available in 10-foot strips and can usually be matched to the color of your gutters.

flow drop outlets that have larger openings with smoothly curved surfaces leading from the gutters to the downspouts. In a conventional system, the water must make a sharp turn around a corner to enter the downspout. With sloped drop outlets, water exits more quickly without forming a vortex. Maximum downspout spacing can be increased to 40 feet, and roof area served to about 1,200 square feet per spout. This method is cheaper and easier than

Most vinyl systems are designed to be owner-installed. If your house has no fascia or rafter tails for bracket attachment, use strap hangers aligned to a stretched string. If the fascia or rafter tails are at an angle, use wedge-shaped blocks between the brackets and mounting surface. Space brackets at maximum 30-inch intervals (24 inches for heavy-snow climes); joints, every 10 feet, the length of gutter sections. Make a sketch to plan downspout locations.

You must allow for expansion and contraction

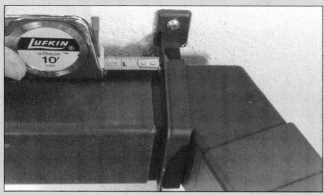

Plastic gutters and downspouts expand and contract more than metal. A 10-foot length of gutter will change in length by as much as ½ inch. Desert areas, where the temperature varies widely from day to night, put the most strain on plastic systems. But you can overcome stresses by allowing for expansion and contraction when you install the gutters.

If you use a system with slip joints, align the ends of gutter sections with the marks inside the joints. Leave ¼ inch for downspout expansion just below the upper spout elbow on the house wall (above left). On a two-story downspout, tuck in another expansion space just beneath the downspout coupling. Some instructions call for a ½-inch space, but ¼

inch works just as well and looks better.

A solvent-welded system requires more space for movement because you are forming it into one long piece. With gutter corners at both ends, put an expansion joint in the run to prevent buckling (above right). Leave at least two inches between the gutter brackets and joints so the gutter can slide adding another downspout.

Other systems are especially slow drainers. Some have drop outlets that are solvent-welded into holes cut in the bottoms of the gutters. Each drop outlet has a flange that is welded to the gutter bottom; this means the downspout cannot be nearly as wide as the gutter. Thus the downspouts must be more closely spaced.

If your house was built with uniform overhangs, you may be able to replicate the downspouts. Make up one, and take it around to the other spout locations to see whether it fits. If so, you can precut all parts on a radial-arm or table saw. A fine-toothed plywood-cutting blade is best. Feed slowly to minimize chipping, and wear face protection.

Runoff from the downspout should empty at least 18 inches from foundations. Some systems offer swing-up extensions to keep water away from your house—one reason for installing gutters in the first place. Or you can connect underground storm drain pipes to your downspout system, if the manufacturer offers a drain adapter.

If you don't like the color of your gutters, you can paint them. Wipe them down with denatured alcohol before you begin. Use exterior latex house paint or exterior enamel. If the surfaces are glossy, you may need a primer that will bond to the vinyl. One manufacturer offers a specially formulated satin-finish brown paint for use as either a vinyl primer or a finish coat.

Remember that if you paint your system, you will have to renew the coating in years to come. Yet even with this inconvenience, vinyl gutters are easy to maintain and will last for years if you install them properly—*by Richard Day. Photos by Richard Day and Phil McCafferty.*

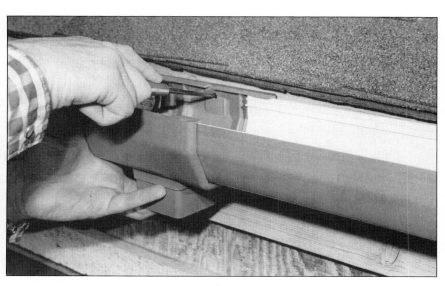

Gutter segments can fit into an inside corner joint. If roof lines don't meet at a right angle, use a saw to take out a wedge or make custom corners. Installing lengths of gutter with a slip joint attached saves having to measure for joint placement. Cut the gutter sections to the proper length beforehand, keeping in mind the clearances needed to avoid buckling. Gutters may be slid, snapped, or solvent-welded together, depending on the brand.

freely. And remember not to weld expansion joints, downspout elbows, and gutter brackets to the gutter.

Ice will not crack a vinyl system, and it won't adhere to gutter sides any better than it sticks to ice-cube trays. But solar heat can be damaging because vinyl is a thermoplastic that becomes soft when it gets too hot. One Phoenix homeowner learned this lesson the hard way: He painted his entire system brown, and the heat it absorbed warped it. The insides of gutters should always be white, to reflect the sun's rays. The outside—the part you see—can be any color you like. Although gutters now come in both dark and light colors, some manufacturers have developed more sophisticated two-tone gutters with dark exteriors and white interiors.

Reflective metal awnings, porch roofs, and patio covers may cause special problems: They reflect solar heat onto the outside of the gutter. Use all-white gutters and accessories above these surfaces. While installing your gutter system, do not lay any parts out on a blacktop driveway. Absorbed solar radiation may deform them.—R. D.

Start the downspout by mounting an elbow in a bracket. Align it with the gutter elbow, as shown, and mark the hole positions for drilling. Measure the gap between elbows, and assemble with a downspout section of proper length. Attach brackets at each elbow, top and bottom, and at any couplings.

add your own casement windows

Y ou've heard of winter waste-lands? That was the dining bay off my kitchen. Its four 18-year-old windows leaked enough winter chill to make the tundra seem a cozy place for breakfast by comparison.

My solution? I replaced the old bay windows with new double-glazed units featuring low-emissivity glass. I also beefed up the insulation in the wall areas and glued rigid foam under the projecting floor. The results were far better than I anticipated: no air infiltration, no fabric-damaging ul-traviolet rays, high energy efficiency in both summer and winter, and—perfect for breakfast—lots of light. Because the new windows *are* more efficient, I could enjoy the benefits of a larger glass area.

Done with mirrors

I selected four clad wood casement windows manufactured by Caradco. Each unit has a left- and right-hinged sash swing and measures five feet high by four feet wide with two 19-inch-wide glass panes. The wood frames are encased in heavy extruded aluminum, and all frame parts are treated with a water repellent, pre-servative, and insect toxicant.

The insulating glass has a ¾-inch dual seal with ½-inch air space to provide maximum insulation. By combining a rigid vinyl leaf weather-stripping on the sash and a flexible one-piece vinyl bulb system on the frame, Caradco virtually shuts down air filtration at 0.03 cubic foot per minute per foot of linear crack.

For still greater comfort and energy efficiency, I specified low-emissivity (low-E) glass. A material with low emissivity resists absorbing energy, so it has a greater ability to reduce heat loss. Low-E glass results in a 20-percent lower U-value, or a higher R-value—meaning greater resistance to the passage of heat through a window unit. Low-E windows pass light and heat from the sun, but once the en-ergy enters the house, the low-E coat-ing keeps the heat from escaping back through the glass.

Low-emissivity glass is highly re-flective, rather like a mirror. In win-ter the coated glass reflects and traps heat created by the home heating sys-tem. In summer or in warm-weather areas the coated glass reflects the sun's rays, reducing the amount of heat entering the room.

Because the surface of the glass fac-ing the room is kept warm, there is less likelihood of condensation. Win-dow drafts caused by cool air falling down the glass surface are elimi-nated. And because low-E glass inhib-its the transmission of ultraviolet light, interior fabrics—curtains and furniture—won't fade.

BEFORE

AFTER
BEFORE

Taller windows transformed this kitchen dinette, both inside and out. Structural headers weren't disturbed—the new windows set closer to the floor. Note in the exterior views that, while he was at it, the author also replaced a plain-Jane window in the living room to the right, installing a handsome four-pane bay. For a floor plan and installation tips, turn the page.

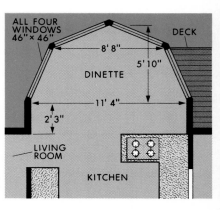

Find a friend

Removing the existing windows and replacing them with the larger Caradco units required careful handling. I took on the job with the help of a professional contractor, Phil Gonsowski. The work is shown in the photos.

We used a long-bladed Milwaukee reciprocating saw to cut through the wall and enlarge the window openings. Cut the rough opening slightly larger than the window—about 3/4 inch along the width and 1/2 inch along the height. The headers that run above windows are structural and should never be cut into. You deepen a rough opening by cutting away the sill, dropping the window closer to the floor. Trim back the cripple studs (2 × 4s installed beneath the existing window), and, after cutting the new opening to size, reinstall the rough sill.

Leave the window's shipping braces in place until the window is nailed squarely in the opening. The braces help support the frame during handling. Use shims or tapered shingles in the corners of the opening to shift the window into a level position, and secure it by nailing flanges all around. (Use galvanized nails so they won't rust.) Stuff fiberglass insulation around the perimeter of each window before adding the casing and sill.

Finish the interior molding and wood frame with paint or stain. Proper exterior repairs must be done to avoid a patched look. Brick and stucco exteriors pose special problems. You might want to hire a professional mason for those projects—*by Marc Brett. Photos by Greg Sharko.*

(1) Reciprocating saw is used to deepen the rough window opening. Cut through the bottom sill, then pry back drywall to make sure no wiring or plumbing is in the way.
(2) Plastic sheet provides a vapor barrier and additional insulation. Wrap it around the opening and staple.

(3) Install the windows from outside.
(4) Be sure the window is level to prevent leaks and possible structural problems. Shim as needed. Dimensions of the dining bay are shown at left. The existing structure wasn't altered; only the window openings were enlarged.

SELECTED MANUFACTURERS' ADDRESSES
Caradco Corp., Box 920, Rantoul, IL 61866 (clad wood casement windows with low-E glass); **Contemporary Shells**, West Hempstead, NY 11552 (upholstered kitchen chairs); **Graber Industries**, Middleton, WI 53562 (vertical blinds); **Morton Jonap Ltd.**, Hicksville, NY 11801 (wallcovering); **Paint Bucket**, Seaford, NY 11783 (lamination)

fast foundations

Footer Blocks can be used with slab-on-grade houses as well as houses with basements. They support foundation walls for additions to one- or two-story houses.

Tom Bertch lives in Floodwood, Minnesota, where the climate limits construction opportunities to a few months a year. When Bertch decided to build a basement addition to his house last year, he didn't want to wait for a cast-in-place concrete footing to cure. Instead, he created the footing from interlocking concrete blocks developed by the Innovative Design Research Division, National Concrete Masonry Association.

Bertch says that preparing a concrete footing "had always been the worst aspect of any new construction." But with IDR's Footer Block System, Bertch and a few friends laid a footing in less than an hour. Heavy rains collapsed the sides of the hole before Bertch completed his project, but the walls were already high enough to protect his work. The same storm buried his neighbor's poured-concrete footing.

According to IDR, even an unskilled laborer can construct the mortarless footing in about half the time of a cast-in-place footing. Because no curing is needed, you can start building a wall at once. Footer Blocks are the first in the U.S., and they meet most standard U.S. building codes. They are lighter than their predecessors, so you can easily arrange them single-handedly.

Footer Blocks are made from the same concrete mix as ordinary concrete blocks. But they're solid—no hollow cores. There are two kinds of blocks: stretchers and corners. The 4-by-8-by-16-inch stretchers weigh about 24 pounds each and make an 8-inch-thick wall. The 4-by-8-by-20-inch stretchers bear 12-inch-thick walls. Square units are grouped four or nine to a corner. They're also used to support isolated piers.

Because the blocks can interlock in endless configurations and are relatively short, you can plan various layouts. Bertch says it will be simple for him to tie in more footing and expand his addition.

To make a block footing like Bertch's, you'll need to prepare a bare earth base, at least one foot below the frost line. Build on unexcavated earth, not on backfill, mud, or snow. If you wish, you may cover the earth with gravel, mortar, lean-mix concrete, or soil-cement before laying the footing.

Stake out the corner points, and run string lines around the perimeter. Lay blocks along the strings, beginning at the corners, and level the stretchers as you go. Unless you're making a mortarless wall, you can do the final leveling for the first course of block with a mortar bedding.

Grooves in the tops of the stretcher units form key slots. Mortar or grout in the keys helps to resist horizontal forces that might be encountered during backfilling and some earthquakes. You may also choose to place steel reinforcing—"re-bars" or 6-by-$\frac{3}{16}$-inch trusses—in the keys. In areas subject to earthquakes, you'll have to lay steel re-bars in a course of bond-beam block just above the footing. Steel-reinforced footings and walls are usually built to an engineered design or a building-code-required plan. You may also reinforce walls by pumping core-grouting into the blocks, filling them level with the top of the wall.

The National Concrete Masonry Assn. licenses local concrete block plants to make Footer Blocks. A 16-inch stretcher costs about $1. If you can't find the blocks, contact IDR (Box 781, Herndon, VA 22070) for the name of the nearest maker—*by Richard Day. Photos by Photo Darkroom. Drawing by Mitchell J. Abala.*

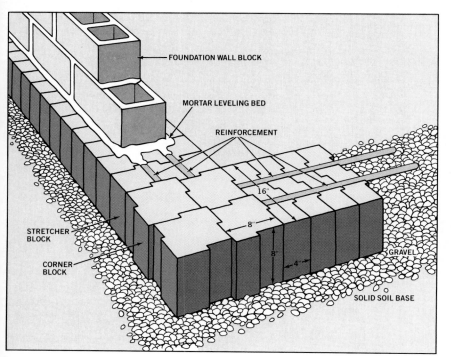

FOUNDATION WALL BLOCK

MORTAR LEVELING BED

REINFORCEMENT

16"

8"

8"

4"

STRETCHER BLOCK

CORNER BLOCK

GRAVEL

SOLID SOIL BASE

Each block dovetails with its neighbors, preventing dislocation under lateral loads. Place trusses or rebars in keys before laying wall blocks.

repairing exterior masonry

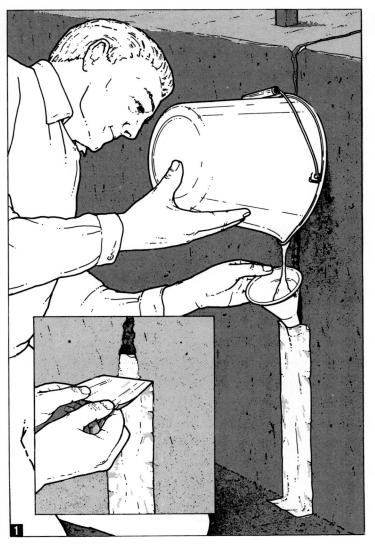

Masonry repairs aren't usually the first projects that come to mind when homeowners contemplate working on their houses; available cash is more likely to be invested in interior decorating and remodeling. But the stresses of successive winters leave many homes with unsightly cracks in foundations, steps, and driveways that only get worse—and far more expensive to fix—when left unrepaired.

Cracked masonry should be repaired promptly, especially in regions where winters are severe. Even a small crack allows moisture to penetrate the concrete, where subsequent cycles of freezing and thawing soon cause further deterioration.

The effective cure for cracked masonry, however, isn't the obvious one. "Slapping concrete into a hole won't solve your problem," warns Murray Steinberg, research chemist at Red Devil in Union, New Jersey. "Concrete surfaces can't be repaired with concrete because the coarse gravel elements in the new mix prevent bonding between the patch and the damaged area."

Cracks in concrete or cinder-block foundations, Steinberg advises, should be quickly repaired with a commercial patching material that is specially formulated to form

1 **Clean vertical cracks** in concrete or cinder-block foundations with a cold chisel and brush to remove loose material. Moisten exposed area, then cover lowest segment with a strip of duct tape and insert a funnel at the top. Prepare a thin mix of patching material and pour into the crack. Remove tape when patch sets. *Don't try to repair more than 3 feet of crack at once.*

a strong bond with concrete. Fine cracks in steps, drive-ways, or garage floors can be filled with cartridge-pack-aged, ready-mixed repair material that is dispensed from a standard caulking gun. If rock salt and ice have loosened the foundations of wrought-iron railings, anchor cement is what you're looking for. It sets rock hard in just 15 min-utes—*by Stuart F. Brown.*

Use a putty knife or old screwdriver to scrape loose fragments out from between fieldstones. Fine cracks up to ⅛ inch wide can be readily filled with premixed concrete and mortar repair material from a cartridge gun.

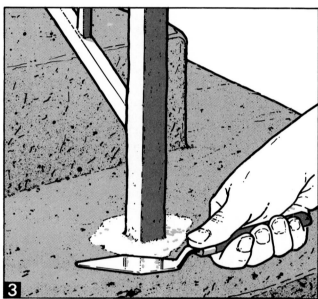

You'll find that a putty knife is also good for removing debris from around iron railings. It's also an excellent tool for applying anchor cement, as shown here.

Once you've applied a patch, finish off by smoothing out your work with a sponge. Then, once the repair has set completly, you can smooth it further by rubbing it with a coarse abrasive.

wood-staining ceramic tile

Matching floor tiles to wood cabinets can become a time-consuming game of compare-and-contrast. To reduce the guess-work, you might consider laying unglazed ceramic floor tiles and staining them with the same wood stain you have chosen for the cabinets. Here's our variation on the technique. For brevity's sake, we've assumed the cabinets are in place and the tile is set in mortar.

Unglazed ceramic tile comes in imperfect 8-inch or 11½-inch squares. Sun- or kiln-dried, their surfaces are usually rough, with blotches, divots, deviations, and ridges along the edges. Sand (without scratching) any imperfections that may chip after the sealer is applied.

1. Using a float, apply grout in joints flush with tile surfaces. When grout has completely set (recommended drying time: 72 hours), clean joint edges and remove any excess pieces.

2. With 120-grade sandpaper, sand off any ridges or unsightly blemishes prior to setting tiles in mortar. After they're set, lightly sand any unwanted imperfections; avoid deeply scratching the soft clay surfaces.

3. The proper sealer is a water-based silicone penetrating sealer for unglazed tile; the wood stain should also be water-based. Mix the solution at a two-to-one sealer-to-stain ratio, slightly increasing or decreasing the amount of stain depending on the final shade you desire.

Supplies: some grout, water-based sealer, 120-grade sandpaper, grout float, mortar trowel, paint brush, and a soft-bristle brush.

Brush-applied sealer-and-stain coating matches unglazed ceramic tiles with wood cabinets, as shown below. Before staining whole floor, test color on individual tiles.

Apply the mixture with smooth, easy strokes, thoroughly coating both tile and grout. Each tile will absorb the mixture at varying rates; avoid puddling or over-saturating, and sponge up any unabsorbed solution after three minutes.

4. Each subsequent coating (you should do at least three) should be applied after the previous coat has completely dried (two to three hours later). Keep applying coats, increasing or decreasing the amount of stain, to match the look of the cabinets.

It's a good idea to apply a coat of sealer every six months or so to protect the tiles from water, food spills, and scuffing—*by Charlie Posoneil. Photos by Dan Borris.*

After setting tiles in thin-set mortar, lay grout into joints. Be sure it's flush to the surface; use float to press grout into joints and clean around edges. Drying time: 72 hours.

Sand tiles twice with fine-grade sandpaper: once, before setting tiles in mortar to remove major imperfections, and again, after tiles are set in place. Use brush to remove dust.

After grout is damp-cured, brush the first coat of 2:1 sealer-to-stain mixture over the entire floor, including tiles and grout. Keep strokes consistent; avoid puddling or oversaturation.

Apply second and third coats a few hours apart. Continue applying coats, with slightly less or more stain, to match cabinet color. Three coats will protect tile from food spills.

how to buy a used car

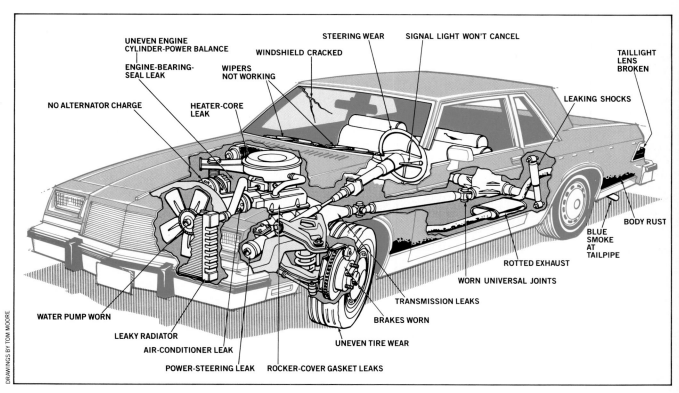

DRAWINGS BY TOM MOORE

UNEVEN ENGINE CYLINDER-POWER BALANCE

ENGINE-BEARING-SEAL LEAK

WINDSHIELD CRACKED

STEERING WEAR

SIGNAL LIGHT WON'T CANCEL

TAILLIGHT LENS BROKEN

WIPERS NOT WORKING

NO ALTERNATOR CHARGE

HEATER-CORE LEAK

LEAKING SHOCKS

BODY RUST

BLUE SMOKE AT TAILPIPE

ROTTED EXHAUST

WORN UNIVERSAL JOINTS

WATER PUMP WORN

TRANSMISSION LEAKS

BRAKES WORN

LEAKY RADIATOR

AIR-CONDITIONER LEAK

UNEVEN TIRE WEAR

POWER-STEERING LEAK

ROCKER-COVER GASKET LEAKS

If you're planning to buy a used car, you're not alone: Almost 17 million of the 26.9 million cars that were recently purchased were used. With the price of the average new car hovering around $10,000, it's no wonder that so many people choose to take the used-car route.

To make an intelligent purchase, however, you have to assess the risks in buying a particular car. The drawing above points out common problems that can plague a used car, and on the following pages I list the major areas I check when a client brings a car to my garage for evaluation. You can make most of these checks yourself. The accompanying checklist helps you tally up a car's approximate value as you look over its components.

Road test. Get behind the wheel and start the engine. The starter shouldn't make any grinding sounds. The car should start easily. Drive the car forward, and test the brakes. Will it stop safely? OK, then head onto a quiet road for a transmission-shift test. Starting from a standstill, accel-

erate modestly. With an automatic transmission, listen for shift changes from first to second and from second to third gears. At about 35 mph, shift the gear selector to the next lower range. You should feel a smooth gear change if the transmission is working properly. If the car has a standard transmission, run through all the gears. Observe how easily you can select each gear. Make sure you can accelerate without jerking or slipping. Finally, any loud whine or grinding noise that changes as the shifts occur indicates a transmission problem.

Now check the brakes. Hold the steering wheel loosely, and hit the brakes. The car should not pull to one side. There should be no squeal or grind, and the pedal should feel firm. The parking brake should keep the car from rolling.

Next, consider how the car steers. Holding the steering wheel loosely again, check for steering pull to either side. (You must be on a level road; a crowned road will cause the car to pull to the side.) The car should steer straight. There should be no binding or grinding when you turn the wheel. The steering-wheel position should be centered when you're on a straight road. Finally, check to be sure there is no noticeable free play in the steering wheel. Now you're ready to take a look at the car's various systems.

Engine checks. The engine should hum; any clicking noise from the top part of the engine indicates probable valve-train troubles. With the transmission in neutral, race the engine momentarily. If you hear a loud knocking noise, it could mean worn bearings. Watch the color of the exhaust. Blue smoke from the tailpipe is a clue to a costly-to-repair oil-consumption problem; black smoke indicates a fuel problem. White vapor may mean a leaking head gasket. Check the engine-oil dipstick. A dipstick covered with a blackish, creamy substance can tip you off to moisture in the crankcase.

If you have a pair of insulated spark-plug-wire pliers and a dwell tachometer, you can do a cylinder power-balance test. This essential test will tell you whether any cylinders have problems that could be expensive to fix. Connect the tachometer to the running engine. Using the insulated pliers to protect you against an electrical shock, disconnect and ground each of the spark-plug wires, one at a time, for a few seconds, then reconnect them. As you remove each wire, engine speed should decrease by 25 to 50 rpm. If it doesn't change, you've found a cylinder that isn't firing.

Fluid leaks. Look carefully at the engine rocker-arm-cover gaskets, the engine front and rear main seals, the oil-pan gasket, the steering gear, and power-steering pump. What may seem like just a bit of fluid could be the sign of a costly-to-repair oil leak.

Transmission. It's important to check the transmission and differential for leaks. Also, remove and check the transmission fluid-level dipstick. One of the first signs of impending transmission trouble is dark brown and foul-smelling burnt transmission fluid.

Steering and suspension. Irregular tire wear is the best clue to a wheel alignment problem, but odd wear on the tires can indicate steering-linkage problems as well. A tire with half the tread in good condition and half nearly bald would indicate a wheel-alignment problem. Front tires with bumpy or gouged treads could indicate a steering problem. Look for worn upper and lower control-arm bushings. Check upper and lower ball joints. Remember to look over the springs and shock absorbers. Broken leaf springs must be replaced. Broken or oil-soaked shock absorbers or Mac-Pherson strut-type shocks will also need replacement. Don't forget to check for excessive power-steering free play while the engine is running.

Brake checks. Pump the brake pedal with the engine off. Then press down on the pedal and start the engine. If the power brake is working, the brake pedal will drop just a bit. Press firmly on the brake pedal again, holding it for 60 seconds. The pedal shouldn't sink. If it does, you may need a brake master cylinder. Examine the thickness of the brake pads or brake shoes. Check the brake drums or disc rotors for scoring. Check for binding disc-brake calipers by placing the car on jack stands and having an assistant press the brake pedal. You shouldn't be able to turn the wheels. When the brake is released, the wheels should turn freely. If they don't, the calipers are binding and need repair. Look over the brake hoses for cracks. Make sure the parking-brake cables work freely.

Cooling system. With the engine warm, look over the hoses, radiator, and engine for leaks. Any powdery, greenish-white residue is a sign of coolant leaking. Look around the base of the water pump and under the engine for leaks. Also check for leaks around as many of the engine's core plugs as you can see. With the engine off, grasp the engine fan and try to rock the water pump. If the water-pump pulley moves, you will need a new pump. Drops of antifreeze on the passenger-side rug signal a heater-core leak.

When the engine is cool, remove the radiator cap and look at the coolant. Rusty coolant warns of a serious corrosion problem. A strawberry-milkshake color indicates a transmission-cooler leak.

Battery and electrical system. Some batteries have a built-in hydrometer; when a yellow warning eye shows, it means that the battery is tired and must be replaced.

You can perform a simple test to tell whether the alternator is charging the battery by connecting a voltmeter across the terminals of the battery. With the engine shut off, the voltmeter should read 12 volts. With the engine running, the voltmeter should read 13 or 14 volts—if not, the alternator isn't charging.

Switch on the headlights. Check the high and low beams. Make sure the parking lights work. Check all the signal lights. Make sure the signal-light switch cancels after the steering wheel is turned back to the straight-ahead position; the switch is expensive to replace. Test the brake lights. Be sure the emergency lights flash.

Generally, a new light bulb will correct most problems with a car's lights. However, an inoperative four-way flasher or a malfunctioning brake light can mean a costly repair. Dim lights or burnt fuses nearly always mean wiring trouble that will have to be traced and corrected. Parking-light, taillight, and back-up-light lenses must be in good condition to pass inspection in several states.

Turn the key to the "ignition" position. Both the oil-pressure light and the alternator light should glow until the engine is started. The engine-temperature and brake warning lights should illuminate when the key is at the "start" position. On General Motors cars built since 1981, a yellow CHECK ENGINE light should come on when starting and should go out when the engine is running.

Heater and air conditioner. Flip on the heater to be sure it produces hot air at all blower speeds. Check the defroster—and the rear-window defogger, too, if the car is equipped with one.

Switch on the air conditioner, if equipped, to see whether cold air comes out of the dashboard louvers. This air should be about 20°F lower than the outside temperature. The air-conditioner evaporator inlet pipe should be ice cold to the touch when the system is cooling. If the air conditioner is empty of refrigerant gas, the compressor, condenser, evaporator, or a line may be leaking.

Body checks. Look for signs of rust around wheel wells, window trim, and at the base of doors. Rust is a cancer that is difficult to control; if a door panel or fender is rusted through, the only sure cure is a new one.

Dents and scratches can be deceiving. You cannot simply spray paint over a scratch. It must be primed, sanded, and reprimed before the final

To buy or not to buy

Using this checklist, tally up the defects you find during your inspection. It will help you determine whether the car is a good buy, a possibility for a do-it-your-selfer, or a clunker to steer clear of.

Compare the total number of points with the values listed below. There are always exceptions, but generally the guide should tell you which cars to consider—and which ones to avoid.

Areas where repairs are needed

Overall body condition					
Minor body work	20	☐	Steering gear	25	☐
Side glass, each	30	☐	**Air conditioner/heater**		
Windshield	35	☐	AC control	10	☐
Major body work	50	☐	Blower motor	10	☐
Repaint body	50	☐	Heater core	10	☐
Seats/carpets	50	☐	Hoses	10	☐
Vinyl top	50	☐	Condenser	30	☐
Rusted sheet metal	100	☐	Compressor	35	☐
Transmission			Evaporator	35	☐
Fluid leaks	15	☐	**Cooling system**		
Differential	25	☐	Hoses	5	☐
Torque converter	25	☐	Radiator	10	☐
Overhaul	55	☐	Water pump	10	☐
Mileage			Core plugs	15	☐
Over 70,000	50	☐	**Oil leaks**		
Over 100,000	100	☐	Differential-pinion seal	5	☐
Over 150,000	200	☐	Valve-cover gaskets	10	☐
Engine			Timing-cover seal	15	☐
Major tuneup	5	☐	Engine main seals	25	☐
Camshaft	25	☐	Oil-pan gasket	25	☐
Timing chain	25	☐	**Exhaust**		
Valve job	25	☐	Muffler	5	☐
Carburetor	30	☐	Tailpipe	5	☐
Crankshaft/bearings	35	☐	Engine pipe	10	☐
Low oil pressure	50	☐	Exhaust manifold	10	☐
Rebuild	100	☐	Catalytic converter	25	☐
Brakes			**Electrical**		
Reline brakes	10	☐	Battery cables	5	☐
Calipers/cylinders	15	☐	Interior lights	5	☐
Master cylinder	15	☐	Signal lights	5	☐
Rotors/drums	15	☐	Alternator	10	☐
Steering/suspension			Battery	10	☐
Ball joints	10	☐	Starter	10	☐
Power-steering hoses	10	☐	Taillight lens	10	☐
Shock absorbers	10	☐	Wiper motor	10	☐
Steering linkage	10	☐	Radio	25	☐
Bushings	15	☐	Electric windows	30	☐
Power-steering pump	25	☐	Major wiring	75	☐
			Total points	—	

How it all adds up

Total points

0 to 20	Excellent value, may be worth more than top book value.
21 to 30	Good value, worth top book price.
31 to 75	Pretty good at trade-in price.
76 to 150	OK if body is clean and rust-free, and price makes cost of repair worthwhile.
151 to 375	Fair value, but only if price of car is a few hundred dollars less than book value minus cost of repair.
376 to 500	Poor value, risky to buy if you don't do most of your own major repairs. Price must be low even for experienced DIY to consider.
501 to 599	OK if you do your own major repairs and get car for less than ⅓ of book price. Otherwise, forget it.
600 and up	Do not accept this clunker, even as a gift from a little old lady who only drove it to church on Sunday.

spray. Fixing even the smallest scratch or dent takes time, and this means money. Also, remember that a cracked windshield will not pass inspection in many states.

Exhaust system. The entire exhaust system—from the engine to the tip of the tailpipe—should be checked. Rotted-out exhaust parts will soon need to be replaced. If there are any loud noises, find out where they are coming from. Don't overlook the possibility of a cracked exhaust manifold. Check to see that the catalytic converter hasn't been removed; it's a particularly costly item to replace.

When to rely on a pro. If you don't perform a cylinder power-balance test yourself, have one done by a professional mechanic. It tells you whether any cylinders have costly defects. Using an engine analyzer, a competent mechanic can determine whether the car is firing evenly on all cylinders, and can warn you of bad valves, low compression, carburetion problems, defective ignition wires, vacuum leaks, and a host of other conditions. A passing grade on the cylinder power-balance test is undoubtedly the most important element of your used-car check.

Your mechanic can also test the car's exhaust emissions. It's important to know that it will pass your state's emissions inspection. Flunking the test could mean fuel-system repairs that could wind up costing you hundreds of dollars.

Further information. Recently enacted regulations require dealers selling used cars to attach a sticker to each car stating the terms of any repair warranty that is included in the price of the vehicle. Look for this sticker; it also advises the buyer to have the car checked by an independent mechanic. The Federal Trade Commission (Box 37041, Washington, DC 20013) offers a guide to used-car warranties and mechanical inspections called "Used-Car Buying: A Checklist." It is available free from the commission.

Prices of used cars are listed in the "NADA Used Car Value Guide," which is available from the National Automobile Dealers' Association (NADA—8400 Westpark Dr., McLean, VA 22102-9985). A subscription costs $29 per year.

The federal government also maintains a toll-free hot line providing information on car models affected by safety recalls. The telephone number is 800-424-9393—*by Bob Cerullo. Drawings by Russell von Sauers and Tom Moore.*

what to know before you're towed

As I stepped from my car, a chill Manhattan wind smashed icy rain pellets against my cheek and carried snatches of an argument between an angry young woman and a tow-truck driver to my ear.

The woman had called for help for her disabled Datsun 280ZX. The tow truck that arrived was the typical sling-type wrecker. The shivering woman refused to allow the tow operator to hook up her Datsun. She hotly demanded a flatbed truck. Muttering angrily, the disgruntled driver sped off. Sensing a story, I offered the woman shelter in my car.

She told me that the Datsun had a cold-start problem and had been towed several times. Each time the wrecker had caused expensive dam-age to the car. First it was the fuel tank; then it was the rear fender; the third time the grille was demolished.

The woman's plight illustrates a growing problem: Newer cars are in-creasingly tough to tow without caus-ing damage. And it's no longer enough to rely on the tow operator's expertise. In this article I'll tell you why new towing methods have been sought, what the three most often used tow methods are, and what to look for in a damage-free tow.

The background

For many years, passenger-car towing was simply a matter of getting a solid hold on the car. A rugged steel tow bar was pressed against the bumper, and J-hooks on the ends of steel chains were attached to any solid parts of the suspension or chassis. The strong front and rear bumpers, beefy suspension designs, and body-on-frame chassis could easily stand up to the strain.

Today, the familiar rubber-sling towing system, generally known as a Holmes sling, is used by more than 90 percent of wreckers. And for older models and most of today's cars, it's an excellent way to lift and tow. But every year there are increasing num-bers of cars with soft, aerodynamic noses; sophisticated but delicate sus-pension designs; and lightweight chassis technology. These cars are tough to tow, even for the rubber-sling-equipped wreckers.

Experts from three domestic manu-

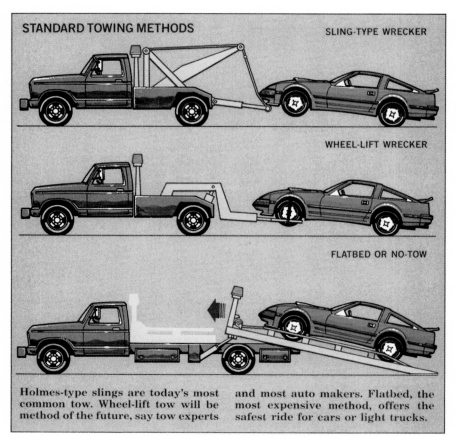

STANDARD TOWING METHODS

SLING-TYPE WRECKER

WHEEL-LIFT WRECKER

FLATBED OR NO-TOW

Holmes-type slings are today's most common tow. Wheel-lift tow will be method of the future, say tow experts and most auto makers. Flatbed, the most expensive method, offers the safest ride for cars or light trucks.

facturers gave me the impression that car makers are making the best of a bad situation. Although they claimed that most cars can still be towed with a sling-type rig, special wooden adapter blocks must be used, and the manufacturer's towing manual must be followed to the letter.

According to Gus VanderDonck, senior project coordinator at General Motors Service Research Center in Warren, Michigan, "The wheel-lift and the flatbed are the future. The sling is dying. There's no doubt in my mind about it. Cars don't have bumpers anymore; they have moldings."

The safe but intricate sling-and-chain hookups recommended by the American Automobile Association (AAA) and car makers are complicated and require special spacer blocks and tow beams. To find out whether operators in my area were using the all-important spacer blocks, I made a quick check of more than a dozen wreckers. Result: I didn't find a single set of the prescribed spacer blocks. Apparently, on the street, the chances of a towtruck driver using a maker's tow manual and all of the necessary

WHEEL-LIFT TOWING PROCEDURE

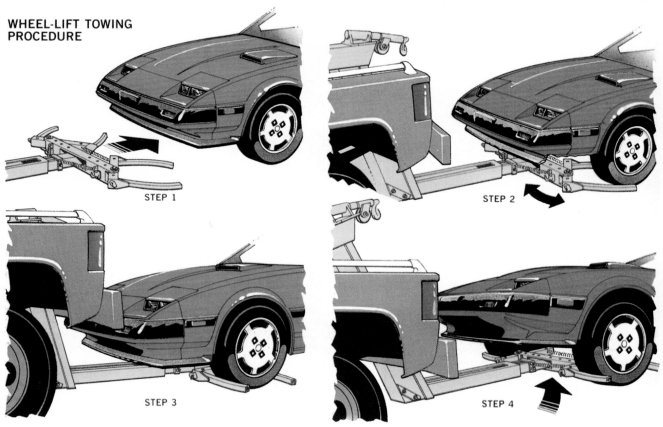

STEP 1

STEP 2

STEP 3

STEP 4

The wheel-lift wrecker backs up to the disabled car and lowers its "stinger" to within a few inches of the pavement (1). The driver then backs up farther, slipping the stinger's claws under the nose of the vehicle (2). The wrecker backs up gently, slipping the spring-loaded claws around the tires (3). The stinger then rises, lifting the car (4).

equipment are slim. Your best insurance against damage is to become an expert on towing your own car.

Slings and tows

If you have a new import or one of a growing number of domestics, the sling-type tow technique is probably inadequate for your car. One of the sling's main drawbacks is that either the front or rear wheels must remain on the ground during the tow. This is a problem when the wheels on the ground are the drive wheels because most makers recommend speed limits (as low as 30 mph) and distance limits (as short as 15 miles) to protect transmissions and differentials from damage. For long tows, the drive shaft on most cars must be disconnected.

A second type of car transport is the flatbed. As its name implies, this is a truck with a movable, flat steel deck, or bed. Hydraulic motors move the flat steel bed rearward and then tilt it to provide an inclined ramp. A winch hauls the vehicle onto the bed, which is then tilted back, leveled, and moved forward against the cab. Flatbeds are also known as roll-backs, tilt-beds, and no-tows.

This is one of the best methods of car transport. An important factor in its favor is that the entire vehicle rides on the bed, so there is no possibility of damaging transmissions or drive trains. The flatbed is also less prone to instability at higher speeds than is a wrecker.

But there are some problems for operators. First, flatbeds are longer and more difficult to maneuver, especially on narrow streets. Because of their height, they cannot be used inside most garages. And a car parked between two other cars is a more difficult job for a flatbed because the truck lacks the shorter wrecker's maneuverability and boom. Most tow-truck operators I polled said they charge more when the job requires a flatbed. The woman with the 280ZX, for example, paid $45 to be towed by a conventional wrecker. Later, she paid $90 to be hauled home from the same location by a flatbed.

A third type of wrecker is the wheel-lift. It tows a disabled vehicle by its front or rear wheels. Used in Europe for a few years, I've seen increasing numbers of them on the streets in the United States. The idea is not new. The Ernest Holmes Div. of Dover Corp. (2505 E. 43rd St., Chattanooga, TN 37407) developed a wheel-lift wrecker back in the 1930s. And many years later, in response to the introduction of delicate energy-absorbing bumpers, a Canadian firm, Vulcan Equipment Co. Ltd., promoted a revolutionary wheel-lift device called the Vulcan Cradle Snatcher. Today, almost every wrecker manufacturer offers some type of wheel-lift adapter for its existing sling-type wreckers—or even entire wreckers designed around the popular wheel-lift concept.

With the wheel-lift, there is no need for J-hooks, spacer blocks, crossbeams, or chains. The design also eliminates much of the need for operator expertise or tow manuals. Short of punching a hole in a tire, it's hard to make a mistake with the equipment. And the lifted weight of the vehicle is supported by its suspension, which also absorbs shocks from bumps and rough roads.

I recently had an opportunity to watch a wheel-lift wrecker with the Eagle Claw Self-Loading Wheelift System (American Wheelift Systems, 999 Serramonte Blvd., Colma, CA 94014) at work. It looks much different than the standard wrecker. There's no boom, cables, or hook. That means there's nothing to stop the wrecker from going into a low-ceiling garage. In place of the sling and boom there's a hefty square steel tube called a stinger.

I watched veteran tow-man Joel

Merksamer grab a vehicle in 12 seconds flat. And nothing touched the vehicle except the slender claws that cradled the two front tires. As a precaution, Merksamer attached two heavy nylon hold-down straps over the wheels to keep the tires from bouncing out of the claws' grip.

This method has many advantages, but, as with the sling-tow method, one set of wheels must remain on the ground. Naturally, all of the speed and distance cautions for automatic and manual transmissions still apply.

When you're hooked

Towing recommendations for your car can be found in the owner's manual in the glove compartment, but here are some general cautions. First, ask the operator to tow the vehicle with the drive wheels off the ground. Excessive towing speeds may damage both manual and automatic transmissions. If the vehicle must be towed on its drive wheels, make sure that the transmission is in neutral, that low speeds are maintained, and that the hand brake is released.

A high-speed or long-distance tow usually requires that the drive shaft be disconnected. Use either chalk or a crayon to index the drive shaft and companion flanges: That ensures proper alignment at reassembly. Improper shaft-to-flange alignment can result in severe vibration. To avoid disconnecting the drive shaft, many wrecker operators carry a small wheeled dolly that they insert under the vehicle's drive wheels.

If you have a car with a soft front or rear fascia, deflection may occur when the car is lifted. Don't panic. Most makers say that some deflection is normal. The plastic panel should return to its original shape without any scuffing or deformation.

If the vehicle is a rear-drive type and must be towed with its front wheels on the ground, don't rely on the ignition steering lock to secure the wheels in the straight-ahead position. The lock isn't strong enough to withstand the shock transmitted during a hard bounce. Special clamping devices are available for tow operators. Make sure the driver uses one.

General Motors recommends that towed vehicles be raised until the lifted wheels are a minimum of four inches from the ground to ensure adequate ground clearance. Care should also be taken to ensure adequate ground clearance at the opposite end of the vehicle. Remember the 280ZX's gas tank—*by Bob Cerullo. Drawings by Russell von Sauers.*

Cars that are tough to tow*

Make and model	Front	Rear
Alfa Romeo GTV6, Spider	W	S
Aston Martin Coupe, Vantage, Volante	W	W
Audi 5000	S	W
Bertone X1/9	W	S
BMW 318i, 325e, 635CSi	W	W
BMW 528e, 535i, 735i	S	W
Chrysler Fifth Avenue, Gran Fury	S	W
DeLorean	W	W
Dodge Challenger	S	W
Dodge Omni GLH, Shelby Charger, Conquest	W	S
Honda Civic	W	S
Honda Accord	S	W
Honda Prelude	W	W
Isuzu I-Mark	S	W
Jaguar XJS	W	S
Jeep Cherokee/Wagoneer, Sport Wagon	S	W
Mazda GLC	W	S
Mercedes-Benz 380SL	W	S
Mitsubishi Tredia, Cordia, Galant	W	S
Mitsubishi Mirage, Starion	W	W
Nissan Maxima (sedan, wagon), 2WD pickup	S	W
Peugeot 505 turbo gas/turbo diesel	W	S
Pininfarina Spider	S	W
Porsche (all)	W	W
Renault Alliance/Encore, Fuego	S	W
Rolls-Royce/Bentley	W	W
Saab 900S	S	W
Saab 900 turbo	W	W
Subaru GL & hatchback 2WDs, Brat 4WD	S	W
Subaru sedan & station wagon	W	W
Toyota Cressida, 4 Runner	S	W
Toyota MR2, Corolla	W	S
VW Vanagon	S	W
Volvo 740, 760	W	S

* Compiled from the AAA towing manual, this table includes only those vehicles that AAA research indicates require wheel-lift or flatbed towing for a damage-free tow; S: sling-type wrecker; W: wheel-lift or flatbed

troubleshooting oxygen sensors

Bud Robinson put his hand loosely over the carburetor of the idling engine. As the engine began to shake a bit more than previously, the digital voltmeter in Robinson's other hand read 0.8 volt. When he took his hand off the carburetor, the idle smoothed and the voltage reading dropped to 0.3 volt.

"See, when I make the gasoline mixture richer by restricting the air intake with my hand, almost one volt is produced," Robinson said. He did it again for effect—0.8 volt with his hand on the carb, 0.3 with it off. The veteran mechanic was demonstrating an oxygen sensor at work.

Oxygen sensors, a recent addition to automotive technology, have made a previously complicated task easier. Engineers can now design an engine that performs well without producing illegal amounts of harmful pollutants. Better yet, it will stay in tune for 50,000 miles or more with only minor maintenance. This is quite a change from the early 1970s, when primitive emissions controls resulted in engines that ran roughly no matter how carefully they were tuned.

Although an oxygen sensor looks like a spark plug, its function is entirely different. And unlike a spark plug, which is practically indestructible, oxygen sensors can be easily damaged by the wrong fuel or improper repairs. The result can be an engine that idles roughly, lacks power, pollutes the air, and uses too much fuel.

An oxygen sensor is also far more expensive than a spark plug—some cost up to $100—so it's not something to routinely replace as part of a tuneup. Yet the truth is that a lot of units are replaced unnecessarily. An understanding of how these sensors work and how you can keep them working properly—as well as how to tell if they *are* indeed working—will not only help keep the air we breathe clean, it will save you money.

Clean air and the O₂ sensor

Prior to the passage of clean-air laws during the 1960s and 1970s, automo-bile engines were designed with little regard for the pollution they caused. Today, however, the amount of by-products produced—specifically carbon monoxide (CO), hydrocarbons (HC), and oxides of nitrogen (NO_x)—is limited by law. Engineers, after trying out various ways to limit emissions, have settled on a strategy that first lowers the production of harmful gases, then converts the rest into less noxious compounds like water vapor and carbon dioxide.

The key was the catalytic converter, a muffler-shaped device that uses platinum, palladium, and other catalysts to oxidize and reduce harmful gases. Beginning in the mid-1970s, an oxidation catalyst was installed on some cars to oxidize hydrocarbons and CO into CO_2 and water vapor.

These catalysts did nothing to control NO_x emissions, however, so most cars produced since the 1981 model year have a more sophisticated three-way catalytic converter that can reduce oxides of nitrogen as well as oxidize HC and CO. One serious problem

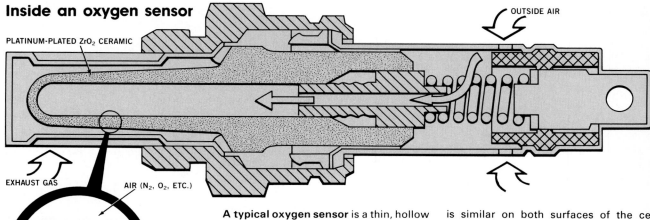

Inside an oxygen sensor

PLATINUM-PLATED ZrO₂ CERAMIC

OUTSIDE AIR

EXHAUST GAS

AIR (N₂, O₂, ETC.)

NEGATIVELY CHARGED OXYGEN IONS

PLATINUM ELECTRODES

EXHAUST GAS (HC, CO, ETC.)

A typical oxygen sensor is a thin, hollow finger of zirconium oxide ceramic, plated with platinum inside and out to form two electrodes. Hot exhaust gas flows over the outside of the sensor; fresh air enters the hollow center. Though solid, the ceramic conducts oxygen ions from one metal surface to the other. When the engine runs lean, there is oxygen in the exhaust gas, so the oxygen partial pressure is similar on both surfaces of the ceramic. When the mixture's rich, the amount of oxygen in the exhaust drops, and the difference in partial pressure is much greater. Negatively charged oxygen ions flow toward the outer surface of the sensor, creating a voltage difference across the electrodes. Sensor output is about 1 V when the mixture is rich, and nearly 0 V when it is lean.

Catalyst efficiency and sensor signal vs. air-fuel ratio

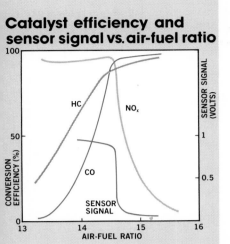

The switching point for an oxygen sensor is when the air-fuel ratio is optimal—which is also where the three-way catalyst is most efficient.

exists with a three-way converter, though. It cleans all three pollutants efficiently only when the air-and-fuel mixture being burned by the engine is at a specific ratio. This point occurs when there is just enough oxygen present to allow for the complete combustion of gasoline—when 14.6 parts of air are supplied to one part gasoline.

An engine can run smoothly over a range of air-fuel mixtures, explained Carlos Barrera, an engineer who designs oxygen sensors at Ford. "The reason for operating at 14.6:1 is not because engine designers like that point. Rather, the catalyst itself is most efficient there."

Because the engine must always operate at the optimal air-fuel ratio, some method is needed for fine-tuning the mixture to compensate for changes in speed, load, fuel quality, and such. "It so happens that an oxygen sensor operates at this optimal ratio, too, so it's a perfect mate for the catalytic converter," Barrera said.

How oxygen sensors work

Barrera explained that an oxygen sensor generates about one volt across its electrodes when the mixture is too rich and there is insufficient oxygen for complete combustion. If the engine is running lean, voltage output drops to nearly zero (see cutaway and caption). This switching point occurs at the optimal air-fuel ratio, and it occurs very abruptly. The on-off signal created as the mixture crosses from rich to lean is a language understood perfectly by computers: The ox-

ygen sensor generates a digital signal.

Ford and other car makers use an oxygen sensor to tell the engine control computer when the mixture is too rich or lean for maximum catalytic-converter efficiency. The mixture is then adjusted by changing the amount of fuel delivered by the carburetor or fuel injectors. If the mixture is too rich, it's made slightly leaner; too lean, and it's adjusted back the other way. This constant fine-tuning keeps the mixture close to the sensor's switching point, which keeps it close to the best air-fuel ratio.

The oxygen sensor, the key component in this feedback loop, is easily spotted in the engine compartment of your car. It's mounted in the exhaust manifold, usually as close as possible to the engine. As previously noted, it resembles a spark plug. Unlike a spark plug, it can have one, two, or three wires attached to it, depending on its design.

A typical sensor used by Chrysler, Ford, General Motors, and European and Japanese imports has only one wire attached. This is its link to the computer. Like most electrical components, the sensor is grounded through the metal manifold and engine block, although some GM sensors have a separate ground wire. A few have three wires, two of which are for a small electric heater.

Like some people, an oxygen sensor doesn't function well when it's cold. Exhaust gas needs to heat it to about 350°C before it produces a reliable signal. That's why an oxygen sensor is mounted close to the engine, where gases are hottest. That's also why the sensor may have a built-in heater to keep it at the ideal operating temperature of about 700°C.

What can go wrong?

An oxygen sensor usually doesn't require routine maintenance. And because it's an emissions-control component, a sensor is guaranteed for five years or 50,000 miles by the manufacturer, provided you service the car according to the maker's recommendations. (Some cars, mostly European, do require a sensor change before they log 50,000 miles. Be sure to check your owner's manual.)

"If you treat a sensor with a little care, it will work fine," said Mark McMackin, product engineer for oxygen sensors at Chrysler. A sensor of recent design should last the life of a moderately driven car, added McMackin. Still, physical abuse, neglect of other engine components, using the wrong fuel or lubricant, or just plain bad luck can relegate an otherwise-

good sensor to the trash.

Physical abuse is easy to prevent. When working under the hood, be careful not to hit the sensor with a wrench or pry bar. Although ceramic is extremely hard, it's also brittle—and a sharp blow will crack it. Also, don't spray the sensor with undercoating, rustproofing, or solvent, which can block the flow of outside air to the inside of the sensor. This can change the calibration because the reference air is blocked or can cause the sensor to fail entirely. Leaking engine oil, brake fluid, or power-steering oil can have the same effect.

Sensor poisoning by lead or silicon is much harder to guard against. It's invisible, and can result from the inadvertent use of the wrong fuel or other chemicals.

"Be careful that you buy gasoline from a reputable retailer," warned Bruce Holleboom, a development engineer for the AC Spark Plug Division of GM. "It's more likely that you will have a problem with an oxygen sensor due to poisoning by bad gasoline than for any other reason."

Lead and silicon are the contaminants in gasoline that cause the most problems. The effects of poisoning vary from slight shifts in the engine's air-fuel ratio to complete failure of the sensor. Slight poisoning may go unnoticed by a car owner. It's only in extreme cases—when the sensor is severely poisoned or fails entirely, for example—that fuel economy or drivability deteriorates to the point where it's noticed by the driver or the "check engine" light flashes on.

Aside from deliberate misfueling by the owner, lead can end up in a car because the gas station is pumping leaded fuel in place of more expensive unleaded. Such practices are illegal but may be difficult for a driver to detect. Sometimes independent operators are innocent: They buy fuel from wholesalers and are unaware of its chemical composition. And, occasionally, fuel is accidentally mislabeled or contaminated during handling.

Whatever the reason for misfueling, the results are the same. Lead deposits coat the oxygen sensor, eventually causing it to fail. How long it takes for performance to be adversely affected depends on the specific engine and its operating conditions.

The harder the engine has to work, the higher the engine exhaust temperature. If leaded fuel is added at temperatures above 900°C, "it's like coating the sensor with a high-temperature varnish," said Holleboom. This permanently blocks the flow of ions between the two surfaces of the sensor; replacement of the sensor is the only cure. Worse, if the car still has leaded gas in the tank, it's possible that the new sensor will also be poisoned.

Oxygen sensors exposed to less hellish conditions can survive several thousand miles of lead contamination. A sensor that hasn't failed can return to normal operation after just one tank of genuine unleaded fuel is used, because the deposits will burn off the exhaust side of the sensor. "A Detroit-area police department provided a classic example," Holleboom said. "Suddenly, patrol cars couldn't go fast enough to catch speeders. But by the time troubleshooters arrived, tickets were again being issued. I think that a new batch of unleaded fuel delivered to the fleet garage had helped restore law and order."

Similar poisoning is caused by silica, the combustion by-product of silicon compounds. Gasoline and RTV (room temperature vulcanizing) engine gasketing material are the two main sources of silicon poisoning.

There is little you can do to guard against silicon in gasoline except to buy from a reputable dealer. If the fuel is contaminated, you won't know it until your engine starts hesitating or missing. In extreme cases, replacing the sensor is the only cure; baked-on silica coats the sensor as if it had been dipped in molten glass.

Servicing is one area where you have more control. RTV is the familiar silicon-based gasket in a tube used by auto makers, service technicians, and backyard mechanics. RTV gaskets are used on engine valve covers, oil pans, and intake manifolds.

Using the wrong RTV during repairs can cause severe sensor poisoning, as the silicon finds its way into the intake manifold and is burned in the engine. Worse still, the engine will poison one sensor after another until the RTV is removed. RTV that's safe for use on engines equipped with oxygen sensors should so state. Check the package.

Even with compounds safe for use with oxygen sensors, apply the material carefully. Don't get sloppy, and don't use more than you need. Also beware of solvents or cleaners containing silicon. Don't use them anywhere they might be drawn into the engine or fuel system.

Diagnosing a bad sensor

Misdiagnosing oxygen-sensor problems is common when working with computer-controlled engines. In fact, misdiagnosis was cited by every manufacturer I interviewed as the number-one reason for sensor replacement. "Most of our returns from the field are the result of diagnostic problems, rather than sensor failure," said McMackin.

This hasn't been a major expense for consumers to date, as most of the sensors replaced were on 1981 and later models and were therefore covered by the five-year, 50,000-mile emissions-system warranty. But oxygen sensors could become an expensive repair item as warranties expire and car owners begin paying for replacements. Care is needed if you are repairing your own car, and skepticism is called for if a mechanic asks you to pay for a replacement sensor.

Unnecessary replacements occur, in part, because of the closed-loop design of engine control systems. "The oxygen sensor is the last thing in the line," said McMackin. "Every other component in the system is in front of it."

For instance, if the fuel injectors are supplying too much fuel, the oxygen-sensor signal won't cycle properly, said McMackin. "People who blame the sensor are like kings who kill the messenger for bringing bad news."

So the tricky part of diagnosing a sensor is separating cause from effect. Good electrical connections, outside air for the reference side of the sensor, and a high-enough exhaust temperature are prerequisites for the switching action. And many problems can develop in an engine control system that can alter the mixture enough to prevent the oxygen sensor from switching. A methodical approach and a good service manual are called for here.

The most common diagnostic sequence involves hooking a voltmeter or dwell meter to a special connector under the hood, then watching for changes as the engine is forced to run lean, then rich. This not only tests the sensor, but the wiring and computer as well. Such procedures are simpler than they sound if you make sure and follow the detailed sequence in a factory service manual.

Ford and some other car makers approve of checking sensor output directly by attaching a digital voltmeter (one with an input impedance of 10 megohms or greater) to the sensor lead. But you run the risk of damaging the sensor if you use the improper voltmeter or try to check its resistance. And you still need to know the proper way to force the engine to run rich, then lean, to check output voltage. Otherwise you may overheat the catalytic converter. Again, I recommend reaching for a service manual that covers your make and model.

Finally, remember that given good fuel and proper engine maintenance, the oxygen sensor should be about the last thing to check when an engine is running poorly. Just because it's easy to remove and looks like a spark plug doesn't make it a candidate for the trash can—*by Kenneth Zino. Drawings by Russell von Sauers*

Typical fuel injection

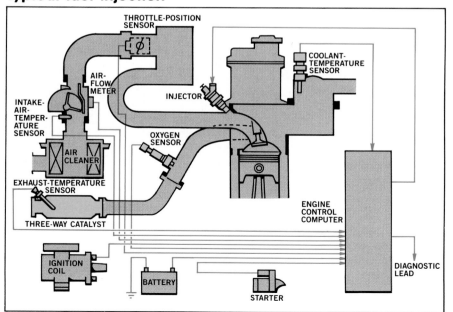

By combining feedback from the oxygen sensor with information from other sensors on the engine, a small computer can adjust the air-fuel mixture to keep the engine running smoothly and exhaust emissions at a low level.

troubleshooting short circuits

First I replaced the battery, then I replaced the alternator. But the battery still goes dead every few days. I give up." Obviously frustrated at his failure to solve the problem after several hours of effort—and quite a few dollars of expense—this car owner had put his pride in his pocket and brought his car to my service garage in Brooklyn, New York.

Raising the car's hood, I asked the driver to describe the symptoms of the problem. "The car starts fine with a boost, or immediately after a battery charge. Then it runs well," he replied. "But if I don't drive it for a few days, the battery goes dead again."

I wish I had a dime for every perfectly good part that is replaced simply because the owner suspects it might be defective, I thought to myself. "The key to success in electrical-circuit repairs is never to assume anything," I explained. "The discharged battery could be caused by a slipping alternator belt, a bad regulator, a loose wire, dirty battery connections, current drain from a defective switch, or any one of a dozen other faults.

"We'll find the problem by methodically running down the list of possibilities," I said. "Without even touching a voltmeter, we already know a few things about the situation. Because the alternator and battery are new, it's safe to assume they are all right.

"My guess is that you may have an unwanted ground, or current drain," I ventured, pulling the cable loose from the positive battery terminal. I clipped the lead of a 12-volt test lamp to the unattached battery cable and touched the probe to the terminal. The light bulb glowed.

"It is a drain," I announced. "Now all we have to do is find the bad circuit." I opened the fuse box and started at one end of the row, removing a fuse labeled "taillight." The

DRAWING BY ROY DOTY

light still glowed, so I replaced the fuse. Then I removed the second fuse from a receptacle marked "dome/trunk." The test light went out. Not bad. On the second try, after less than five minutes of work, we had found the circuit that was causing the current drain.

The next step took a few minutes longer to complete. Searching through my shelf of service manuals, I found an electrical schematic that matched the customer's make and model of car.

"Do your dome light and cigarette lighter work all right?" I inquired. "They've never caused any trouble," the customer answered.

"Then let's have a look in the trunk." I reconnected the battery, then folded the sedan's rear seat forward and peered behind it. The trunk light was glowing brightly, permanently connected to the battery by a switch stuck in the "on" position. "We found the drain," I proclaimed. The customer seemed overjoyed that a new trunk-light switch would cure the dead-battery problem.

Beginners welcome

Problems like the one above can be difficult—and expensive—to diagnose if you don't have a grasp of the basics of electrical troubleshooting. But armed with a modest kit of diagnostic tools, a shop manual, a few basic techniques, and a measure of patience, the weekend mechanic can do as good a job of automotive electrical repair as many professionals.

And this is a category of repairs where learning how to do the work yourself can save a sizable service bill; not all troubleshooting goes as quickly as the previous example, so a simple but elusive electrical problem can run up a hefty tab. Besides the money-saving aspect, the low voltage involved probably makes tracing electrical problems one of the safest repair jobs you can perform.

Just be careful with the secondary wiring—the heavy high-voltage cable that connects the coil and spark plugs. And when working on late-model cars with electronic engine controls, make sure you follow the procedures in the factory service manual

ELECTRICAL SYMBOLS

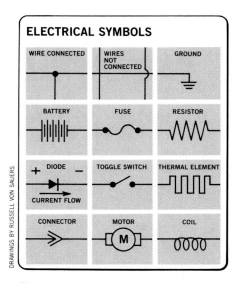

WIRE CONNECTED	WIRES NOT CONNECTED	GROUND
BATTERY	FUSE	RESISTOR
DIODE	TOGGLE SWITCH	THERMAL ELEMENT
CURRENT FLOW		
CONNECTOR	MOTOR	COIL

DRAWINGS BY RUSSELL VON SAUERS

These symbols describe the components found on wiring diagrams.

when you perform any tests on the control module or its sensors and wiring. Mistakes here can damage or destroy expensive components.

Whether confronted with instrument-panel lights that flicker or fuses that blow, you won't have much chance of finding the problem if you don't understand the circuit you're working on. So the place to start isn't under the hood, it's in the schematic wiring diagram for the car. The best schematic is one drawn specifically for your make and model car. These are available from the car maker or in auto-repair manuals sold in auto supply and book stores.

The schematic diagram is your road map through a maze of thousands of wires. As with any road map, you have to know where you are and how to read the symbols. (The legend identifies most of the commonly used symbols.)

The schematic also tells you what powers the component you are checking, and which other components share the same circuit. Your starting point on the schematic should be the battery. Next locate the questionable component. Then trace the route the current takes from the battery to the failed part. Sometimes it can be helpful to highlight the circuit you are working on with a colored felt-tip pen.

You will often find the component shares its wiring and fuse with some other seemingly unrelated part. A good example of this is an instrument-lamp circuit that shares a fuse with the license-plate lamp. In this case, when the wire to the license-plate lamp is shorted, the fuse blows, causing the instrument-panel lamps to go

out as well. Without the schematic to explain it, a connection like this would probably remain a mystery.

Troubleshooting tools

The most basic of these tools is the test lamp. When it glows, you know there is power present in a circuit. You can make a test lamp from a 12-volt taillight bulb and socket with leads and gator clips attached. But you may also want to buy a ready-made light from an auto-parts store. This type usually puts the bulb inside the plastic handle for protection, and its sharp metal tip allows you to probe for current by gently piercing the insulation of a wire.

A battery-powered test lamp is another tool that makes testing isolated circuits for continuity quick and easy. You'll also need an assortment of jumper wires with alligator clips at each end. Use these to bypass dead circuits and to directly connect motors, etc. to the battery for testing. You can save yourself a great deal of grief if you buy a few five-ampere in-line fuse assemblies (available at radio-supply stores) and splice them into your jumper wires. This way the jumper-wire fuse will blow before you can cause damage to most circuits, should you happen to hit the wrong wire.

Cutting pliers, wire strippers, screwdrivers, and electrical tape should also be a part of your basic toolbox. Another important item is a supply of adhesive labels to identify anonymous-looking wires before you forget where they belong. 3M Company makes handy numbered labels for this purpose. Finally, a volt-ohm-

Is there current in the circuit?

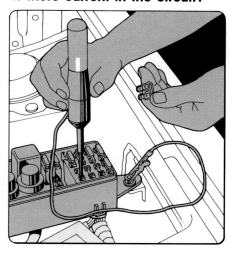

Current reaching the fuse receptacle from the car's battery illuminates the grounded test light. So far so good.

What's draining the battery?

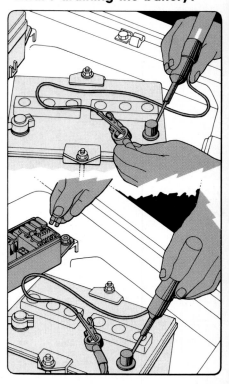

The test light connecting the battery terminal with the disconnected cable clamp glows, indicating a current drain. When the fuse for the offending circuit is pulled, the test light will go out. Check them all, one at a time.

meter, or multimeter, is useful for several tests.

Checking for Current

When a component—the heater blower, for example—doesn't work, the first thing to do is check the fuse for that circuit. If the fuse is OK, the next step is to check for power at the switch that controls the component. Attach one lead of a test light to the heater-blower side of the switch, and ground the other lead. If the light doesn't illuminate, it's time to work backward toward the battery, looking for the place the break occurs.

Make a step-by-step check for voltage between the battery and the switch. Start by removing the fuse and connecting one lead of a test light to the battery side of the fuse socket. When you ground the other lead to the car body, the light will glow if power is reaching the fuse block. If there is no power at the fuse, you know the problem lies somewhere between the battery and the fuse block. If you find you have power at the fuse, start tracing the circuit in the

Does voltage drop across connectors?

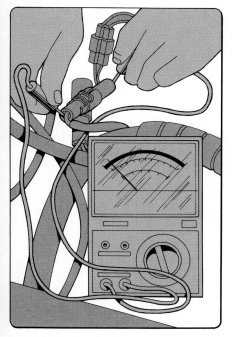

The voltmeter leads tap the wires on either side of the connector. A drop of more than 1 V indicates trouble.

other direction, using the schematic as a guide. At every connector along the way, check for voltage with the test light. If you find a point where the light doesn't illuminate, you know there's an open or shorted circuit somewhere in the section of wire leading to that point.

What if there is power at the blower switch? The test light should glow intermittently when you work the switch back and forth. Now you know the problem is occurring still farther along the circuit.

When the test lamp indicates current at the connection closest to the motor, the motor itself becomes suspect. The first thing to check is the condition of the motor's ground. Often the motor grounds to the car body through its mounting bolts. (This is also common with horns, wiper motors, and so on.) If there isn't a clean connection here, the circuit remains open. By connecting a jumper wire from the motor to a known good ground point, you can answer this question. If the motor runs, the bad ground is the culprit.

Finally, before you start to remove the motor, give it one last chance. Use a jumper wire to connect it directly to the battery. If it's still silent, replace it. If it runs, you missed something along the way.

Detecting a Current Drain

If a car's battery goes dead when the vehicle isn't driven for a few days, it is possible that the battery is simply worn out and won't hold a charge. But if the battery is in good condition, it's likely there is a current drain somewhere. There's a quick and easy test for current drain that requires only a test light.

Remove the positive cable from the battery. Then touch one lead of the test lamp to the battery terminal and the other lead to the disconnected cable clamp. If the lamp illuminates when all the accessories in the car are shut off, this indicates a current drain. A pointer: When performing this test, beware of electric clocks. If the car has one, temporarily remove its fuse to get a reliable reading with the test lamp. (Note: Some cars have computer control circuits that remain continuously energized. In most cases, these chips draw too little current to affect a test-light reading.)

By removing and replacing the

Where's the short circuit?

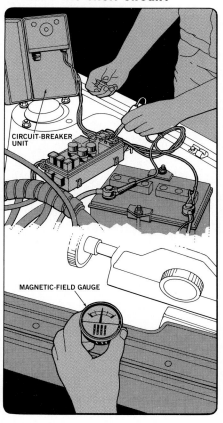

CIRCUIT-BREAKER UNIT

MAGNETIC-FIELD GAUGE

Short-circuit finder's circuit-breaker unit connects to the car battery. It sends a pulsing charge through the circuit from the fuse block. The gauge's needle stops oscillating when it locates a short circuit inside the rocker panel.

fuses one by one as I did for my customer, and repeating this test until the test light goes out, you can isolate the circuit where the drain is occurring. Just think of all the fruitless wire-chasing this eliminates.

Checking for Voltage Drop

Using a voltmeter, you can perform a voltage-drop test that will tell you whether a loose or dirty connection is raising the resistance of a circuit. This is also an alternative method of diagnosing a malfunctioning switch.

Connect the voltmeter's positive lead to the side of the connector or switch that leads to the battery. The negative lead is attached to the other side of the component. If voltage drop across the component reads more than one volt, resistance is probably too high. The most common cause is a connection that is dirty or oxidized.

Short-circuit Detector

Finding a short circuit in a wire that runs through a plastic conduit, behind a trim panel, or under a carpet can be a time-consuming nightmare. A clever short-circuit finder called Shortell is available from Kent-Moore Tool Group (Sealed Power Corp., 29784 Little Mack, Roseville, MI 48066-2298; catalog No. BT 8034-A; about $70). This tool makes the job a lot easier.

Shortell uses a circuit breaker powered by the car's battery that sends pulses of current through a lead connected to an individual fuse socket. If there is a short in that particular circuit, the pulsing current sets up an intermittent magnetic field that can be readily detected with a small handheld meter.

As you move the meter along the area containing the wire, its needle deflects with the pulses. When you arrive at the point of the short circuit where the pulses of current escape to ground, the needle stops moving. Then you know exactly where to begin excavating. This device can save hours of needlessly tearing up the body and interior, as well as reducing the possibility of creating new electrical problems while trying to fix the original fault.

A last word: Don't replace an electrical component unless you are sure it is defective. If, for example, you believe you have removed a defective motor, take the time to attach it to the battery with two jumper wires to make sure the motor is really dead—*by Bob Cerullo. Drawings by Roy Doty and Russell von Sauers.*

quick-change modules and portable radials

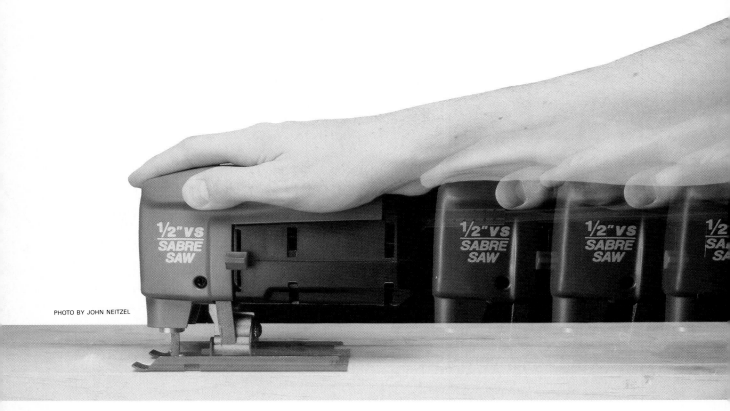

PHOTO BY JOHN NEITZEL

modulars that make sense

It's an idea whose time has finally come: a modular tool system that lets you clip a variety of work heads onto a single power pack so you can tote a portable shop to any job in a compact case. You avoid a tangle of power cords, and because you'd only use one portable at a time anyway, why should you buy a motor for each?

The concept isn't new—manufacturers have previously brought forth modular tool systems, only to drop them later. But now two widely different sources are offering cleverly designed clip-together modulars that make real sense: The system pictured on the facing page comes from West Germany's Kress, while the one on the following page is sold by Sears.

Each system has a red-tipped lock lever on the double-insulated power pack that clips it, in turn, to drill, sander, and sabre-saw heads. But beyond that, the systems differ dramatically. The Sears is lighter weight: The ¼-hp, 2.5-amp power pack weighs 1½ pounds and has a six-foot cord. Kress offers a 1-hp, 4.9-amp power pack that weighs three pounds and trails a 9½-foot cord.

And the two systems have very different switching: The variable-speed, lockable (but not reversible) switch for the Kress system is built into the power-pack handle. In the Sears system, each tool head has its own switch; different trigger linkages provide reversibility and speed variation only where appropriate.

In the Kress system, the hand posi-

tions sometimes required by the way the power pack attaches to the tool heads take some getting used to, especially on the drill, where the handgrip seems upside-down.

In working with both systems, I'm impressed with performance—comparable to dedicated tools of the same power size. The ease of convertibility is what makes both systems viable. Changing from one head to another involves no hand tools—the lock-un-

lock device is built in.

Light-duty work around the home? I'd choose the Sears system—for elegant design and easy handling. But you don't have the option of adding that nifty 6-inch circular saw or grinder-polisher . . . at least not yet—*by Al Lees.*

Kress Tools of America (1698) Post Rd. E., Westport, CT 06880) packages three tools plus power pack (shown at top, mounted on the orbital sander) for $125; drill head and sabre saw (below) are included. Angle grinder-polisher and circular saw are extra, at $40 and $50. The Sears system, next page, has the same basic trio (power pack is here shown on sabre saw, with pad sander and drill heads below). Each unit is about $20 at Sears—all four in a fitted pouch are $85.

PHOTO BY JOHN NEITZEL

Lightweight Sears system , above, includes the same basic components offered by its German counterparts.

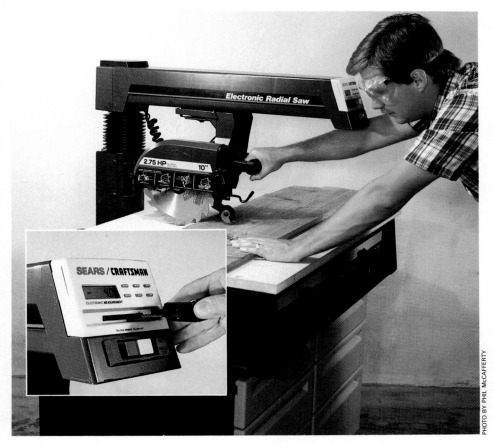

redesigned radials

You don't need to have Arnold Schwarzenegger's muscles to carry Ryobi's new radial-arm saw. It's a 53-pound bench-top model.

The saw, called the RPM 200, is also a space saver: It stores out of the way when not in use. And it's easy to transport to a job site (though the first radial to make that claim was Black & Decker's 65-pound *folding* saw).

I made a nodding acquaintance with the RPM 200 at a press conference but could not get one for testing. "There are only two in the country, and we just can't spare one now," a Ryobi staffer explained.

The tool has a solid feel and a look of quality. The 11-amp (2-hp) motor drives the 8¼-inch blade at 5,000 rpm. Depth of cut at 90 degrees is three inches; at 45 degrees it's 1¾ inches. Crosscut capacity is 15¾ inches; rip capacity: 17¾ inches. An 18,500-rpm accessory spindle takes router bits, sanding drums, and mold-

PHOTO BY PHIL McCAFFERTY

ing heads. Dimensions: 20½ by 27½ by 17 inches (minimum height). Ryobi (1158 Tower Lane, Bensenville, IL 60106) suggests a selling price of $299.

User-designed radial

"Give me a more stable cutting platform."

"I'd like the controls up front, fewer levers and cranks, and more mobility."

These are some of the comments Sears heard in a coast-to-coast survey of radial-arm-saw users, the starting point for a complete redesign of the company's radial saws—the first since 1962.

Heeding the comments, Sears made prototypes, had them field-tested, then subjected the final designs to abuse in the test lab. The result: three new electronic radials and three manuals that, depending on the model, deliver the most-wanted features—and more. I tested the top-of-the-line electronic saw in my shop. It is tagged at $470; the others range down to $280.

All are 10-inch saws with 26-inch rip and 15½-inch crosscut capacities; they cut three-inch material at 90 degrees and 2¼-inch material at 45 degrees. The smooth-running 1½-hp induction motor is said to develop 2½ hp on the three lower priced saws, and 2¾ hp on the top three. The saw I tested handled everything I fed it.

On all of these new saws, you elevate the arm via a folding crank mounted at the front of the base. (Users reported that they wanted more control returned to them, even on electronic models.) Two adjacent toggle levers clamp the fence. Lifting and returning one of four levers unlocks, stops, and locks the rip, miter, bevel, and motor-swivel movement.

On the electronic saws, an LCD readout on the front of the arm (see inset photo) tells you the blade height (from work table or workpiece), arm-angle readout (left or right), and rip-width readout (for in or out rips). Rip and elevation positions are displayed in 0.01-inch increments; bevel and miter angles in 0.5 degree. I checked the claimed accuracy with a dial indi-

cator and precision protractor. They are honest.

I found the system, which can be zeroed wherever you wish, really speeded up and improved the accuracy of my sawing, dadoing, and hole boring. The memory and LCD readout are battery powered. That means the machine doesn't dump its memory should the power fail. The display shuts off automatically if you forget.

The table is 44 inches wide—four inches wider than most. And it's two inches shorter than on older Sears radials. The base cabinet is stable and has six steel drawers with molded plastic fronts. Other models have drawers and a door, just doors, or a shelf. Even the low-end saw with just legs has been reinforced to be rock solid. The saw I tried moved around with the agility of a kid on a skateboard, thanks to excellent hidden casters, and jacks that lock down with a tap of the toe. The saws, except for their electronic control modules, are American-made—*by Phil McCafferty. Photos by John Neitzel, Mike Kelly, and Phil McCafferty.*

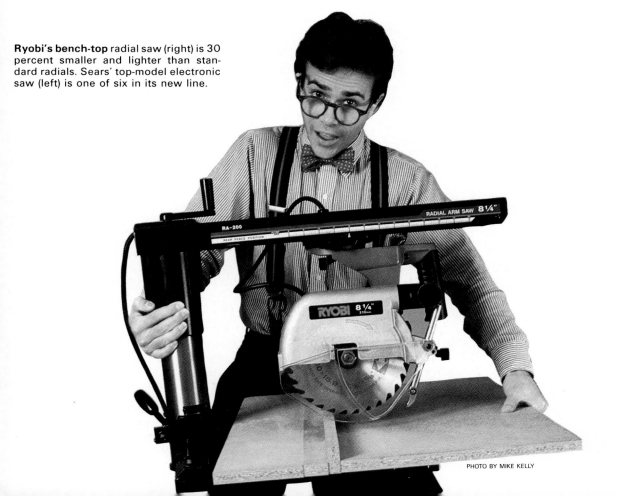

Ryobi's bench-top radial saw (right) is 30 percent smaller and lighter than standard radials. Sears' top-model electronic saw (left) is one of six in its new line.

PHOTO BY MIKE KELLY

power miter saws

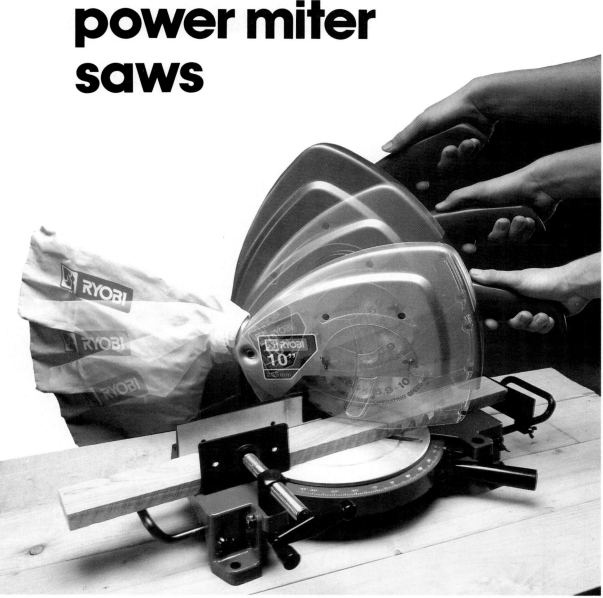

PHOTO BY GREG SHARKO

Zip. A perfect crosscut. Zip. Zip. Two perfect miters. The work of a pro? No. The work of a new tool called a power miter saw. It looks like a circular saw mounted on a short-legged table. But it performs like no other saw you've ever used.

A power miter saw is designed for accurate cross-cutting and mitering on jobs as varied as construction framing and cabinetmaking. Compared with a radial-arm or table saw, a power miter is faster to set up and much more accurate. That's critical when you put two or more corners together: If they aren't perfectly cut (even a ¼-degree error is bad), you have a poor project. And a power miter saw is handier than a table or radial-arm saw: You can't take the totable tool to the job site.

Throw away your table saw? Not yet. Power miters aren't designed to make large crosscuts, and they won't rip stock. But what they do, they do exceedingly well, as I quickly learned after trying several of the newest models. Here's why:

Stock chopper

All power miter saws work much the same way. The saw head is attached to the back of a turntable; the table and head swivel to the desired angle while the stock is held against a rear fence. (Positive detents are provided for common angle settings.) The head is spring loaded—and works like a paper cutter. To make a cut, you pull down the head by its handle and chop the stock in two.

Compared with a table saw, a power miter is more accurate because the work is stationary. And compared with a

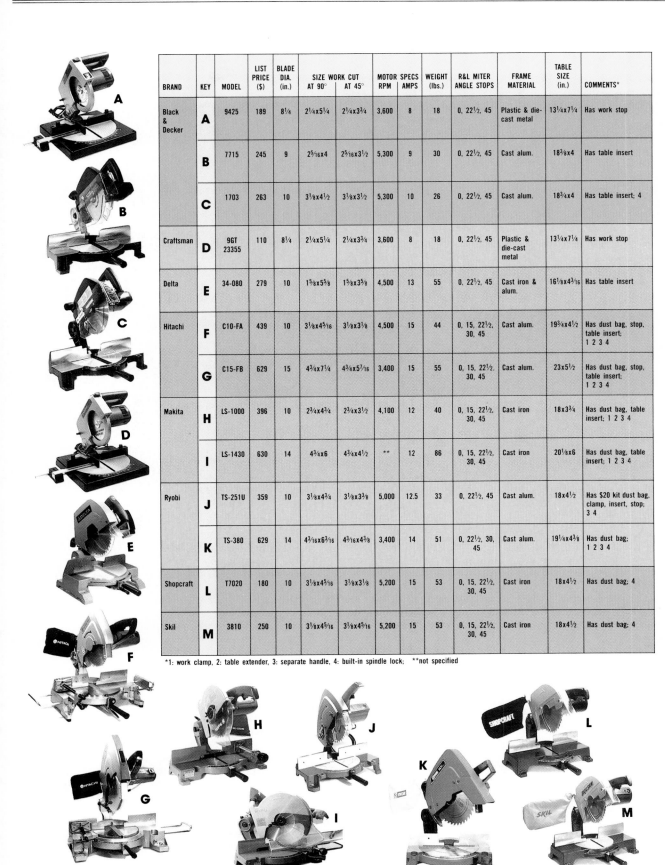

BRAND	KEY	MODEL	LIST PRICE ($)	BLADE DIA. (in.)	SIZE WORK CUT AT 90°	SIZE WORK CUT AT 45°	MOTOR SPECS RPM	AMPS	WEIGHT (lbs.)	R&L MITER ANGLE STOPS	FRAME MATERIAL	TABLE SIZE (in.)	COMMENTS*
Black & Decker	A	9425	189	$8\frac{1}{4}$	$2\frac{1}{4}$x$5\frac{1}{4}$	$2\frac{1}{4}$x$3\frac{3}{4}$	3,600	8	18	0, $22\frac{1}{2}$, 45	Plastic & die-cast metal	$13\frac{1}{4}$x$7\frac{1}{4}$	Has work stop
	B	7715	245	9	$2\frac{5}{16}$x4	$2\frac{5}{16}$x$3\frac{1}{2}$	5,300	9	30	0, $22\frac{1}{2}$, 45	Cast alum.	$18\frac{3}{8}$x4	Has table insert
	C	1703	263	10	$3\frac{1}{8}$x$4\frac{1}{2}$	$3\frac{1}{8}$x$3\frac{1}{2}$	5,300	10	26	0, $22\frac{1}{2}$, 45	Cast alum.	$18\frac{3}{4}$x4	Has table insert; 4
Craftsman	D	9GT 23355	110	$8\frac{1}{4}$	$2\frac{1}{4}$x$5\frac{1}{4}$	$2\frac{1}{4}$x$3\frac{3}{4}$	3,600	8	18	0, $22\frac{1}{2}$, 45	Plastic & die-cast metal	$13\frac{1}{4}$x$7\frac{1}{4}$	Has work stop
Delta	E	34-080	279	10	$1\frac{5}{8}$x$5\frac{5}{8}$	$1\frac{5}{8}$x$3\frac{5}{8}$	4,500	13	55	0, $22\frac{1}{2}$, 45	Cast iron & alum.	$16\frac{1}{8}$x$4\frac{3}{16}$	Has table insert
Hitachi	F	C10-FA	439	10	$3\frac{1}{8}$x$4\frac{5}{16}$	$3\frac{1}{8}$x$3\frac{1}{8}$	4,500	15	44	0, 15, $22\frac{1}{2}$, 30, 45	Cast alum.	$19\frac{3}{4}$x$4\frac{1}{2}$	Has dust bag, stop, table insert; 1 2 3 4
	G	C15-FB	629	15	$4\frac{3}{4}$x$7\frac{1}{4}$	$4\frac{3}{4}$x$5\frac{7}{16}$	3,400	15	55	0, 15, $22\frac{1}{2}$, 30, 45	Cast alum.	23x$5\frac{1}{2}$	Has dust bag, stop, table insert; 1 2 3 4
Makita	H	LS-1000	396	10	$2\frac{3}{4}$x$4\frac{3}{4}$	$2\frac{3}{4}$x$3\frac{1}{2}$	4,100	12	40	0, 15, $22\frac{1}{2}$, 30, 45	Cast iron	18x$3\frac{3}{4}$	Has dust bag, table insert; 1 2 3 4
	I	LS-1430	630	14	$4\frac{3}{4}$x6	$4\frac{3}{4}$x$4\frac{1}{2}$	**	12	86	0, 15, $22\frac{1}{2}$, 30, 45	Cast iron	$20\frac{1}{8}$x6	Has dust bag, table insert; 1 2 3 4
Ryobi	J	TS-251U	359	10	$3\frac{1}{8}$x$4\frac{3}{4}$	$3\frac{1}{8}$x$3\frac{3}{8}$	5,000	12.5	33	0, $22\frac{1}{2}$, 45	Cast alum.	18x$4\frac{1}{2}$	Has $20 kit dust bag, clamp, insert, stop; 3 4
	K	TS-380	629	14	$4\frac{3}{16}$x$6\frac{3}{16}$	$4\frac{3}{16}$x$4\frac{3}{8}$	3,400	14	51	0, $22\frac{1}{2}$, 30, 45	Cast alum.	$19\frac{1}{4}$x$4\frac{3}{8}$	Has dust bag; 1 2 3 4
Shopcraft	L	T7020	180	10	$3\frac{1}{8}$x$4\frac{5}{16}$	$3\frac{1}{8}$x$3\frac{1}{8}$	5,200	15	53	0, 15, $22\frac{1}{2}$, 30, 45	Cast iron	18x$4\frac{1}{2}$	Has dust bag; 4
Skil	M	3810	250	10	$3\frac{1}{8}$x$4\frac{5}{16}$	$3\frac{1}{8}$x$4\frac{5}{16}$	5,200	15	53	0, 15, $22\frac{1}{2}$, 30, 45	Cast iron	18x$4\frac{1}{2}$	Has dust bag; 4

*1: work clamp, 2: table extender, 3: separate handle, 4: built-in spindle lock;   **not specified

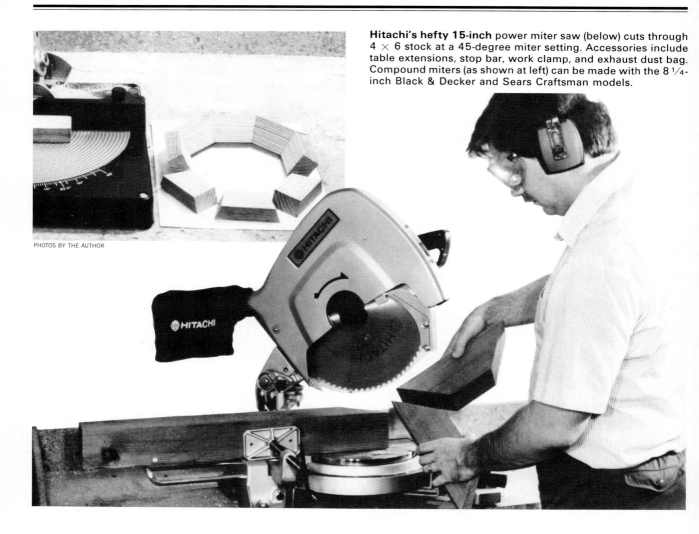

PHOTOS BY THE AUTHOR

Hitachi's hefty 15-inch power miter saw (below) cuts through 4 × 6 stock at a 45-degree miter setting. Accessories include table extensions, stop bar, work clamp, and exhaust dust bag. Compound miters (as shown at left) can be made with the 8 1/4-inch Black & Decker and Sears Craftsman models.

radial-arm saw, it makes a smoother cut: Splintering, caused by pulling a blade through the work, does not occur.

Aside from the 8¼-inch Black & Decker and Sears Craftsman compound miter saws, the saws are similar in design. Most have 10-inch blades, all have sufficient power and quick-stopping blade brakes, and, unfortunately, all are noisy.

The blade size determines the size of the work a saw can handle. Generally, a 10-inch saw will miter (at 45 degrees) a 2×4; a 14-inch saw accepts up to a 4×4; and a 15-inch saw can take a 4×6.

I found all the larger saws to be nearly perfectly aligned as received. Each comes with detailed instructions on how to check and set the saw head square and perpendicular to the table. I also checked the saws with a dial indicator to see how closely they repeat an angle after you swing, detent, and lock a miter setting. All came within 0.003 inch—as measured at the center of the blade—and most were just about zero.

The 8¼-inch Black & Decker and Craftsman saws can miter a 2×4 at 45 degrees, and they can make compound miters, too. The compound miters usually involve odd angles, which you set using a protractor. These saws are not as heavy or as rigid as the others, and I had some trouble accurately repeating angles with them. But if you don't get too pushy with the saws, they work just fine.

While trying these saws, I learned there are lots of features worth considering when you buy. For example, look at the number of angle detents. Some saws have as few as three, others have five. (I also like Delta's vernier scale that lets you make odd-angle settings down to ¼ degree.)

For long work, you'll want table extensions. And for most work, stops and clamps are helpful in holding the stock in place. A separate carrying handle is handy for moving the saw; a built-in blade lock is a real help when changing blades; and an exhaust bag keeps the dust to a minimum.

Finally, a word of caution. These saws are made for cutting *wood*. Although some makers describe how you can cut aluminum molding using the proper blade and procedures, miter saws are not abrasive chop saws for metal, and they should never be used that way. Also, although they're transportable, always fasten down a power miter saw before you use it—*by Phil McCafferty. Photos by Greg Sharko and the author.*

MANUFACTURERS OF POWER MITER SAWS
Black & Decker Corp., 10 N. Park Dr., Hunt Valley, MD 21030; Delta International Machinery Corp., 246 Alpha Dr., Pittsburgh, PA 15238; Hitachi Power Tools USA, 4487-F Park Dr., Norcross, GA 30093; Makita USA, 12950 E. Alondra Blvd., Cerritos, CA 90701; Ryobi America Corp., 1158 Tower Lane, Bensenville, IL 60106; Sears, Roebuck and Co. (Craftsman), Sears Tower, Chicago, IL 60684; Shopcraft, 209 S. Alex Rd., Dayton, OH 45449; Skil Corp., 4801 W. Peterson Ave., Chicago, IL 60646

power paint rollers

Just about every room in my house needed painting. At first, looking over the considerable expanses of walls and ceilings, I was tempted to postpone the project until some indefinite future date. Then I realized that this was a good opportunity to get the job done while testing a new category of painting tools for *Popular Science* magazine: power paint rollers.

Power roller systems pump pressurized paint through a hose from a reservoir to a trigger-activated roller. The units are designed to make painting easier by eliminating—
● stopping to load the roller;
● dripping paint from an overloaded roller;
● climbing down from ladders and stooping to reach the paint tray.

The five systems I tested were: the Wagner Power Roller I'd seen advertised so often; a Power-Flo; the Campbell Hausfeld PaintPal; one I'd never heard of called the Homax; and a little CO_2-powered unit from Black & Decker. The table lists the specifications for the units. Here's what I learned:

Wagner Power Roller. With this system you place a can of oil or latex paint inside a plastic canister, screw on a twist-lock top, and throw a switch. A small air pump pressurizes the canister and feeds paint to the roller. The first Wagner I tried was worthless. I found it difficult to achieve a tight seal between the canister and its top. When I did finally succeed, the pressure was still insufficient to deliver a medium-bodied latex paint at a reasonable rate.

I called Dan Nixa, Wagner's expert on homeowner systems, and found that Wagner had improved the Power Roller at the beginning of 1985. Nixa sent me one of the reengineered models. The difference was dramatic: I could apply paint as fast as I could move the roller.

Even with the improvements, though, the Power Roller wasn't per-

Black & Decker's CO_2-powered roller system is compact enough to take up a ladder. With the paint canister clipped to his belt, the author paints a window soffit 20 feet in the air. Paint reservoir capacity is one quart.

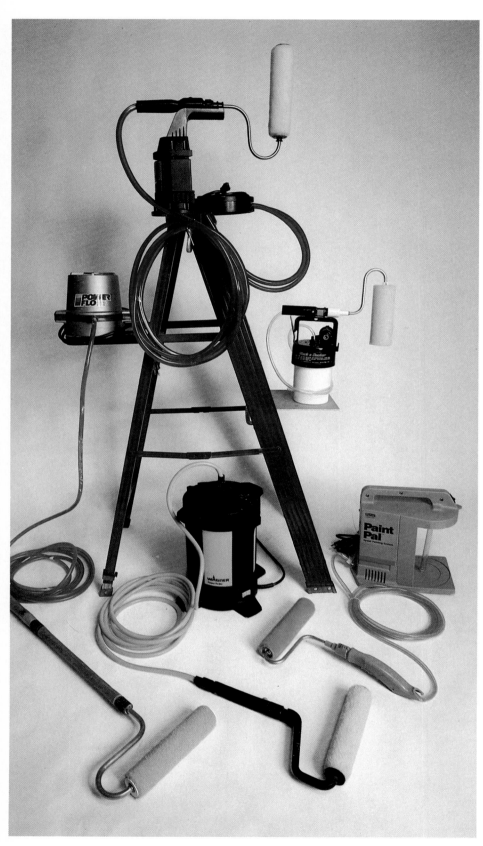

Power paint rollers tested are (clockwise from top) Homax, Black & Decker, Campbell Hausfeld, Wagner, and Power-Flo. Accessories for these systems include pads for trim work and extension handles for longer reach.

fect. First, all the other units I tested had transparent hoses; the Wagner's was opaque, making it impossible to see whether paint was flowing when I started the job. And at the end of the job, it was impossible to tell when the hose had been rinsed clean.

The Wagner does have an impressive list of optional attachments, including a special brush, pad, roller for trim work, and an extension handle. The extension increases your reach and lets you run the roller two-handed. This allows better control and reduces fatigue.

The trim pad is useful for cutting in against straight trim; the 3-inch roller is OK for tight spots, and the brush can be useful for trim and irregular surfaces. But I still prefer an ordinary brush to all these accessories. Because a brush is unhindered by a hose, I find it less tiring, as well as easier to control.

Power-Flo model 800. Like three of the five rollers I tested, this one uses a peristaltic pump to feed paint (oil or latex) to the roller. A small motor turns a pair of little rollers that squeeze a C-shaped section of the paint hose, forcing the paint along using the same sort of action you use to swallow food.

The pump is quiet and effective. If I kept the feed button down constantly, I could roll on a medium-thick wall paint almost as fast as I wanted. But soon my hand began to cramp, so I used a small spring clamp instead.

The Power-Flo comes with a cleanup faucet fitting that lets you force water through the hose and squirt water over the roller at the same time. This system works well for cleaning the hose, but cleaning the roller seems to take forever.

Campbell Hausfeld PaintPal. This is another peristaltic-pump unit. The PaintPal is the cheapest of the mechanical units, and the lightest duty. Still, it manages to move medium-bodied paints about as fast as you can roll them on. The paint-flow trigger is a generous four fingers wide and features a lock. Even with the trigger locked, however, I found that the little pump couldn't keep up with me when I fed it a heavy latex wall paint. The PaintPal is not intended for use with oil-base paints.

Homax Power Painting System. This unit can handle oil or latex paints, and its peristaltic pump seems to run at about twice the rate of the other units. It can feed even heavy paints as fast as you can apply them. Despite its power, it is compact, lightweight, and quiet. It has a smooth,

PHOTO SUPPLIED BY HOMAX CORP.

Pump in Homax unit forces paint to the roller. A thumb valve controls flow.

PS buyer's guide to power paint rollers

Model	Price ($)	Flow rate	Roller size	Noise	Hose type	Trigger lock	Capacity	Accessories
Black & Decker Power Painting System	71	Good	7 in.	None	4 ft., clear	No	1 qt.	Angled trim brushes, pads
Campbell Hausfeld PaintPal	61	Fair	9 in.	Low	12 ft., clear	Yes	1 gal.	Extensions, pads, triangular pads
Homax Power Painting System	110	Excellent	9 in.	Low	18 ft., clear	Yes	5 gal.	Extensions, pads
Power-Flo model 800	100	Good	9 in.	Low	20 ft., clear	No	5 gal.	Extensions, pads
Wagner Power Roller	100	Good	9 in.	High	18 ft., opaque	No	1 gal.	Extensions, pads, brushes, trim rollers

easy-to-use feed button with a lock, and an effective cleanup system. I found the Homax to be a thoroughly professional system.

Black & Decker Power Painting System. This little unit uses CO_2 cartridges for power, has just a seven-inch roller (instead of the usual nine-incher), and only holds a quart of paint. On the surface, these would seem to be limitations—but they aren't. The cartridges supply plenty of pressure. And the quart-sized paint container is small enough to clip to your belt.

I look at the B & D as a compact unit to take to hard-to-reach small- or medium-scale jobs. I used it while standing high on a ladder to paint the soffits around a big arched window on my new addition. It proved flexible and easy to handle in this awkward situation. The small roller performed better than a larger one would have on this kind of work. If you want to use oil-base paints, forget about the B & D, however; it's simply not designed for them.

The bottom line

All of the rollers I tested worked well. But, with the exception of the Homax, they lacked the pressure to feed the thickest-bodied latex paint as fast as I could have rolled it on.

Sometimes the roller ends remained nearly dry so that only the center was putting on paint. This slowed me down and made it hard to trim and paint inside corners. Also, when painting narrow hallways the hoses tended to drag through wet paint.

But the biggest snag is at cleanup time. Even though all the systems came with special hose or faucet attachments for "easy cleanup," they still took an average of 20 minutes to clean. And that's with water-base paints. Cleanups with oil-base paints are even more time-consuming, and often use up a gallon of thinner. It's wise to disassemble the roller and head to give them special attention. And remember: If you neglect to clean a power roller, you've just thrown close to $100 out the window.

All this cleanup time—at least on small-to-average jobs—tends to offset the speed advantage that power rollers have over conventional rollers, which can be cleaned in about two minutes with a garden hose. But if you have a very large room to paint, or perhaps two or more rooms, a pressure system will save you time and will certainly be more convenient than a conventional roller. Whether it's worth the price—as much as $110 in the case of the Homax—is up to you to decide. Note, however, that the units may be heavily discounted (prices in the tables are suggested retail). Homax, for example, says its system is typically sold at prices ranging from $70 to $100—by *A. J. Hand.*

MANUFACTURERS' ADDRESSES
Black & Decker, 3012 Highwoods Blvd., Raleigh, NC 27625; **Campbell Hausfeld Co.,** 100 Production Dr., Harrison, OH 45030; **Homax Corp.,** Box 5643, Bellingham, WA 98227-5643; **Power-Flo Products Corp.,** 1661 94th Lane N.E., Minneapolis, MN 55434; **Wagner Spray Tech Corp.,** 1770 Fernbrook Lane, Minneapolis, MN 55441

index